Toward an Inclusive Creative Writing

Toward an Inclusive Creative Writing

Threshold Concepts to Guide the Literary Curriculum

Janelle Adsit

BLOOMSBURY ACADEMIC
LONDON • NEW YORK • OXFORD • NEW DELHI • SYDNEY

BLOOMSBURY ACADEMIC
Bloomsbury Publishing Plc
50 Bedford Square, London, WC1B 3DP, UK
1385 Broadway, New York, NY 10018, USA

BLOOMSBURY, BLOOMSBURY ACADEMIC and the Diana logo
are trademarks of Bloomsbury Publishing Plc

First published 2017
Paperback edition first published 2019

© Janelle Adsit, 2017

A version of a section in Chapter 2 has been previously published in Stephanie
Vanderslice and Rebecca Manery's tenth anniversary release of a second edition of
Can Creative Writing Really Be Taught? (Bloomsbury Academic, 2017). Some content
appears in "What Is a Writer? Historicizing Constructions of the Writing Life in Composition
and Creative Writing," dissertation submitted I partial fulfillment of the doctoral program in
English at the University at Albany, SUNY and "Resisting the Last Word: U.S. Creative
Writing Pedagogy's Exclusionary Tendencies Revised," thesis submitted in partial
fulfillment of the master's program in English at Colorado State University.

A version of Chapter 3 has been previously published in *New Writing: The International
Journal for the Practice and Theory of Creative Writing* vol. 14 (Mar. 2017): 1–12.

Janelle Adsit has asserted her right under the Copyright,
Designs and Patents Act, 1988, to be identified as Author of this work.

For legal purposes the Acknowledgements on p. ix-x constitute
an extension of this copyright page.

Cover design: Eleanor Rose
Cover image © Getty Images

A catalogue record for this book is available from the British Library.

Library of Congress Cataloging-in-Publication Data
Names: Adsit, Janelle author.
Title: Toward an inclusive creative writing : threshold concepts to guide the
Literary curriculum / Janelle Adsit, Humboldt State University, USA.
Description: London ; New York, NY : Bloomsbury Academic, 2017.
Identifiers: LCCN 2017003740| ISBN 9781350023864 (hb) |ISBN 9781350023871 (epub)
Subjects: LCSH: English language–Rhetoric–Study and teaching. | Creative
writing (Higher education)
Classification: LCC PE1404 .A37 2017 | DDC808/.0420711–dc23
LC record available at https://lccn.loc.gov/2017003740

ISBN: HB: 978-1-3500-2386-4
PB: 978-1-3501-0722-9
ePDF: 978-1-3500-2388-8
ePub: 978-1-3500-2387-1

Series: Social Theory and Methodology in Education Research

Typeset by RefineCatch Limited, Bungay, Suffolk

To find out more about our authors and books visit
www.bloomsbury.com and sign up for our newsletters.

For our students

Contents

Acknowledgments   ix

Introduction   1
    Discussions of diversity and inclusion in creative writing   3
    Threshold concepts to guide the literary writing curriculum   9
    Toward an inclusive creative writing pedagogy   11

1 Privileged Assumptions and Assumptions of Privilege   13
    What the VIDA Count tells about teaching   15
    Exclusionary constructions of the writer's life   17
    Finding a voice   21
    The lonely writer   23
    Leisure and unalienated labor   26
    The writer as exceptional   30
    Mapping pedagogical constructions of the writer   31
    Progressive pedagogical approaches   32
    Humanist pedagogical approaches   34
    Professionalizing pedagogical approaches   36
    Auditioning pedagogical approaches   38
    Experimental pedagogical approaches   39
    Therapeutic pedagogical approaches   41
    Elitism in creative writing   42
    Exclusionary assumptions about writers and writing   47

2 Marginalized Aesthetics   49
    Policing intention: Polemics against polemics   51
    Policing taste: Ideologies of craft   57
    Policing emotion: Scorn of excess   68
    The diversity of the textual landscape   72

3 Threshold Concepts in Creative Writing   75
    Concept 1: Attention   83
    Concept 2: Creativity   88

Concept 3: Authorship   91
Concept 4: Language   94
Concept 5: Genre   96
Concept 6: Craft   97
Concept 7: Community   98
Concept 8: Evaluation   101
Concept 9: Representation   104
Concept 10: Resistance   107
Concept 11: Theory   108
Concept 12: Revision   110
Threshold concepts and learning outcomes   112

4   Toward an Inclusive Pedagogy   117
Starting points   117
Reading   124
Workshop   126
Evaluation and grading   134

Coda: Reimagining Creative Writing's Institutional Practices   137
Appendix A—List of Craft Texts Surveyed in Chapters 1 and 2   145
Appendix B—Sample Syllabus   148

Notes   163
Index   191

Acknowledgments

My abiding gratitude goes to the teachers who have modeled thoughtful critical pedagogy. Thanks to Tamika Carey who has shaped my thinking in many ways; to Laura Wilder for continued collaboration and support; to Deanna Ludwin for friendship and for providing my first teaching experiences in creative writing and for putting so many opportunities before me; to Todd Mitchell for his teaching about creative writing pedagogy; to Lisa Langstraat for all she has taught me over the years; to Charles Shepherdson for exegesis of the aesthetic tradition; to Robert Yagelski who provided guidance that has been essential to my process. Underscored thanks to Sue Doe who saw me through the first sputtering iterations of the concerns that populate these pages. I count myself exceedingly privileged to have her investment in my work. She has trekked through snowstorms and crowded airports to support me. The examples of her deep commitment to teaching and mentorship are countless. To her, most deserved thanks.

My research on the history of creative writing's instructional practices was supported by a University at Albany Benevolent Association grant award. The award enabled me to conduct research at several library collections in Massachusetts, Vermont, New York, New Jersey, Colorado, and California. I would like to acknowledge the librarians and archivists who maintain the following collections, which I visited: the Howard Gotlieb Archival Research Center at Boston University; the Middlebury College Archives; the Yaddo Records at the New York Public Library; the University Archives at the Carl A. Kroch Library of Cornell University; the P.E.N. American Center Records at Princeton University; the University Archives at the University of Denver; the University Archives of Stanford University. These resources have contextualized the historical information provided in the following pages, and I have been fortunate to have access to these collections.

Thanks also to the editors at Bloomsbury—David Avital, Mark Richardson, and Lucy Brown—for their belief in this project and for their collaboration and collegiality. And much appreciation to the creative writing studies community, especially Stephanie Vanderslice, Graeme Harper, Dianne Donnelly, Tonya

Hegamin, Rachel Himmelheber, James Ryan, Trent Hergenrader, Joe Rein, Chris Drew, Michael Dean Clark, Ben Ristow, Rebecca Manery, and James Shea.

The pages that follow would not exist without the education that I have been provided in venues such as the Creative Writing and Race conference, organized by Prageeta Sharma, and the panel sessions dedicated to the topic of inclusion that I attended at the Association of Writers and Writing Programs Conference and elsewhere. This book is also inspired by the work of workshop facilitators such as Omi Osun Joni L. Jones, Lisa L. Moore, and Sharon Bridgforth's *Austin Project* and Elee Kraljii Gardiner's Thursdays Writing Collective.[1] These are a reference point. I find most useful Sharon Bridgforth's belief that a creative writing workshop can break assumptions and provide a space for unpeeling, unmasking, and witnessing.[2]

Deep gratitude belongs to Conchitina Cruz for generous discussions, insights, reassurances, and models for how to move forward with this work. Thanks to Kathryn Hulings for demonstrating to me so much about what it means to be an engaged teacher of writing. Thanks to Patty and Michele Bratschun for their faithful friendship and care. And to Shawn Hargan for the time, conversation, and support he has given to this work over the years. I am fortunate indeed for these sustaining friendships.

Warm thanks also to friends and colleagues at Humboldt State University. Thanks also to my students who challenge me, inspire me, and offer meaning. I want to acknowledge especially Mirabai Collins, Angela Compton, and Jan Calderon who have contributed to this book through conversation and critical reflection.

My love and heartfelt appreciation also goes to my parents, Eric and Lisa Adsit, for their unfailing encouragement and help. Thank you does not suffice, but thank you. And to John Johnson whose commitment to students moves me and heartens me and makes me want to do better. I am honored to witness your work and I have been blessed to be part of your life.

Introduction

On its organization website, the Association of Writers and Writing Programs (AWP) makes the boast, "Our member programs have provided literary education to students and aspiring writers from all backgrounds, economic classes, races, and ethnic origins." In such a claim, diversity becomes a means of marketing an institution, a way of branding and authorizing an establishment. Diversity becomes something akin to points on an institutional scoreboard. "How are our numbers?" the administrator asks. Much more difficult are the questions: What do writers from these backgrounds, classes, races, and ethnic origins experience when they come to the creative writing classroom? What forms of alienation and exclusion characterize the writing workshop? The tokenism underlying AWP's claim to "all backgrounds, economic classes, races, and ethnic origins" and the ways that many of the writers to which it refers have been met with invalidating and insulting practices in creative writing is what demands our attention as a field.

To give this adequate attention is to excavate the discourses that circulate in our discipline, that define our discipline. What stories does creative writing, as a discipline, tell about itself? How does creative writing distinguish and define itself as a field? What assumptions does it rest upon? What narratives do we tell about what it means to do creative writing, and what histories do these narratives rest upon?

In a 2011 article, D.W. Fenza, Executive Director of AWP, tells one defining narrative. He recounts the history of democratization in creative writing and construes the success of its institutions as "a modest emulation of Promethean gift-giving."[1] Consistent with the Promethean story, the powerful protagonist (creative writing as institution in this case) becomes rendered as victim. Fenza writes, "the powers that be must punish the creative writing program for its generosity, for its willingness to share and multiply literary authority."[2] The rhetorical moves made in this statement indicate much about the orientation of contemporary creative writing. The creative writing program is here personified as a philanthropist, paternalistically doling out access to riches, multiplying the loaves to share with the masses. In this discourse of paternalism, Fenza renders the creative writing program as giving access and authority to those who would not otherwise have it. That this gifted authority is only gained through the creative writing program demonstrates the field's role as gatekeeper, embedded in hierarchical power relations. But Fenza's rhetoric sidesteps this fact, attaching the word "power" to the "powers that be" that punish the good philanthropic creative writing program for dispersing literary authority to the "have-nots." These rhetorical maneuvers, which disavow the creative writing program's circulations of power, hint at a disciplinary denial. That denial is the subject of this book.

The power dynamics at play in the creative writing workshop are obscured in the story Fenza tells about creative writing. These power dynamics render some writers as guests, generously invited to a table that is maintained as being not theirs. It is as Sara Ahmed finds in her book about racism and institutional life: some of us "are welcomed *on condition.*"³

Fenza's words reveal a disciplinary self-identity that is tied to what Claudia Rankine has called "a benevolent form of meritocracy."⁴ Creative writing fantasizes itself as a meritocratic and benevolent enterprise, elevating the most accomplished writers, regardless of identity, and giving access to the written word to all. But, as the pages that follow stand to show, this is only a disciplinary mask. The notion that the creative writing program benevolently multiplies literary authority is specious. While the students who can afford enrollment in the Master of Fine Arts (MFA) program (and we know that even well-funded programs require significant affordances from their students) may be authorized to produce pages, this is not all it takes to secure literary authority. As Junot Díaz famously put it in his *New Yorker* article from 2014: "There's nothing about creative writing programs ... that leads me to believe ... that the diversity found at the institutional level even begins to equal the diversity not only of our ... country, but of our readerships."⁵ Multiplying literary authority comes up against a limit.

Fenza prefers to think of the "elite" and the "gatekeepers" as being old and obsolete—helpless to staunch the deluge of literary production happily brought on by the creative writing program. But in constructing the "elite" as obsolete, Fenza obfuscates existing elitism in creative writing—and thereby naturalizes the hierarchies in contemporary writing classrooms and the conceptions of literary culture those hierarchies reflect. His construction neutralizes the fact, well documented by the VIDA Count, that some identity categories consistently remain underrepresented in creative writing programs and in established literary publications. Since 2010, the organization VIDA: Women in Literary Arts has orchestrated an annual tally of the gender and racial disparities in a range of bestselling journals, literary magazines and book reviews. With specific data, VIDA has documented the "sloped playing field" in the literary industry, with white men consistently dominating the pages of almost all mainstream literary publications studied.[6] Again, as VIDA shows, multiplying literary authority comes up against a limit.

The chapters that follow make the argument that creative writing stands upon problematic assumptions about what counts as valid writerly selfhood and valid artistic production, and these implicit beliefs result in exclusionary pedagogical practices. To counter this tendency of creative writing, this book proposes a set of principles upon which a curriculum can be built. These principles, which I offer as twelve threshold concepts for creative writing, can serve to transform the teaching of literary writing craft into an opportunity for critical reflection on cultural production in its diversity and range. This book attends to the constellation of assumptions about the writer-as-subject and who has access to this subject-position. They offer a direction forward that acknowledges the exclusionary history of creative writing and transforms it into a more inclusive approach to art-making and the teaching of literary production.

Discussions of diversity and inclusion in creative writing

The topic of inclusion in creative writing has been present in venues ranging from National Public Radio (NPR) and *The New York Times* to recent issues of the *Writer's Chronicle* and the *Journal of Creative Writing Studies*. Yet the topic remains to be given its due time and attention. Too often it is left to the margins, or pushed off the table of the workshop conversation. When issues of inclusion are not foregrounded in the creative writing classroom, the space loses value for the writers who come to it.

Ayana Mathis, in an interview with NPR, speaks of an experience that many have had, or have witnessed, in the workshop conversation. She describes presenting her writing in workshop only to have her story dismissed because it included a racial identifier. "There was a person in the workshop who said they had been reading happily up to that point," Mathis recounts, "but then felt like they were reading a story about race—which somehow invalidated what they'd been reading up to that point."[7] The colorblind racist assumptions allowed to play out in that workshop conversation—namely, that race can be neutral or invisible, that a mention of race means that a story has become politicized and therefore bad—all need to be interrogated in the creative writing classroom.

The argument of this book is that they are best interrogated in a holistic and scaffolded way, throughout a course—guided by readings in craft-criticism, written by and addressed to writers regarding the most pressing concerns of the craft. This book shows how diversity and inclusion can be priorities from day one in the classroom and that conversations about these topics are essential to a literary writing education. The creative writing curriculum can provide deep learning about the issues that are at stake in any form of cultural production, including identity politics and the relationship between art and activism. The creative writing curriculum can provide a writer-centered analysis of what it means to represent the world and how these representations affect the world.

This book follows from the writers who have raised the consciousness of the field, pointing out what is wrong with the culture of academic creative writing as it stands: Claudia Rankine, Beth Loffreda, Fred D'Aguiar, Toi Derricotte, Junot Díaz, Aminatta Forna, Tonya Hegamin, Cathy Park Hong, Anna Leahy, Shirley Geok-lin Lim, David Mura, Adrienne Perry, Richard Teleky, Dorothy Wang, Mark Nowak, being among these writers.[8] I write this book with these authors' articles and books as a continual point of reference. Because of their work, the racism and oppressive structure of our academic creative writing programs has been documented and exposed. The introduction of the hashtag #MFAvsPOC, following Junot Díaz's article of the same title, marks a continuing conversation that these authors have shaped and galvanized. In response, and with explicit reference to Claudia Rankine's call "to address the status quo that often makes our MFA programs and other literary institutions difficult, unwelcoming places for writers of color and others from outside the dominant culture," the AWP Board of Trustees announced in 2016 a new committee on Inclusion and an Inclusion Initiative that is under the leadership of Trustee and Executive Committee member David Haynes.[9]

These are hopeful signs. But that there is still something amiss in our discipline. Our students know it. They know it in ways that they can not always speak about. They might see it in their instructors' discomfort over the mention of race in a story. They might feel it in the conflicting messages they receive about artistic freedom and the responsibility to write according to craft principles. They might notice it in the absence of writers that look like them in the hallways of the English department or in the writers on stage in their campus auditoriums. They might wonder if they have a place in the literary community—if the doors look open only so that they can be closed.

I can remember feeling deep frustration with my experiences in undergraduate creative writing, despite the privileges I had as a white person in a predominantly white institution. I was assigned writing by white people who represented a particular type of literature. I had been raised in a middle class community, but I could feel that the creative writing curriculum was acting upon me, trying to reform my tastes, my sense of the world. The semester began with a long list of genres we were not allowed to write—horror, myth, fairy tales, fables, young adult, thrillers, mysteries, romance, and many others—presented on the syllabus along with classroom management policies and warnings about what would happen to us if we plagiarized. In class, we were told to find our voices as we read through a syllabus of almost all white and American authors. We were condescended to when we spoke about our love of poetry slams, video games or romantic comedies. We were to accept the tastes presented to us as "right" and become embarrassed about our interest in the literature that was dismissed in the creative writing classroom. Resisting the disciplining force of creative writing was not offered as an option.

As an undergraduate, I wrote a satire of the creative writing curriculum, in imitation of Daniel Orozco's "Orientation." To me, university creative writing felt as restrictive and oppressive as the workplace depicted in "Orientation." My teacher wrote notes in response to my story, covering the pages with penciled cursive. She cut some of her comments away from the 8.5 × 11″ stapled packet of paper. What she handed to me looked like a craft project, with uneven S-shapes cut at the papers' borders, removing words that I imagine were more corrective than the ones I received. My parody was no doubt badly rendered, and my project was likely hurtful to a teacher who was doing her best to relay the discipline as she knew it. I think back on my poor attempt at curricular reform with embarrassment, but, a decade and a half later, I have not lost the impulse that brought me to scrawl that initial attempt at critique, that urge to converse about what is happening in creative writing.

As a creative writing student, I sensed that I was being kneaded, rolled out, and reshaped. And I knew that many of us were not perceived as workable clay. I wanted to be a pliable student, to learn how to fit in to the literary community, but it was clear to me that my unwieldy self would not take the right shape. We were told again and again that creative writing is very competitive; as students, our belonging was not assured. I wanted to be the right kind of subject to get my golden ticket of belonging, and it took me a while to learn that this meant demonstrating a worldview and taste that would be accepted. I remember feeling angry at how inaccessible this subject-position seemed. I was frustrated by the rules of this community, which were rarely made transparent. The implicit rules that I was able to identify seemed to narrow the field of literary production to the smallest subset of literature—short stories, poems, and a few essays published by white men about depoliticized issues, written in a style that demonstrated white middle-class values: respectability (mandating against oppositional discourse, polemics, parody, resistance, or critique); decorum (holding good writerly character to be equivalent to good writerly style); moderation and temperance (avoiding excessive emotion, such as melodrama and sentimentality); thrift and efficiency (valuing simplicity and minimalism in craft aesthetics).[10] While I had familiarity with many of these values, they felt oppressive to me in the context of the creative writing class. After all, I loved literature that did not demonstrate these values. That literature often sold well, so I knew that other people loved literature that did not demonstrate these values too.

Soon after writing the unfortunate parody, I left the creative writing major and sought other parts of the curriculum. I enrolled in a graduate-level critical literacy course where I was introduced to critical pedagogy and found language to describe the violences that can be inherent in writing instruction, through the work of Elspeth Stuckey, Lisa Delpit, Jacqueline Jones Royster, and Patrick Finn, among others.[11] This scholarship in composition and rhetoric continues to inform my perspective on creative writing. I obtained a doctoral degree with a dual emphasis in rhetoric and aesthetics. Now I teach fiction and creative nonfiction at a state university in California.

I have taken the seat at the front of the creative classroom. I facilitate the courses that made me angry as an undergraduate. The pedagogical practices I have inherited as a creative writing practitioner are limited and limiting in many ways. My job now is to remake them with and for my students.

I teach at a Hispanic-Serving Institution (HSI) that has historically been a predominantly white space, a "PWI" as many US universities have come to be known. The campus is located in a predominantly white community that likes to think of itself as progressive, but racism, xenophobia, and homophobia shape the experiences of students on and off campus. Microaggressions (i.e., occurrences that communicate hostility, that insult and do harm, and that police legitimacy) shape students' experiences in and out of the classrooms. Students of Color are regularly treated as guests to be accommodated, rather than as rightfully belonging as central members of the institution. This is communicated in behaviors and white-centered course content, among many other factors. It may be communicated even in the campus architecture that students encounter; almost all of the building and room names on my campus invoke a white person.

Our students speak up about their experience of the campus. Their work has made their faculty and administration more critically conscious of the ways we contribute to our campus environment and what we are responsible for. But the campus is slow to transform.

My institution is just one example of the larger culpability of higher education in sustaining structural inequality, and the field of creative writing needs to attend to the urgency of these problems. These circumstances condition my writing, sharpening my awareness of my complicity and how much work there is to be done. I hold to the belief, expressed by Fiona Probyn-Ramsey, that "complicity can be a starting point; if we start with complicity, we recognize our proximity to the problems we are addressing."[12] I write from this acknowledgment, with awareness that my many blindspots will no doubt show through the pages that follow. The book is, for example, largely grounded in a US context, and fails to fully account for a transnational perspective. We all have sites of ignorance, but we need to keep talking and listening—so that these points of ignorance can be addressed with and for our communities.

I benefit on a daily basis from my students' patience with me—patience that is structured by a system where privileges are not evenly distributed. I can be seen by my students as well-intentioned because of this privilege, even as my praxis has at times fallen short of the education they deserve.

This book is an outgrowth of frustrations I have had in my own classroom, as I have inherited a discipline that serves to exclude and police literary expression. This discipline is anxious to maintain its status hierarchies, its sense of what is inside and outside. The deeply held beliefs of creative writing hold sacrosanct the freedom and immunity of those imaginative writers whose subject-positions are read as legitimate; any interrogation of this writer's choices may be fearfully read as a prohibition on that freedom. Out of this fear, creative writing practitioners may characterize critical theory as deadening, when that theory has galvanized and supported vital forces for change (think Angela Davis, Audre Lorde, Adrienne Rich). What would it mean to expose this disciplinary subconscious? How might that exposure transform the discipline toward an open field of possibilities? What could critical theory and thought bring to the discipline? What might antiracist pedagogies, feminist pedagogies, critical pedagogies have to teach us as practitioners of literary craft? What would it mean to redraft a curriculum that not only teaches literary production in its range, but also takes responsibility for exposing white supremacy, sexism, ableism, xenophobia, and heternomativity in society-at-large, as well as in its own education and publishing organizations?

This book is a response to some of these questions. It is a response that is ongoing, extending beyond the book's pages. It is a response that we, as instructors of creative writing, work out in every class session, every meeting in office hours, every assignment prompt. I check my pedagogical choices against what my students and I hope is possible for the discipline. It is a continual process of self-reflexivity and criticality about the implications of my choices.

I believe that Tonya Hegamin is right that there is an "inevitable sea change" occurring in creative writing, which focuses "on the need for meaningful and radical inclusivity in and beyond the classroom, to incorporate different perspectives of religion, social class, language, gender, identity, nationality/immigrant status and physical/learning (dis)ability in all arenas of Creative Writing."[13] This book has hope in that sea change.

In focusing on the exclusionary tendencies of the creative writing workshop, I do not mean to overlook the important work of many faculty members who have taught the craft in inclusive ways. Many writers and organizations like the Asian American Writers' Workshop, Cave Canem, CantoMundo, Institute of American Indian Arts, Lambda Literary, Mestizo Arts & Activism Collective, Native American Literature Symposium, PEN America, and VIDA: Women in Literary Arts have moved creative writing toward greater inclusion. At the same time, the white-centrism and exclusions of the discipline must be uncovered, made stark and therefore inexcusable.

When the history of creative writing instruction is narrated,[14] it is often narrated as primarily a history of white people; we need to rewrite the history of creative writing instruction to address how "the modern academic creative writing classroom is a direct product of grassroots community activism found in the Harlem Renaissance, the Black Arts Movement, Beat Poetry, Spoken Word, Feminist, Queer and Disability studies."[15] To expose the white-centrism of scholarship that documents the history of creative writing is to expose the forces and counter-forces that have been at work since the discipline's inception.

This book focuses on the present state of creative writing, but also historicizes how we got here, how the assumptions of the discipline became entrenched. While my analysis is focused on the past and present, the orientation of this book is "toward"—it is about the future of this discipline. I submit this book to the conversation because it is a conversation I want to forward, a conversation that involves all of us—as teachers, students, and practitioners of creative writing.

I write to listen and to learn more how to shed the oppressive discipline I was educated in and to bring a new set of practices into the creative writing classroom. As Claudia Rankine notes, "'Segregation Forever' was part of the ideology that reared us and put in place the institutions in which we were taught and in which we teach."[16] This book seeks to uncover how this history remains alive in the ideas we proffer in creative writing. It then suggests a way of dealing with this history, addressing it in the classroom, evacuating it of its insidious power.

This examination of the assumptions undergirding our curriculum is necessary to fully address the exigencies articulated by Rankine and many others. These writers signal the need for a new pedagogical theory of creative writing. *Toward an Inclusive Creative Writing* seeks to draw out the possibilities of such a pedagogy, as it also uncovers exclusionary assumptions that this pedagogy must address. Creative writing now stands upon problematic beliefs which result in harmful pedagogical practices and limited relevance for the field. To craft an inclusive pedagogy is to work against the discipline's entrenched ideologies. As articulated in the pages that follow, creative writing has operated with a hidden curriculum of prejudice. Discrimination is part of creative writing's central philosophies and practices. The difficult task of changing "the basic mindset of so many white writers, a mindset with both conscious and unconscious components"[17] will require examining the structure of the creative writing curriculum.

Having identified these problematic tendencies in academic creative writing, it is necessary to seek an alternative. Seeking transformation, this book aims to make the most of creative writing's unique ability to shape cultural production and to make the field vital for the students who come to it.

Because my argument interrogates creative writing primarily at the level of its core assumptions, seeking to dismantle exclusionary principles that govern much of what is said in the creative writing course, it becomes imperative to offer a set of core concepts that can guide us forward. As we refuse creative writing's longstanding problematic assumptions, we need to find a new set of concepts that will sustain an inclusive curriculum. Here I turn to the idea of a "threshold concept" because it is a tool that has been associated with transformation.

Threshold concepts to guide the literary writing curriculum

The term "threshold concept" has recently come to prominence in Scholarship of Teaching and Learning (SoTL). Mobilized by researchers Jan Meyer and Ray

Land,[18] the term challenges instructors to name the forms of knowledge that a curriculum forwards. Key to the idea of the threshold concept is the belief that learning means undergoing a change. Threshold concepts stand to challenge or solidify a learner's sense of the world. Threshold concepts transform a learner's way of seeing, way of schematizing what they know, or way of engaging with a subject matter.

Every discipline carries with it a set of principles that focus its scope and practice. Students learning a discipline are asked to adopt these principles as they proceed with work in the area of study. Historically, these principles have been left implicit in the curriculum, but the threshold principle, as a tool, has prompted instructors to see the value of making these principles explicit—in order to check students' learning and to check the assumptions that are being forwarded in a curriculum. My purpose in this book is to read creative writing's disciplinary beliefs in this regard—to identify and name the concepts that are coded in creative writing's pedagogical discourse. I read craft textbooks assigned in the classroom and teacher-to-teacher articles on creative writing instruction and examine the beliefs found there, in order to expose the exclusionary implications of these beliefs. I then shift to offer a set of threshold concepts that are meant to actively keep open the field of creative writing, to include the broadest range of literary production. The concepts presented in this book are meant to forward a rigorous writing curriculum that engages the diversity of the literary landscape and the diversity of the world.

This book explores how exclusion happens at the level of concept, in the assumptions we make in our course content; this is, of course, just one of many ways that exclusion happens. I argue that we can not achieve an inclusive creative writing without changing these assumptions, without finding a new set of concepts to guide us. However, examining these assumptions is just one step. What an antiracist, inclusive, and critical pedagogy looks like for creative writing is a topic that necessitates continued discussion, and many topics relevant to this question lie beyond the scope of this book.

My adoption of the term "threshold concept" may give one pause. What does an academicism like this have to offer us? Is not the term itself exclusionary, as it is far removed from the language that people outside of academe speak? And consider the metaphor: the threshold erects a boundary; the threshold foregrounds the status of insider or outsider. You cross the threshold to come inside, to become an insider. The threshold divides us. The threshold concept may seem anathema to an idea of an inclusive creative writing. Ultimately, however, the discipline of creative writing is a particular discourse community with a specific set of concerns, institutions, and practices. My interest is how to identify this set of concerns, institutions, and practices so that they can be made available for transformation. The threshold concepts I list are meant to give us, as members of what is (for better and for worse) an academic discipline, a sense of what that discipline stands to teach. While my aim is to make the creative writing curriculum accessible to the students who come to it, issues of diversity and inclusion demand rigorous attention and interrogation. The creative writing curriculum has the potential to be both accessible and rigorous. Creative writing, as a discipline, can foster the literary production and artistic self-reflexivity of any student who comes to it.

Toward an inclusive creative writing pedagogy

The book is about opening up the discipline of creative writing to consider the wide range of ways that diverse peoples engage with the literary word. My central argument is that students in creative writing should learn how to write difference and identity in ways that demonstrate critical consciousness. As Hegamin argues, "We all need creative discourse in order to validate our own internalized 'isms' and differences, to textualize otherness as a valuable part of the human experience."[19]

The chapters that follow historicize the aesthetic orientation of creative writing and identify how criteria and craft principles used to discuss "good writing" are culturally contingent. They show how creative writing has remained discriminatory and uncritical of the tendencies it reinforces. They then seek to provide a way of turning from this past, presenting a framework to increase the relevance and rigor of the field.

Chapter 1, "Privileged Assumptions and Assumptions of Privilege," makes the case that creative writing operates with several core unexamined beliefs that produce systemic barriers for some students to access the creative writing curriculum. Creative writing forwards inequities that limit students' capacities as cultural producers. The forms of underrepresentation identified in the VIDA Count bear upon not only the publishing industry, but the creative writing curriculum as well. VIDA's findings call into question the myth of aesthetic meritocracy, which continues to undergird the creative writing curriculum. Additionally, constructs of the literary writer and the writing lifestyle in the creative writing curriculum belie forms of privilege that may marginalize students who do not share them. Analyzing the constructions of the writer forwarded by creative writing craft textbooks, aesthetic theory, and institutions of creative writing like the writing residency, this chapter uncovers the forms of privilege that shape creative writing pedagogy.

Chapter 2, "Marginalized Aesthetics," traces how creative writing polices its boundaries through the aesthetic tradition and pedagogical discourses. This chapter argues that creative writing forwards forms of elitism, as large groups of literary practitioners are systematically excluded from the creative writing course. This chapter identifies the racist, sexist, heteronormative, and classist literary beliefs that remain operative as craft texts continue to malign activist writing, genre fiction, popular mass-market texts, "Oprahfied" literature, spoken word and slam poetry, and so-called "sentimental" literature. The chapter suggests that naturalized aesthetic values in creative writing serve to create a false hierarchy of literary practice that, upon closer examination, has no grounding or consistency.

Having identified several significant problems in academic creative writing pedagogy, Chapter 3 takes up the question of how to transform the curriculum. This chapter lists and defines twelve threshold concepts that can transform what is taught in creative writing. Building from the arguments established in the preceding chapters, these concepts foreground the contingencies of literary value and the importance of conceiving creative writing as a form of cultural production.

Chapter 4, "Toward an Inclusive Pedagogy," elucidates the responsibilities of writer-teachers in the academy today. To identify what an integrated creative writing curriculum can be, embracing the diversity of the literary landscape and providing tools for navigating its terrain, this chapter makes several core recommendations. Among these recommendations is that creative writing should refuse deficit-model instruction and should adopt a set of classroom practices that foreground literary diversity as a core value. This chapter describes pedagogical choices in the university setting that are a step forward in undoing the problems of the creative writing curriculum identified in the preceding chapters.

The book concludes with a summary of what we can do to promote the aesthetic development of diverse artists in the academy. The final chapter takes up the question of hiring practices and faculty retention, believing that improving the diversity of the profession is essential for improving the experiences of its students.

1

Privileged Assumptions and Assumptions of Privilege

In *Academic Instincts*, Marjorie Garber emphasizes the importance of the "genius" to cultural fantasy life. The genius—constructed as the bearer of authenticity, the "real thing"—is representative of creative writing as much as other disciplines.[1] Regularly invoked in constructions of the literary writer—from the so-called "genius grants" provided by the John D. and Catherine T. MacArthur Foundation to the Lamont Poetry Selection/Laughlin Award, administered by the Academy of American Poets, that promotes "the discovery and encouragement of new poetic genius"—the figure of the literary genius provides a window into some of creative writing's foundational assumptions. Regularly in discourses of creative writing, the figure of the genius is blended with the figure of the craftsman (a tellingly gendered noun). William Herbert Carruth exemplifies the close coexistence of these terms in his creative writing craft text from 1934. He claims that "those with the best natural gift are often the ones who take most pains in filing and polishing."[2] Charles Raymond Barrett's 1921 craft text provides another example, as he admonishes his readers: "do not therefore consider yourself a genius and so exempt from work."[3] In creative writing, the genius possesses a natural gift accompanied by the work ethic of a craftsman— doing the work of "filing and polishing" a page, as a craftsman would do to his material.

The ideal of the genius is a specter in creative writing. Its presence conditions the way the field organizes itself, and it conditions what it means to belong to the field. Stephanie Vanderslice addresses the field's attachment to the figure of the genius, warning that:

> Yet, if we continue to support a culture that continually reinscribes the notion of the artist as an individual genius who springs miraculously and fully formed virtually from birth (and only coincidentally from a middle or upper class background) at the expense of deliberately cultivating writers from among a

burgeoning youth culture that ranges across race and class . . ., the very idea of a literate culture will die on the vine.[4]

To move toward an inclusive creative writing is to identify and analyze the assumptions that the field carries about the figure of the writer. Creative writing instruction—which comes in many academic and extra-academic forms— teaches students not just the *skills* of craft. Creative writing's institutions teach— and, in so doing, continuously *construct*—the writer and the *lifestyle* of writing. This sets the terms by which a writer can find belonging in the field. Creative writing's institutions—from the academic MFA to the writer's residency to the craft textbook—exist to help writers "take care of themselves" as writers, in the Foucauldian sense. What is at stake here is how one comes to be recognized as writer-subject, which is about much more than simply putting words on a page. To participate in creative writing entails performing versions of subjectivity that are made valid. The field is structured to produce a certain kind of writer-self, and many assumptions are embedded here that are more or less accessible to potential members of the field, based on their positionalities. Paul Dawson notes that creative self-expression is "a technology of the self whereby language . . . is a device for discovering and developing the expressive potential of one's own human character."[5] What norms determine or shape what a writer ought to be?

The field's practices might remind one of a humorous (and not-so-humorous) anecdote told by Foucault at the beginning of his seminars on Subjectivity and Culture at the University of California, Berkeley:

> In a dialogue written at the end of the second century A.D., Lucian presents us a certain Hermotimus who walks mumbling in the street. One of his friends sees him, crosses the street, and asks him, 'what are you mumbling about?' And the answer comes: 'I am trying to remember what I have to tell my [teacher].' Through a conversation between those two, we learn that Hermotimus has been visiting his [teacher] for twenty years, that he is nearly ruined by the very high cost of those precious lessons, and we learn that Hermotimus may need 20 years more to arrive at the end of his training. But we learn also what those lessons are about: Hermotimus is taught by his [teacher] how to take care of himself in the best possible way.[6]

As Foucault notes, we all can recognize the figure of the present-day Hermotimus: people give their money to learn how to be the identity they seek. Teachers, of various kinds, tell others how to take care of themselves, how to constitute themselves, as more ideal subjects in particular fields. But this comes at a cost, and the cost is not equitable.

Foucault's story of Hermotimus can highlight a cost, which student-writers pay in coming to the creative writing class. It is a cost that some pay at a higher price than others. It is a cost that comes from the assumptions that creative writing makes about who belongs to the field and what forms of living as a writer are valid. Creative writing has become an industry built from the practice of constituting selves, helping students to configure themselves as writers. Creative writing, understood as a discipline and a culture that extends beyond academe, is a set of organizations and discourses that teach writers how to achieve a life that is aligned with its own constructs. From the craft textbook that instructs writers how to cultivate daily writing habits, to the writer's retreats that provide, and in doing so define, the perfect set-up for getting writing done, to the university MFA program that promotes itself as helping students find what it takes to *be writers*, these institutions demarcate the writing life. They limn what a writer looks like—the writer's daily habits, dwelling space, relationship to community, and behavior—the horizon of subjectivity that constitutes the creative writer as a type.

Today, the writing life is sold as an experiential commodity: it is sold in the proliferation of residencies, retreats, and summer schools with their admissions fees; it is sold in the ever growing body of craft textbooks and "how to become a writer" books. The writing life and the writer's identity are sold to a wide market.[7] The irony here is that the popularity of the writing life fosters a particular kind of consumerism even as it preserves an ascetic identity of the writer that is inherited from the aesthetic tradition. The writing life is bolstered by a consumer identity; this fact also raises the question of who has access to the writing life.

In this chapter, I show how such constructions of the writer and the act of writing reinforce a type of exclusion. If writing is first of all a way of life, as May Sarton is known for saying it is, then we should be mindful of the ways of living that become foreclosed in what we say about writing.

Constructions of the literary writer and the writing lifestyle belie forms of privilege that may marginalize students who do not share them. As creative writing teachers, our question should be: Who has access to the subject-positions called "writer" that are constructed by creative writing?

What the VIDA Count tells about teaching

There is a growing conversation about inequity in the field of creative writing. Thanks to the reach of the VIDA Count (i.e., the annual "count" that measures disparities in representation in literary publications, which has been performed by the US organization VIDA: Women in Literary Arts since 2010), much of this discussion about inequity in creative writing focuses on what gets published and what gets read. However, given the proliferation of MFA programs in the academy and the extent to which literary practitioners are involved in university work (whether as former or current students, teachers, visiting writers, lecturers of creative writing, editors of literary journals housed in an academic setting, or otherwise), discussions of the literary publishing industry have a connecting line to the higher education curriculum in creative writing.

The VIDA Count of identity representation across a set of literary publications presents a data-based picture of the marked imbalances in the field. Women, and in particular women of Color, are underrepresented in the pages of major literary publications. The disparity is clear, and these numbers presented in the VIDA Count tell us not only about representation in literary publications; they also indicate something about how the field has constructed the figure of the writer. Institutions of creative writing sustain a set of assumptions about what and who can be valued in creative writing. As I show in what follows, creative writing sketches a portrait of the good, productive, and capable writer-self who lives with a particular set of enmeshments. This writer represents a self on the page in a way that is valued by the field. The field's constructs of selfhood foreclose possibilities for actual living writers, as these writers' material circumstances and positionalities may make conformity to the (masculinized, elite) constructed writer-self an impossibility.

Writing is not evaluated with neutral or universal terms. Rather, as Barbara Herrnstein Smith insisted in the eighties, following Bourdieu and others: literary value is contingent. The VIDA Count exposes some of the biases that shape our contemporary literary landscape—forms of what VIDA has called "literary nepotism" and the rejection of a plurality of voices. In light of the VIDA Count, the meritocratic belief that the market will sift worthy literatures from the slush pile is shown to be a naive myth. Because this myth of aesthetic meritocracy has traditionally been influential to creative writing pedagogy, the VIDA Count asks for a pedagogical change in practice, as much as it asks for a response from the publishing industry. As teachers of creative writing, it becomes our responsibility to move toward a more inclusive creative writing pedagogy by uncovering the ways that the myth of aesthetic meritocracy has blinded us to inequity.

Exclusionary constructions of the writer's life

Before we can move toward a more inclusive creative writing pedagogy, we must uncover and expose the forms of privilege that have sustained this myth of aesthetic meritocracy, which is a defining part of creative writing's legacy to date.

One way I have begun to bring this question into my own teaching is to use a tool that I have created, borrowing from Peggy McIntosh's well-known heuristic "White Privilege: Unpacking the Invisible Knapsack."[8] Early in the semester of a creative writing workshop class, I offer the following list in a hand-out, and I ask the students to circle statements that they find to be "somewhat true" or "very true" of themselves.

UNPACKING PRIVILEGE IN THE CREATIVE WRITING CLASS

1. I have never noticed when an anthology, literary journal, or magazine consists primarily of white or male writers.
2. I assume that the works that don't get published or canonized are always examples of bad or lesser writing.
3. I grew up admiring heroes from movies and books that shared my race or gender.
4. I have never experienced censorship.
5. I have never received punishment for something I wrote.
6. To my mind, only less important or less skilled forms of literature are political or politicized.
7. I assume that my experiences and my writing can reach a universal audience.
8. I believe that the people who really have something to say are the people that get large audiences.
9. I believe writers are born and not made.
10. I believe that writers should not make money from their writing.
11. I rarely feel the need to examine the ways I present race, gender, sexuality, class, nationality, or religion in my writing.
12. I rarely feel the need to examine the ways I present the body or ability in my writing.
13. I feel comfortable writing about characters of political/cultural/linguistic/ social/ethnic identities that I do not share, and I do not go out of my way to check my representation of these characters against perspectives other than my own.

14. I often don't name the race of my characters because I assume readers will know the characters are white, or I feel that race doesn't matter.

15. I can be sure that the curricular materials I receive in a creative writing class will present characters and narrators that share my racial, ethnic, gender, sexual, class, national, linguistic, or religious identity or that have bodies that look like mine.

16. I do not consider how audiences of differing identities, backgrounds, and experiences will experience the texts I produce.

17. I feel comfortable writing in genres (e.g., haiku, slam poetry, etc.) that have cultural legacies of which I am unaware.

18. I feel comfortable portraying the speech patterns of characters from cultural backgrounds that I don't know well. I feel comfortable using a vernacular, code, or language that I do not speak and have never sought to learn.

19. Readers do not expect me to speak for all people of my racial, ethnic, gender, sexual, class, national, linguistic, or religious group in my writing.

20. I have never considered how my first or last name might be perceived by publishers, literary agents, or application review committees.

21. When I name the great authors of the literary tradition, most of the names that come to mind are white or male writers.

22. I do not worry that my peers or teachers will be disapproving of my taste in literature.

23. I am largely unaware of contemporary writing by people of Color.

24. I am largely unaware of contemporary writing by people from countries around the world.

25. I have experienced writing courses or literature courses that have given attention only to people of my race.

26. I do not worry about cultural appropriation in my storytelling or poetic practices.

27. I can note bias in the creative writing workshop without being accused of displaying extreme emotion, being irrational, or being too self-interested.

28. I do not sympathize with requests to preface literary texts with trigger warnings about racism and other forms of prejudice, abuse, anti-trans views of bodies, dismissal of lived oppressions, marginalization, illness or differences.

29. When readers are offended by something they read, I believe it's the reader's individual problem—and not the writer's—because it's the reader's individual emotions that are being activated.

30. I do not fear being seen as a cultural outsider to creative writing.

The exercise is meant to spark conversation, but the conversation should be guided and scaffolded by readings such as *The Racial Imaginary,* Dorothy Wang's *Thinking Its Presence,* or the series of responses to Claire Faye Watkins' "On Pandering," which was published on the website of the literary magazine *Tin House.*[9] Some of the statements in this list may not be immediately clear to students. Students may not know about residencies and writing conferences, for instance. And students may be uncertain about how some of the statements relate to the concept of privilege. The survey is not meant to be a simple exercise; it is meant to reveal the complexities of how power and privilege operate in the literary landscape. Our central question in discussing this exercise is: How does privilege get expressed in creative writing classrooms, publishing practices, evaluations of literature, and guides to craft? When I run this exercise, I ask students to write a 2–3-page reflection response to this question and to the experience of circling statements on the survey. In the response, students are welcome to interrogate or question any of the statements and to think about what the heuristic might offer them going forward in their careers as writers.

Each statement on this knapsack exercise has a history, and these histories are creative writing's inheritance, so a critical discussion of this history is necessary. There is congruence between mass-market representations of the literary writer and what we find in the pages of magazines and journals of the field of academic creative writing. Harry W. Pope's contribution to a 2013 issue of the AWP *Writer's Chronicle,* for instance, assumes that the lifestyle of the writer is one of solitude: "Solitary days, weeks, and even months spent struggling with a work," he writes, "causes many writers to suffer feelings of angst."[10] Such a construction naturalizes the assumption that one needs the time and space for solitariness to get writing done and, in turn, excludes the possibility that some get writing done at a kitchen table with a child on the lap, some get writing done at a bedside in-between caretaking responsibilities, some get writing done on a lunch break at one of the two or three jobs they maintain to make ends meet. The solitary writer working in a garret is etched into the mind with well-worn grooves. What images of the writer writing are we less likely to encounter in our journals, our films, our writers' conferences?

The type of excavation prompted by this question requires thorough and careful analysis. It requires a holistic rethinking of the field. It requires a thorough evaluation of how our field's inherited lore and values create the hierarchical conditions we see today, where only certain writers, with certain embodiments, are respected for what they bring to the craft.

It is not sufficient to refuse one or two clichéd elements of the lore that the field has established; it is not sufficient to merely reject one or two commonplaces of the field. A thorough appraisal is needed. In *Uncreative Writing*, Kenneth Goldsmith, critiques craft texts that uphold the idea that "creative writing is liberation from the constraints of everyday life."[11] Yet he then immediately invokes three male "giants" in the artistic sphere—de Certeau, Cage, and Warhol, specifically—as those who best exemplify the tie between art and the mundane. In this gesture, Goldsmith ignores the ways that creative writing's assumed relationship to "everyday life" may be gendered, classed, and raced. He is right to critique the construct that to write is to be without everyday responsibilities, but he does not go far enough in thinking about the identity politics that are at work in this belief—a belief that has a long history in an aesthetic tradition that has privileged the white male writer. This Western aesthetic tradition has had a particular writer-subject in mind when it has made its pronouncements about literary art-making; in turn, creative writing's inheritance from this aesthetic tradition tends to marginalize writers who represent "difference" from that writer-subject. The assumption about the writer's liberation from everyday life marginalizes writers with significant caretaking, domestic, medical, or financial responsibilities. The heroic genius writer's special status as liberated outsider to mass society becomes his cultural capital when the assumption remains unexamined and unchanged.

When a student-writer sits down with a text that forwards an idea that to write requires liberation from the constraints of everyday life, and when this idea goes unquestioned in the classroom, the student-writer who does not have the privilege of such "liberation" may believe that their access to the literary sphere is barred from the start. If a student-writer sits down with a text and sees only white males listed as "giants" of the artistic sphere, a student-writer who does not have this subject-position may again feel barred from the start. These students are being subjected to an invalidating educational experience, a form of hostility that works to keep the student-writer from the page. This hostility is insidious because it is cloaked in commonly held beliefs. It is hidden just well enough that the student-writer may be read as irrational or needlessly sensitive if they speak of the hostility they feel. So the invalidation comes in at all sides.

The onus is on all of us to be vigilant in addressing the core beliefs in creative writing that marginalize and foreclose possibilities for writers. A thorough analysis of exclusion in creative writing turns up an ever ramifying network of assumptions about the literary artist that police the boundaries of who can be considered "in" the field of literary art-making. My purpose here is to begin to identify some of these assumptions.

Finding a voice

Consider, for instance, the construction of the writer's voice—the unique signature that must be "found" by the writer and made visible to readers. *Find your voice*, launched into the workshop as a command, is about achieving a goal. This presumption of singular individuality (the voice—uniquely singular—is the individual's ostensible possession) sends the writer on a quest to find or recover that one thing which is the writer's own. If we each have only one true voice this regime risks erasing the complexity of an identity. It elides the way that writers code-switch in different spheres, which is always an issue of embodiment as much as it is a rhetorical skill. "Find your voice" assumes that what one puts to page is entirely one's own, not conditioned by the world that has formed the self, the history and culture that condition its thought patterns, or what the writer knows about their listeners.

Not all voices can be equally accessed. Constructions like "find your voice" reflect an individualist orientation as it celebrates the under-appreciated heroic genius writer, a writer who is racially coded and gendered, however implicitly. The specter of the genius writer would have us believe that the process of accessing one's born-not-made voice is an innate process, unencumbered by the world. If a writer is minoritized in this paradigm, this minoritization is read as the writer's internal issue, again unencumbered by the world, as it is read as being an issue of "finding one's own voice."

While many writers of varying backgrounds find the discourse of "finding voice" to be empowering, it is important to note also that these discourses can also be felt as pathologizing. To fail to express oneself becomes rendered as a failure in self-actualization; this focus can be marginalizing when it is not accompanied by a deliberate look at the question of recognition—how one not only has to find a voice, but has to be recognized as having found it. To have found a voice is to have found what can be *recognized* as "one's own voice," but this recognition comes from outside, from "those who know," or those who have the power to determine whether the voice has been found. Such powers—whether they come in the form of literary agents, editors, teachers, or readers—can giveth and taketh away, as it were; they make the designation about whether a voice has been found. Such constructions ignore the problematic role of audience in accepting or rejecting a piece of writing as demonstrating "authentic voicing."

McGurl shows that the mandate to "find your voice" becomes weighted "[f]or the ethnically-marked or woman writer ... [for whom] the voice ... might have to be 'claimed' in defiance of the silencing forces of social oppression and cultural standardization."[12] McGurl writes:

> Not ... all identities are equally claimable, an identification with female experience alone ... will not typically succeed in finding a place for a given writer in the high cultural pluralist system, and this is perhaps because, as detailed by Sandra Gilbert and Susan Gubar, 'woman writer' was precisely the category against which modernist authorship had originally defined itself. Without the affective intensities of race and ethnicity, or the prestige associated with aggressive experimentalism ... women's writing ... is apt to be perceived in terms of the middlebrow sentimentality of 'daytime' culture.[13]

The feminized, ethnically-marked, or minoritized writer's claimed voice then becomes, problematically, "a synecdoche for the voice of the (variably defined) social collectivity from which it emerged and into which it feeds back."[14] It is in this context that debates about an author's "legitimate ethnic consciousness" (and, in turn, the potential typecasting and pigeonholing of the woman writer or ethnic author as doing only one thing: representing their group) arise—debates that have been freshly brought to public awareness in a recent National Public Radio (NPR) Code-Switch segment.[15]

The writer becomes typecast if they reflect the essentializing representation of a subject-position or culture as it exists in the popular imaginary, but this typecasting is the only path to legibility when an uncritical readership dominates, a readership that has not self-examined its sexist, racist, ableist, xenophobic, and heteronormative assumptions. The writer becomes typecast by this readership, as the writer is read as possessing an authentic voice. If the writer subverts these essentializing representations, then they risk remaining illegible and not being read at all. This double-bind is created and perpetuated in institutions of creative writing, which do not thoroughly engage the biases of the literary sphere. And this double-bind is embedded in admonishments to "find your own voice." The question should not be whether one's own voice is found, but rather which voicings are possible and for whom. Who has access to which voices? Which voices are recognized by whom? Who and what is silenced, and who stands to gain—who stands to lose—from these regulating forces?

Importantly, the answer to the problems with "find your own voice" outlined above is not to do away with voice altogether. The move toward a "post-identity" poetics, forwarded by both Conceptual and Language poets, among others, carries with it clear blindspots of privilege. As Amy King and Cathy Park Hong have argued, the "belief that renouncing subject and voice is anti-authoritarian" is specious and "clueless that the disenfranchised need such bourgeois niceties like *voice* to alter conditions forged in history."[16] We must keep the idea of voice, but pluralize it, and accompany it with the question of recognition. The concept of a writer's voice requires a corresponding concept of readerly bias. What voicings are possible in the conditions as they stand? How can we describe and make visible the silencings that occur? How can we be vigilant in revealing how power works upon members of the literary sphere? These should be our questions.

The lonely writer

The value of individualism embedded in constructions of the writer's voice extends further as the writer is regularly constructed as necessitating separation from the masses. In Shelley's famous metaphor: "A Poet is a nightingale, who sits in darkness and sings to cheer its own solitude with sweet sounds." Shelley's nightingale-poet is alone—physically, mentally, and spiritually apart from community—he (and I use the gendered pronoun purposefully, reflecting Shelley's language) is overheard:[17] He has auditors who are "entranced by the melody of an unseen musician, who feel that they are moved and softened, yet know not whence or why."[18] Admonitions that the poet should separate himself from society are articulated repeatedly in the Western aesthetic tradition (e.g., Shelley, Schiller, Emerson). This construction brings with it assumptions that the lonely, contemplative writer in his solitude offers more to society than direct community engagement would. This serves to produce a conception of the writer as gloriously alienated, and this alienation is a direct reflection of privilege, tied to the genius writer. "At first, the concept of alienation came from the Romantic artist's sense of his divine mission, and special endowments—his superiority to other men," Monroe Beardsley writes. "Later there was added the sense of being rejected by society, as superfluous in a political and economic system running by its own hard and self-sufficient laws."[19] It is this image of the poet as alienated by society that Charles Baudelaire prized in his representation of Edgar Allan Poe as a quintessential poet. As Vincent Leitch recounts, "Baudelaire was immediately smitten by the image of a poet rejected and misunderstood in his own country."[20]

Discourses of creative writing reinforce the idea of the rogue writer who resists social conformity and mainstream values, saying, as Lopate does in a craft essay intended for the creative nonfiction writer, that "Literature is not a place for conformists." In warning against "try[ing] so hard to be likable and nice, to fit in," Lopate asks writers to construct an *ethos* that does not entirely "fit in" to bland social convention.[21] What Lopate's construction overlooks is how this issue of "fitting in" has different consequences for writers based on subject-position. Lopate presumes a writer who has inherited a sense of belonging. That belonging, taken as a given, enables the departure from convention: the writer can choose to not "fit in" since the writer is already "in." For this writer who already belongs, being a non-conformist is something different than it is for the writer whose belonging is always in question or the writer who persistently experiences microaggressions that render them a second-class citizen. For the writer who persistently experiences microinvalidation—defined by Derald Wing Sue as "communications that exclude, negate, nullify the … thoughts, feelings, or experiential reality of a person"[22]—non-conformity means something different from what it means for the writer who is not harmed in these ways. The field's lauding of the outsider does not consider how this outsider status differs for those who have been subjected to disenfranchisement.

Creative writing upholds a form of privileged individualism that is accessible to those who have inherited a secured status. Captured in the symbol of the "garret" is an imagined writer who is, in Paul Dawson's words, "cut off from society, defending his or her integrity against it, but also is able to observe the world from on high." Dawson continues, "The metaphor of the garret assumes that writing takes place outside society."[23] The garret, as a retreat from the world, functions in a metonymic way to signify the material conditions that allow for what Kelly Ritter describes as "the notion of the author as an entity somehow above the common person … separated from mass society by his or her innate, mysterious talents." Ritter goes on to remind us that this "is a decidedly modern construction that has been supported mightily by the enterprise of (the pay, or by patronage) writers' colonies, writers' workshops, and, ultimately, MFA programs" which—from their marketing materials to their studio curricular structure—serve to reinforce the separateness of the writer.[24] The symbol of the garret has materialized in many structures associated with creative writing: the studio creative writing program, the professorship in the ivory tower, the writer's residency, and constructions of the writer's working space. Each of these structures carries a set of values and assumptions that figure the writing life as a particular kind of life, which is naturalized but is actually exclusionary in its function.

The university, for instance, is sometimes imagined to be a more permanent version of the writers' residency. Indeed, many universities use the formal title of the "writer-in-residence" (and these positions may be found not only in English departments but also in the hard sciences and health professions, such as the Hellman Visiting Artist Program at the University of California-San Francisco Memory and Aging Center). The university is regarded as, in Beardsley's words, "a sanctuary where, away from the politicians, the police, and the money-hungry people, the artist might polish away at his verse, might weigh every syllable (as Flaubert did) to create his finished work of art."[25] The classism in this idea that the writer must be kept away from the "money hungry" is illustrative. The university writer is here imagined to be one who can retreat from society, one who is provided the material resources to carry out the difficult toil of art. The ivory tower—with its so-called town–gown divide—has also been figured as a place that is above the everyday workings of mass society, despite the exploitative labor practices of the contemporary corporate university.[26]

Writers' residencies and colonies likewise provide a physical place for the writer to reside apart from society. The creative writer is thought to require withdrawal from the busy, crowded world of the masses, which the residency provides in the form of quiet for contemplation and meditation meant to foster inspiration. This intention is clear in Hermann Hagedorn's 1921 description of the architecture of the MacDowell Colony. Hagedorn reports, "Mrs. MacDowell determined that the forest solitude which had been an inspiration to her husband should be granted, if possible, to every member of the Colony. [...] Each was given its own corner of fragrant seclusion in the great pine woods; no two were in sight of each others, or, better yet, within hearing."[27]

The necessity of solitude that we find in contemporary representations of the writer is laced through the Western aesthetic tradition from centuries past. The lonely, contemplative writer in solitude offers more to society by being, in Schiller's words, "untainted by the corruption of the generations and ages wallowing in the dark eddies below."[28] Yet writers may have responsibilities to caretake for these generations and ages. We need to reexamine what we have inherited from the aesthetic tradition, the ways that this inheritance shapes what is said in creative writing classrooms and what is written in creative writing craft texts. The presumption that a sustained space apart and structural loneliness are essential to the writer's craft indicates that the field has tied the material considerations of lifestyle to the aesthetics of textual evaluation. In presuming that writing only happens when the writer's life looks a certain way, it becomes clear that the spaces a writer has access to—and the degree to which the writer is able to access solitude—is tied to the field's constructs of literary success. Such assumptions are class-based, and they prioritize the privileged experience, made normative in the constructions of the writer outlined so far, of being exempted from domestic and social responsibilities to one's community. The solitary writer working in the woods has the privilege of being unconcerned with issues of safety, poverty, or access to resources. This writer's enfranchisement is a given, so much so that they do not have to fight to maintain it within society. The lonely writer in the wooded landscape has been afforded privileges that are taken as givens when this representation of the writing life is forwarded.

Leisure and unalienated labor

Embedded in the field's constructions of the writer is an implicit insistence on leisure that enables the contemplative life. The leisure is imagined to be outside of the economic system of exchange, uncorrupted by a capitalist mass-market. In turn, the field's emphasis on craft fantasizes a form of unalienated labor that belongs to the writer-as-craftsperson.

To privilege the writer who is outside the economic system of exchange is to privilege the writer who has access to the resources to sustain this outsider status. This comes with little criticality regarding issues such as poverty, housing insecurity and, food insecurity. A certain bohemian "poverty" may be celebrated in creative writing (the trope of the "starving artist") without attention to the ways that this lifestyle is tied to whiteness and comes with little of the vulnerability that people of Color experience in an inequitable and racist society.[29]

To presume that the "good" or valid literary writer eschews economic concerns is to perpetuate inequity within the literary sphere, which rewards privilege with more privilege: the writer who has the privilege to envision a residency for themselves—the writer who has the privilege to be able to pay the application fee and escape responsibilities to work, family, community to attend—is the writer who is afforded the residency.

Moreover, to presume that the literary writer can avoid economic concerns is to ignore the ways that writers have had to secure their access to the practice of writing by participating in the industry as an industry. Katherine Adams describes women in the late nineteenth and early twentieth centuries who used the economic system as a tool to justify their writing. Demonstrating that they knew their place as "non-authors," these women made their writing practice palatable to a dominant society by making it a form of money-making for the family. These women legitimized their work by identifying writing as an activity that could bring resources to the family, while still enabling their full attention to homemaking.

Contrast this with male-dominated constructions of the ideal literary artist. Whereas the ideal literary artist constructed by male writers such as Tolstoy renounces any financial motive, US women writers in the late nineteenth century used financial need to provide an "excuse or justification for writing and publishing."[30] As Adams explains, "Using financial exigency as a form of protection and legitimacy, these few women writers of the nineteenth century began to occupy an accepted place in society, as modest souls supporting themselves and their families, as 'literary domestics,' a label suggested by literary scholar Mary Kelly in *Private Woman, Public Stage*."[31] Being excluded from the subject-position of the literary writer/author—a subject-position that is constructed as apart from the concerns of the marketplace—these women writers were explicitly putting forward their fiction, articles, and poetry as commodities. Reminding the reader that the woman writes to support her family and not for any other motive, these women were able to justify their texts in a social milieu that would not allow them the status of "author." By explicitly commodifying their texts, these female writers present themselves as not threatening to the status quo.[32]

Today, the field of creative writing reflects the ideal of the writer set apart from consumerism. Except in professionalizing pedagogies of creative writing, discussed below, the question of money-making is beyond the scope of the workshop. The self-sustaining leisure of the ideal literary writer who escapes embroilment in the economic system is coupled with an emphasis on the *toil* and *craft* of the written word.[33] The figure of the literary writer as "Modernist craftsman" (to use Paul Dawson's term, which underscores the masculinization of the writing life) is represented in creative writing's chosen vocabulary. With terms like "craft" and the "workshop," creative writing associates itself with the unalienated labor of the artisan—one who produces something with skill. This is echoed across a corpus of twentieth and twenty-first century craft texts:

"A writer works with his hands." "A writer has the need to groan and sweat over his measures and his rhymes."[34] The labor of writing is understood to be a physical labor of crafting and shaping an object. And to not put in this labor of writing is not to have earned the position of the "writer." In Esther Schwartz's words, from a craft text published in 1936, "There ought to be a law against anyone's calling himself a writer unless he writes fairly regularly."[35] Thus, labor becomes one of the ways that the status of the literary writer is maintained. As R. V. Cassill puts it: "Writing is hard work. [. . .] It always will be. Therefore all the practical details connected with the craft ought to be reduced to system and disposed of with minimal effort."[36] The craft of writing requires a laborious devotion and requires that the writer remove all distractions that would take away from the writing—that is, writing requires a type of leisure that minimizes external demands.

With these constructs comes the idea that only the select few are capable of the exertion that the writing life requires, as Charles Irving Glicksberg asserts in a chapter titled "The Romantic Myth of Inspiration": "The art of writing demands a degree of diligence and devotion which few of the many who are called are capable of sustaining."[37] "Few of the many" are capable of sustaining utmost devotion because their material circumstances prevent it. This is the "problem of living" for the literary writer; the lives of all but the exceptional few are rendered as ill-suited for writing.

Charles Raymond Barrett's 1921 craft text identifies the writer's "call is but a summons to labor—and to labor the severest and most persistent." He continues, "To one who comes to it half-heartedly, illy prepared, shirking its requirements, I can predict certain failure; but to the earnest, serious, conscientious worker, I would say a word of hope."[38] The assumption that the status of the "author" will be granted to those who just work hard enough neglects the many other factors that contribute to the construction of the author, the factors that contribute to one's access to publication, that contribute to how a writer is read and valued in an inequitable and oppressive society, etc. Such discourses of labor in creative writing's tradition perpetuate the myth that authorship can be fairly earned through a meritocracy-based on work ethic.

Such assumptions are not only present in creative writing craft texts; they are also underscored in the existence of residencies like MacDowell and Yaddo. These organizations' marketing materials and foundational missions emphasize the toil that is associated with the writing life. Spencer and Katrina Trask established Yaddo with the toil-leisure dyad specifically in mind, as they write of their reasons for establishing Yaddo:

Those who in working for their art have not laid up material possessions for themselves and those who are starting in life are making a brave fight to guard and augment and meantime earn their bread by labors prosaic and oppressive are so often unable to obtain the rest and refreshment so sadly needed. It is such as these whom we would have enjoy the hospitality of Yaddo their sole qualification being that they have done, are doing or give promise of doing good and earnest work.[39]

The Trasks' remarks demonstrate the value of "good and earnest" work. Society does not adequately value this "good and earnest work" and therefore a retreat must be established that will provide an adequate situation to sustain this work. The Trasks were careful to note in their will for Yaddo that: "We do not intend this as a home for those who would lead a life of Ease." The residency should inspire the hard work of writing. The MacDowell Colony, as another example, is described as "beyond a doubt the worst loafing place in the world."[40] Hagedorn entices the writer by claiming that at MacDowell: "The impulsion to work is in the air. It is easier to work than to resist its persuasive influence." The MacDowell Colony has, since its early years, been advertised as a place that creates a sense of leisure that is conducive to writing: "Peterborough is, in fact, a great place of liberation. There the shackles of ordinary existence are, for a season, removed."[41] The anxiety that the writer's energies will be "frittered away" on meaningless pursuits, when all of the writer's energies are needed for the craft, produces a need for a retreat into a type of leisure, distanced from extraneous demands.

Both sides of this leisure-and-toil dyad in creative writing involve a form of class-based exclusion. On the one hand, the need for a life of leisure limits the ways that writers think about where and how writing gets done; on the other hand, the expectation that the writing life demands complete devotion to the toil of writing craft presumes an "if you just work hard enough" mythology (lore which is pronouncedly called into question by data like that which is provided in the VIDA Count, which shows that hard-working writers do not have equal access to top-tier publications). Such mythology in creative writing excludes writers who may have responsibilities additional to the work they do with their pens. Writing is regularly associated with an escape from what is conceived as the soul-sapping, work-a-day lives of the masses, and thus it becomes difficult to imagine how writing can have a place in a life made up of multiple responsibilities. Such discussions of the writing life naturalize the privileged few as belonging to the literary sphere. Those who can afford to devote themselves to the extreme toil of the craft and exempt themselves from responsibilities and everyday concerns, financial or otherwise, are rendered as the only legitimate inheritors of the writer identity—the only ones who can access the writing life as it has been constructed. Writers are thus silenced by their circumstances in this dominant discourse of creative writing. They are marked as not rightfully belonging to writing because they do not have inherent access to the privileges of the ideal literary artist. They are excluded before they have even begun.

The writer as exceptional

The "problem of living" is a key consideration for discussions of creative writing, because it circumscribes who belongs to the identity of writer. Consider, for instance, two seemingly conflicting passages from Nathaniel C. Fowler's *The Art of Story Writing*. On the one hand, Fowler writes, "So long as this world has a material side to it, and while the possession of money is necessary to feed the material boiler, without which the mental engine will not run, it is well for one to consider the material … before he looks up into the clouds, which, however beautiful they may be, are not sufficient to sustain life." On the other hand, Fowler claims this about the would-be writer: "If he has in him the stuff that authorship is made of, he will win in the end, if he lives long enough."[42] The second claim seems to neglect the first. In the second claim, Fowler forwards an idea of the writer as one who has "the stuff of authorship" naturally born within him. Given sufficient time, no material conditions can stop this authorial interiority from being brought forth. Yet Fowler's prior statement indicates that the writing life is dependent upon material considerations, such as access to adequate funds.

The demands placed upon the writer's imagined material life (e.g., the expectation that the writer will create a life of utmost dedication to the craft for its own sake, renouncing other responsibilities—social, financial, domestic, or otherwise) coexist with conceptions of the writer that promote exceptionalism. Echoing Shelley, William Herbert Carruth lauds the literary writer: "There is no higher office on earth" than that of the author.[43] These may be inspiring words for a reader of a craft text like Carruth's, but they also establish the writer as the very definition of the elite. We can trace this "conception of the poet as a higher order of being" in Longinus' conception of the "great soul"; in Emerson's claim that the poet is "the true and only doctor," is a liberating god; and in many other statements across the Western aesthetic tradition.[44] We can see this conception in "Mallarmé's view that the artist practices a mystery, which cannot be revealed to the masses who are not initiated to its rites."[45] We can find it in Wordsworth's aesthetic theory that puts the poet in the language of the "common folk" with the assumption that the poet will not be inherently among them—that is, the poet will not be a commoner by birth, but will do well to join the commoners, to ethnographically "express himself as other men express themselves" for the good of his work. While some aesthetic theorists believe that all have the capacity to be poets, literary writers are elevated to become greater than human, or most quintessentially human—possessing of a greater capacity to feel[46] and a greater capacity to imagine[47]—making the writer a member of a special class.

Sustained by a belief that some are endowed with exceptional capacities, the elitism of the Western aesthetic tradition's constructions of the writer is evident. To the extent that these constructions of the writer remain operative in academic creative writing instruction, they can serve to marginalize student-writers who do not find themselves reflected in these beliefs about what it means to be a literary practitioner.

Mapping pedagogical constructions of the writer

To gain a clearer picture of how some of these constructions of the writer shape the field's pedagogical practices, we need to account for the different pedagogical schemas that have shaped academic creative writing.

We may take for granted that creative writing does indeed belong in the classroom, but such a premise remains a contested issue in creative writing, even as the field has a presence in many institutions throughout the world. The question continues to be asked: Does creative writing belong in the classroom at all?[48]

The ambivalence about creative writing's place in the academy manifests in a question that has continually preoccupied the discussion about creative writing pedagogy: "Can it be taught?" Indeed, the question traces back to the earliest moments in the Western aesthetic tradition. Horace poses the query: "Do good poems come by nature or by art? This is a common question," he writes.[49]

This question has everything to do with the idea of inclusion in creative writing. At stake in the question "can it be taught" is who is teachable? What does it mean that those who access higher education can also access creative writing? Who belongs to the subject-position called "writer"? If creative writing is a teachable art, then who are its students? Do *all* people have access to the literary arts, to the subject-position of the literary writer? Any attempt at defining an inclusive pedagogy in creative writing must reconcile the history of this line of thinking.

Various answers to the question of who has access to the literary subject-position have been formulated over creative writing's history, and it is essential to mine these answers and examine the pedagogies that have arisen around them. An inclusive creative writing pedagogy is not something that can be painted atop of the field; rather, an inclusive reorientation requires digging into creative writing's roots, exhuming the assumptions about the writer we find there.

Investigating a range of source materials that give evidence of teaching practices in creative writing—including craft texts, archives of course materials, teaching handbooks, histories of writing instruction and examples of pedagogical theory—I find six general creative writing pedagogies that have been formative for the field, and each poses a different response to the questions of "can it be taught?," "should it be taught?," and "who belongs in creative writing?" The following six orientations represent both the means and the ends of creative writing pedagogy: that is, each pedagogical approach is not only a praxis, but is also a justification for why creative writing is a legitimate area of instruction.

Notably, any given example of teaching might incorporate several of these approaches at once. The following list is meant as a heuristic that identifies trends of thought in creative writing pedagogy; it is not meant to reduce the actual practice of creative writing instruction or individual teachers as belonging to one "camp" or another. The list provides context to the discussion of what it means to consider "inclusion" in creative writing pedagogy. Where can inclusive instruction locate itself in the landscape of pedagogical thought in creative writing?

The six pedagogical approaches to creative writing I outline below—progressive, humanist, professionalizing, auditioning, experimental, and therapeutic orientations to the teaching of literary writing craft—each entail a set of assumptions about who belongs to the field of creative writing and what it should teach. The list I outline below is meant to provide a tool for identifying the practices and corresponding beliefs that are mobilized in classrooms today, based on instructors' inheritance of the field's history, which involves these six movements and orientations. This of course is only one way of mapping the pedagogical practices of creative writing.[50]

Progressive pedagogical approaches

Creative writing, as an academic discipline, has origins in progressive education. This pedagogical movement, which began in the late nineteenth century and was promoted by educators such as John Dewey, sought to reform aspects of the classicism embedded in educational practices of the day. Progressive education draws out the creative and expressive capacities of every human. The goal is to use the instinctive creativity of all human beings to further equip a critical democratic citizen. Progressive approaches to creative writing pedagogy rest upon a belief that all people have the capacity for creative expression and that creative writing is an important part of a quality educational experience, which emphasizes critical thought, social responsibility, creativity, and experiential learning.

Progressive education in this regard is to some extent an inheritor of Romanticism, which was to make "genius" the imaginative power available to every poet.[51] This belief that imagination or creativity is common to all was enabled, Paul Dawson notes, "by modern psychology and the concept of the unconscious, which provided the ground for a belief in the latent creativity in every child."[52] The progressive education movement endowed every student with both the right and the ability to express themself. As McGurl recounts, "educational progressivism ... had assumed the inborn presence of an artist in every individual, who needed only to be set free from external constraints to flourish."[53]

The progressive education movement was one of the primary forces that contributed to the growth of creative writing. Creative writing was central to Deweyan pedagogy. As D. G. Myers writes, "Creative writing was perhaps the most widely adopted of the curricular reforms instituted by progressive education; in many ways it was the model progressive subject."[54] Indeed, it was in the Deweyan educator William Hughes Mearns' edited book *Creative Youth*[55]—a book published in 1925 that demonstrated the success of the experiment in "creativist" literary study—that "the phrase 'creative writing' was used for the first time to refer to a course of study."[56] The book had far-reaching influence. Indeed, "little more than a decade after the first news of Mearns' experiment, creative writing had become one of the most popular subjects in the curricula, receiving the official sanction of the National Council of Teachers of English."[57]

In 1894, Dewey joined the University of Chicago where he formed the Laboratory Schools in 1896. During his ten-year tenure at the university, in 1899 he published *The School and Society,* which advocates that a child's "capacity to express himself in a variety of artistic forms"[58] be fostered and developed in the school setting. By 1903, the so-called "Chicago school" was firmly established as an influential pedagogical force, emphasizing the role of self-expression in experiential learning.[59] This individualist strain of progressivism that "held neoromantic or 'expressivist' views of writing instruction ... began just after the turn of the century and continued through many versions to the present."[60] Progressivism, despite its stereotypes,[61] was not an inclusive pedagogy. "Like other whitesteam thinkers," Sandy Grande writes in *Red Pedagogy*, "Dewey's vision for an educational system presumed the colonization of indigenous peoples." Grande cites Katharyne Mitchell who analyzes Dewey's use of the term "frontier" as a "metonym" for the expansion of democracy.[62] These constructions are part of creative writing's history.

The belief that "anybody can write" is not necessarily inclusive of actually *anybody*, and it is not necessarily coupled with the claim that writers can be taught. Indeed, Mearns, as a figure of the progressivist education movement, believed that although we all have the capacity for writing, writing cannot be taught. In his words, writing "must be summoned from the vasty deep of our mysterious selves. Therefore, it cannot be taught; indeed, it cannot even be summoned; it can only be permitted."[63] These progressivist claims continue to hold sway in creative writing. We see Mearns' influence, although it is not acknowledged as such, in Colin Bulman's more recent claim, "I do not think we so much teach students *how* to write as encourage them to use a potential they already have and which has germinated from the reading they have done since infancy."[64] The progressivist philosophy that combined a belief in the generalized, inborn capacity for creative expression with a desire to see creative writing practiced in the schools is one instantiation among many of creative writing's deep ambivalence regarding the question: "Can it be taught?"

Humanist pedagogical approaches

Attacks on the progressive claim that "anybody can write" helped to establish an exigency for humanistic creative writing instruction that fostered standards of literary taste. Humanism crafted a response that reseated standards as central to the curriculum. Indeed, one of the landmark books of the new humanism in creative writing is a text by Norman Foerster titled *Toward Standards* (1928).

Representative of this shift, Carruth's 1934 craft text complains that:

> Poetry is the only art for which no definite preparatory training is deemed necessary or even desirable; at least this seems to be the warrantable inference from our school curriculum. The musician, the painter, the sculptor, must usually go through a long and more or less systematic apprenticeship or novitiate. They find schools and academies established for their better training. [...] The

acquisition of a style in language is as distinct and difficult an art as any other. But while a master like Stevenson spends half his life at developing a good style even in prose, it is a common assumption of the uninitiated that 'anybody can write,' or that a style is a 'knack' to be acquired by a few months' experience. . . .[65]

Dedicated US arts schools for sculptors and painters were available by the nineteenth century. The type of instruction Carruth favors would teach students the difficult art of writing, while also instilling a sound judgment of what constitutes quality literature. Carruth's argument soon became moot, with the rapid proliferation of graduate-level creative writing programs in the second half of the twentieth century, beginning with Iowa's establishment of a degree in creative writing in 1936.[66]

Under Foerster, the University of Iowa began to accept the creative dissertation, which was to demonstrate literary study in a way that paralleled the critical dissertation. Foerster's curriculum was designed to put creative writing in service of literary study, as was the case in both of the earliest PhD programs in creative writing—the programs at Iowa and at Denver University. The humanist approach of Denver University's creative writing program, which was founded by Alan Swallow in 1947, is exemplified in a 1972 flyer advertising the undergraduate creative writing program:

> The program is designed for the student whose primary interests are the study of literature and the act of writing. The student who completes the program will not necessarily be a successful writer, but he will have a fuller understanding of the nature of the creative act and a sharpened awareness of the critical act; hence, he will have a better grasp of the nature of literature. Though the program is not designed in explicit ways as a vocational program, it does provide the background for careers in such fields as editing, freelance writing, public relations, communications and teaching. Most importantly, however, it is our hope that this program will develop in large measure each individual's mastery of his language. We believe such mastery is essential to the civilized man.[67]

The humanist orientation emphasizes the critical acts and literary appreciation that are "essential to the civilized man." A humanist pedagogy of literary appreciation tends to privilege reading over writing and tends to imagine an ideal subject of a "cultivated human" with refined tastes, rather than a "recognized author" with a long publication record. As Sharon Crowley explains, "The point of a humanistic education, after all, is to become acquainted with the body of canonical texts that humanists envision as a repository of superior intellectual products of Western culture."[68] Humanist approaches understand creative writing instruction to be an opportunity to study literature as a mode of aesthetic and spiritual cultivation, claiming that creative writing is a worthwhile endeavor because it produces more refined citizens with a more thorough understanding of literature. Within humanist pedagogies, students learn to write as a means of achieving a refined aesthetic taste, spiritual sensitivity, and cultivated judgment. They seek the "best that has been thought and said." From this belief that literature is a means of spiritual cultivation comes a faith in the inherent goodness of the literary word, which we see in Smock's 2007 article for the AWP *Writer's Chronicle*. Smock insists, "We can trust poetry." And he quotes Mary Oliver, claiming that: "No poet ever wrote a poem to dishonor life, to compromise high ideals, to scorn religious views, to demean hope or gratitude, to argue against tenderness, to place rancor before love, or to praise littleness of soul. Not one. Not ever."[69] The optimism of such a view is beside the point: the devotion to literature as a spiritual good remains an important assumption of creative writing. May Sarton goes so far as to assert that poetry is "holy."[70]

Under humanists like Norman Foerster, creative writing set to the task of fostering the becoming of persons—over the coming-to-fruition of the literary calling. As D. G. Myers puts it, "The aim of a humanistic education was to produce human beings, not poets. It wasn't adverse to producing poets, but in the humanistic order of things one became a poet in order to become a more complete person, not the other way around."[71] A humanist approach to writing instruction puts writing in the service of living better with a more enriching understanding of the world. Within the humanist paradigm, it is literary appreciation—not the production of great literature—that can be taught, and its teaching is nothing short of a gift to humanity.

Humanism, this "bourgeois project of self-improvement,"[72] in which "ethical instruction was conducted under the pedagogical heading of taste,"[73] pursues a particular kind of social and cultural capital as it affirms its ideal subject-positions. As Crowley notes, "humanism has tended to be an exclusive educational tradition, insofar as the humanist impulse is to impart instruction to a select few who are considered able to inhabit a humanist subjectivity."[74]

Professionalizing pedagogical approaches

Beginning in the 1940s, more academic programs in creative writing began to emerge. Some of these shifted away from the humanist goal and instead considered graduate education as a form of professional development and preparation for the vocation of writer. Once considered a professional-vocational course of study, McGurl writes, creative writing's "sponsors and practitioners began to care more for the quality of the works created than for the quality of the educational experience of which they are the occasion."[75] Rather than provide a particular educational experience to prepare citizen-subjects, professionalizing programs sought to foster the cultural capital entailed by a publication record, a strong network of fellow writers, connections to the publishing industry, and professional experience with literary editing. Professionalizing approaches seek to equip students with writing and creative skills that will prepare them for industry—whether the publishing industry, professional writing, gaming, digital storytelling, film and TV, marketing and communications, or any other.

Professionalizing programs may be closely aligned with visual arts and graphic design, journalism, and communications departments, as well as computer science programs. They may be part of interdisciplinary programs in creative studies or writing practices. Or they may be stand-alone programs that emphasize professional development in some way. Stephanie Vanderslice's *Rethinking Creative Writing*, for example, provides a number of case studies of professionalizing programs in creative writing.[76]

This professional orientation for creative writing has been with the discipline from the start. It is an orientation exhibited in some of the earliest creative writing craft textbooks.[77] At the turn of the century, the profession of "writer" was becoming established in America, and this provided a reason to offer advanced professionalization in writing at Harvard and other universities.[78] As Adams writes, "Creative writing may have been recognized as an academic specialty because its practitioners could earn a living by 1900."[79] With the writer profession came the emergence of associated occupations—such as the literary agent[80]—and trade publications intended for writers: for instance, *The Writer* magazine was established in 1888.

Professionalizing approaches tend not to regard literary writing as exceptional, but rather provide practical instruction on writing as a marketable skill among skills. Some professionalizing approaches may be less concerned with maintaining hierarchies of "high" vs. "low" art, and instead seek to provide student-writers the potential for wage-earning careers in the craft of writing. As such, professionalizing approaches hold that writing can be taught broadly, as a specialized but not exclusive skill. It is a skill that belongs not to the geniuses among us but to the practitioners.

This calls up what Clint Burnham calls "the subjectivity of the poet as bourgeois artist"[81]—the artist who is imagined as a producer, writing for a specific market. The skill of being able to produce pleasurable commodities that are considered beautiful is one that, according to Daniel Pink, is becoming more marketable. He writes in a *Harvard Business Review* article titled "The MFA Is the New MBA": "An arts degree is now perhaps the hottest credential in the world of business. [. . .] [T]he master of fine arts is becoming the new business degree."[82] The employers who value the MFA as a credential imagine that the MFA identifies the degree holder as a particular kind of person—an artist who is able to creatively appeal to the consumers of her craft. Seeing this crossover between the MFA and MBA, one may speculate, along with Mary Ann Cain: "Perhaps it is no coincidence that the expansion of MFA programs in creative writing came at roughly the same time as the rising popularity of MBA."[83]

Auditioning pedagogical approaches

Auditioning approaches are interested in assessing, whether implicitly or explicitly, who among a body of students are primed to become the best writers of the next generation. Rather than provide a generalized educational experience to prepare democratic citizens, cultivated readers, or industry professionals, auditioning approaches seek to be a clearinghouse where the "talented" earn recognition and access to the literary sphere. These orientations prioritize the production of great works of contemporary literature. The production and preservation of literature as a unique aesthetic form is primary in this orientation, as it sustains a restricted definition of the "great."

Within the auditioning approach, the university MFA program is conceived as an opportunity to, in Jesse Lee Kerchval's words, "share an elevator with someone famous for a little while"[84]—to be in the presence of greatness and to find out if one has that quality of greatness as well.

While both the professionalizing approach and the auditioning approach centralize the production of texts, auditioning approaches resist some aspects of the professionalizing orientation. Auditioning approaches may be characterized by an assumption—inherited from the aesthetics of Emerson, Schiller, and others—that the artist must be set apart from the trappings of the commercialized world, from economic concerns, and from the realities of mass society. Stephanie Vanderslice elucidates the divide between the artistic life and the practical/professional life, as it has been constructed in the popular imaginary and manifested in creative writing pedagogy. Drawing from Carol Lloyd's *Creating a Life Worth Living,* Vanderslice explains,

Western culture tends to hold a narrow, either/or conception of the artist's life. Either we spend our days painting masterpieces . . . or we abandon our creative needs for the 'practical' livelihood our parents warned us we'd need to fall back on. Largely because of these parental admonitions and black-and-white cultural expectations, we rarely explore the area in between.[85]

The anti-commercialism of the auditioning approach can be linked with conceptions of the writing life as a life of leisure.

Courses and programs that take an auditioning approach may not advertise themselves as such, since a program's branding is meant to attract prospective students and cast a wide net. But within the walls of a classroom, the auditioning approach becomes evident as teachers feel greater responsibility to engage those writers who show "promise," and unevenly distributed institutional support goes to those writers who are determined best among their peers.

Experimental pedagogical approaches

An experimental approach to creative writing—which may be variously known as innovative, avant-garde, etc.—favors teaching that manifests the unpredictability, specificity, and vigor of art. Pedagogical form reflects artistic form in this sense. Messages about an artistic mindset are embedded in pedagogical craft.

Craig Dworkin describes what he calls a "mycopedagogy"—using the prefix "myco" for its connotations of the slippery and the combinatory—to describe a "mode of teaching that itself has learned from literary innovations." He explains, "If avant-gardes are not, in the end, 'always pedagogical,' they can indeed present a challenge to the modes of communication at play in the classroom, and they can provide a model of how a truly radical pedagogic practice might more successfully correspond to the theoretical critiques offered by recent trends in the study of . . . teaching."[86] This pedagogy responds to the fear that experimental literature "will be taught with an inadequate pedagogy: that it will be familiarized, domesticated, inoculated, neutralized, and counteracted—in short: professed."[87]

Dworkin's key reference points in articulating this theory are John Cage, for his own experimental pedagogy, and recent theorists in rhetoric and composition including Victor Vitanza, Gregory Ulmer, Geoffrey Sirc, Thomas Rickert, and Paul Kameen. Little attention is paid in these theorists' work to the embodiment of a teacher and how positionality matters. The writers of these pedagogical approaches typically have an embodiment that is already associated with "one who professes," so they have access to thinking beyond this form of authority.

The specter of the literary "genius" who violates norms is present in this pedagogical orientation, a figure made popular in the Enlightenment period in western Europe. The genius, in Alexander Pope's words can "snatch a grace beyond the reach of art."[88] In the *Spectator,* Addison lauded "the production of a great genius" and found that the "many lapses and inadvertencies" that might characterize a rule-breaking work of genius "are infinitely preferable to the works of an inferior kind of author, which are scrupulously exact and conformable to all the rules of correct writing."[89] It is this image of the poet as subversive agent that Charles Baudelaire prized in his representation of Edgar Allan Poe as a quintessential poet. Such is the power of this image. Yet the image is eminently white, masculinized, and class-based. Because of inequities that are intersectional in nature, writers do not experience rule-breaking in the same way. Those whose circumstances offer the most security and privilege have less to lose in breaking the rules and are less likely to have their conduct policed.

Experimental approaches take seriously the idea that in the literary realm, "To succeed beyond mere adequacy," Katherine Coles notes, there is an expectation that one "must finally escape, not adhere to, our prescriptions and proscriptions."[90] This is what might be called the paradox of the "rule of the non-rule" in creative writing. The Poundian-concept-turned-workshop-cliché "make it new" is an imperative to break established imperatives. The writer receives the mandate to break the established mandates of craft. In adopted craft principles such as "make it new," institutions of creative writing serve to conventionalize unconventionality.[91] In other words, creative writing is the *institutionalization of anti-institutionality.*[92] This paradox can help to shed light on the apparent contradictions in representations of the creative writer. On the one hand, the creative writer is a vanguard artist who bucks "the system" in order to emancipate his imagination; simultaneously, the creative writer is disciplined in a workshop community that favors a particular workshop aesthetic. Experimental approaches seek to reconcile these two sides of creative writing's coin by making the workshop aesthetic itself experimental, and layering this experimentation into pedagogical practice.

Experimental pedagogies open up the performance of art in the process of making. They make creation, in all its startling messiness, the focus, providing an enactment of the mind at work. Art comes into the classroom in the process of its unfolding. This might include deformative criticism, alternative "wreading" (to use Charles Bernstein's term), or unconventional forms (e.g., writing on "sex dolls, mice, and mother's suitcase"—as Derek Owens describes of his class).[93] These experimental approaches are interested in art as an immersive experience that should shape what happens in a classroom, if the walls of the classroom remain intact at all; these approaches defamiliarize the conventions of academe to the extent that the teaching may parody other forms of instruction and the space where work is done may be a distortion of the conventional classroom.

Therapeutic pedagogical approaches

Therapeutic approaches, sometimes eschewed in academic circles, represent another significant orientation of creative writing pedagogy. Therapeutic pedagogies see creative writing as a means of healing. These pedagogies may borrow from scholarship about art therapy, with the goal of using writing to achieve self-awareness, health or empowerment. Representative works in this orientation include Louise Desalvo's *Writing as a Way of Healing*, Geri Giebel Chavis' *Poetry and Story Therapy: The Healing Power of Creative Expression*, Deborah Philips and Liz Linington's *Writing Well: Creative Writing and Mental Health*.[94] The therapeutic mode extends beyond books that have explicit titles regarding the intersection of art and healing, however. Jim Collins' study of contemporary reading practices finds that literary reading in popular culture has become "a sophisticated form of self-help therapy."[95] He finds "early nineteenth-century notions of reading as self-transformation" to be still prevalent in popular book clubs, like Oprah's.[96] Creative writing has been correspondingly influenced by these trends. Some writing texts—such as Goldberg's *Writing Down the Bones*—have been identified as belonging to the genre of self-help, read by writers and non-writers alike, for reasons that may or may not have to do with the production of circulating literary texts. Some use such texts as a means of generating writing for the self, rather than writing for readers.

Locating craft texts in the genre of self help is not a new phenomenon: D. G. Myers claims that craft texts written by women writers in the 1930s and 1940s would "now be shelved among the self-help books."[97] Myers is here referring to texts such as Marguerite Wilkinson's *The Way of the Makers* (1925), Adele Bildersee's *Imaginative Writing* (1927), Dorothea Brande's *Becoming a Writer* (1934), Esther L. Schwartz's *So You Want to Write!* (1936), Margaret Widdemer's *Do You Want to Write?* (1937), and Brenda Ueland's *Help from the Nine Muses (If You Want to Write)* (1938).[98] Several of these women—Bildersee, Brande, Widdemer, Ueland—taught college-level writing.[99] Creative writing was an important site where many women were afforded access to a profession, and that access sometimes came through the justification of writing as serving a purpose of self-betterment or well-being.

Adams identifies how creative writing provided a gateway to the academic sphere for women as, in the first two decades of the twentieth century, a high percentage of women's colleges offered creative writing,[100] and by 1930 around 45 percent of American colleges had at least one creative writing course, with many of them offering two or three on different genres.[101] In a complementary study to Adams', Kelly Ritter notes that the type of academic work that women did in creative writing was in "sharp contrast to the negatively feminized work in rote theme correction for composition." Ritter continues that "creative writing opened the door for women to be not only *teachers* of writing (in the classroom, or in the home), but also *producers* of literary work—ergo *art*—themselves, and to be recognized both inside and outside the academy for their pursuits."[102]

Therapeutic approaches to creative writing pedagogy have been important in opening the field to not only women writers. A therapeutic orientation to creative writing aligns with approaches that prioritize self-actualization and empowerment. These methods can be politicized in certain spaces, to work toward social justice. The Austin Project, for example, centers the experiences of writers of Color, women writers, transgender writers, and gay, lesbian, bisexual writers by focusing on truth-telling that is at once empowering, healing, and affirming. The workshop exists to dismantle racism as it also invites participants to open the self, "going in deep, articulating, and returning. The writer's job is to *feel*," the organizers of the Austin Project write. The Find Voice circle and workshop provides "help, support, and nurturing in this process."[103]

Therapeutic approaches to creative writing have something to offer an inclusive pedagogy, which should be inclusive of the whole self. A holistic approach to creative writing accounts for the body, for spirituality, for emotion because all of these parts of the human condition are at stake in an oppressive system. We should pause when therapeutic approach to creative writing are generalized and demeaned, as they sometimes are in academic circles. Certainly therapy requires a specialized skillset that is not necessarily part of the creative writing instructor's expertise, but this pedagogical orientation can be a compatible framework for the teacher who seeks an inclusive model.

Elitism in creative writing

As each of these pedagogies has been important to the formation of creative writing as an educational enterprise, each of these pedagogies also can carry conservative, deleterious, and exclusionary features. There is the "the essentially conservative and didactic mission of humanistic [approaches]: to honor and preserve the culture's traditionally esteemed objects … and to illuminate and transmit the traditional cultural values presumably embodied in them."[104] There is the inherent colonialism of progressive approaches, as discussed above. In addition, those pedagogies that elide concerns of professionalization may assume privilege where material needs and employability are not of concern— failing to acknowledge that: "There are economic conditions for the indifference to economy."[105] On the other side, the professionalizing approach can too easily take the economy and salability as a basis, without offering students a criticality toward the destructive and ruinous results of capitalism and without offering the tools for an art-activism that intervenes.

This schema of six common pedagogies—each uniquely instrumental in the emergence of the field of creative writing in the twentieth century—provides a heuristic for analyzing some of the controversies that continue today in discussions of creative writing instruction. For instance, when, as McGurl notes, "the usual insults hurled at the creative writing program stem from the rejection of the value, even the possibility of, a general human creativity,"[106] we can see how these hurled accusations might emerge from an auditioning orientation that believes creative writing exists to lift the genius figure out from the masses.

As we trace the histories of these pedagogical orientations, we can see ebb and flow, a kind of seesaw motion, moving between populism and elitism. From creative writing's roots in progressive education, we can trace the idea that all humans have a generalized capacity for creative writing, that "anyone can write"—a view that is emphasized in several craft texts from the 1930s and early 1940s.[107] This is countered with a tradition that upholds literature to be the best of what is thought and said, as determined by those who are imbued with the authority to make this designation.

Is the writing of literature like any other skill, or is it unique and preserved for the worthy few? Does literature belong to the many or the exceptional? Is literary writing an inherent or learned ability? Or is it that, in Paul Engle's memorable and place-based words, "good poets, like good hybrid corn, are both born and made."[108] Does creative writing exist to cultivate taste, or are all forms of creativity equally valuable? Should the literary writing apprenticeship be available to all or to only the talented few?

Table 1.1 schematizes vacillating views regarding these questions. Each row represents a spectrum of thought with two opposing poles, with the left column representing more populist orientations and the right column representing

Table 1.1 Spectrum of perspectives in creative writing pedagogy

Generalist:	*Exclusivist:*
Everyone should have access to creative writing instruction.	Only the talented should have access to creative writing instruction.
Writers are made.	Writers are born, not made.
Democratic:	*Selectivist:*
Anybody can write.	Only the genius can write.

more elitist orientations. Of course, this schema is an oversimplification and is meant only as a resource for tracing tendencies in creative writing's pedagogical thought.

Notably, each line of thinking entails a different situation for creative writing in the academy. Nancy Welch's 1999 article "No Apology: Challenging the 'Uselessness' of Creative Writing" is an example of a pedagogical argument that advocates the generalist perspective. Welch's article describes her "English 252 Introduction to Fiction Writing" course, which fulfills an intermediate-level composition requirement for students in education, criminal justice, and nursing at a large Midwestern university. She advocates courses that promote creative writing across the curriculum.[109] Likewise, Hans Ostrom in "Undergraduate Creative Writing: The Unexamined Subject," argues that creative writing should be an essential part of the undergraduate English curriculum as it enables students to make use of multiple genres, styles, and codes as well as assimilate other subjects and improve reading abilities. He contends that: "Creative writing should, in fact, be central, not peripheral, to an undergraduate education. It should be thought of as a course from which many different kinds of students can benefit, not as an eccentric course for counter-culture students, nor as a course for the gifted."[110] For Ostrom, creative writing can be a course utilized by students from across the disciplines, much like composition. It can be a practical course of study for students with any career track in mind.

The exclusivist rebuttal to such proposals is, of course, that literature is a special type of writing, and only a special few are able to produce the genuine thing—a view that is expressed by creative writing instructors such as Doris Betts, who emphasize a concern that "once 'everybody's doing it [creative writing],' perhaps nobody will do it very well."[111] Notably, this exclusivist position was in creative writing discourse before "everyone was doing it" via the proliferation of MFA programs. Fowler's 1913 craft text bemoans, "Thousands of would-be writers believe that they have been called to write fiction and they write; and occasionally gain the appearance of success."[112] Fowler warns his novice readers, "The mere call to write should not be considered as *prima facie* evidence of literary ability, until the call comes from several disconnected directions."[113] The novice writer, Fowler advises, needs to be sure that she is the right type of person, that she is truly *called* to the vocation of the literary writer. Contrast this construction of the writer—as one with a lofty, spiritual "calling"—with the arguments that try to generate broad participation, to get more people writing, to encourage community literacy as a form of empowerment.

Ostrom, as an advocate of the generalist position, counters the exclusivist claim: "I don't think there was ever a time when writers did not feel that there were too many other writers, and the 'creative glut' prejudice simply uses creative-writing courses as a convenient scapegoat."[114] The exclusivist claim emphasizes the gate-keeping role of creative writing instruction—"holding the masses back from storming the garret doors" to use Vanderslice's apt phrase.[115]

Several permutations of pedagogical thought in creative writing cross between columns. The selectivist claim that only the genius can write may coincide with the generalist claim that everyone should have access to creative writing. Whether writers are born or made is almost beside the point within humanist pedagogy, since humanist approaches aim to produce not writers but cultivated citizens who can appreciate literature. In the humanist orientation, the selectivist claim may coincide with the generalist claim that everyone should have access to creative writing instruction, since that instruction fosters literary understanding more than it aims to produce the figure of the genius writer.

Take the example of Ron McFarland's "Apologia," cited as the sole creative-writing-focused article published in *College English* in the nineties. Countering the common exclusivist lament that broadening access to MFA programs damages the art, McFarland argues that the institutionalization of creative writing does no harm because it does not "make people into writers." Creative writing instruction can only impart craft, McFarland claims, and craft is only one of the "five essentials of a serious writer"—the others being desire, drive, talent, and vision. Of these five essentials, "only craft can be taught."[116] Craft, McFarland assumes, is a skill that can be acquired through formal instruction, whereas the other four essentials are innate or otherwise acquired characteristics of the artist-as-subject. The generalist claim that "everyone should have access to creative writing" can coexist with the selectivist claim "writers are born, not made" in McFarland's argument. Open-access creative writing instruction is not deleterious for McFarland because he believes writers are born and not made.

Similar to McFarland's assertions, Dave Smith, who served as chair of the Writing Seminars at Johns Hopkins, offers this response to the question: "Can it be taught?":

> Writing can and always has been taught. One may teach both the forms and formulas of literature. One cannot teach how to write masterpieces of great art. Art history, art appreciation, and studio instruction teach a great many valuable things about painting. There has never been a course which could teach even the most talented apprentice to be a Michelangelo.[117]

The genius artist will be a genius artist regardless of whether he enters the classroom, Smith and McFarland claim. While appearing to give everyone access to artistic production, the creative writing course, as Smith conceives it, actually maintains the divide between literary genius and the formula-following student who can be taught only how to *judge* great literature, not how to make it.

The classroom in these constructions has no ultimate effect on literary *production*. Rather, the creative writing classroom, in Smith's view, is well equipped to teach *appreciation* to the masses. If creative writing teaches only appreciation, then a generalist view can coexist with the selectivist position that only the genius can write. In this case, everyone should have access to creative writing instruction—not to produce literature themselves but to appreciate the genius of others. A diagonal line is drawn to represent this view (See Table 1.2).

This is a way of schematizing creative writing's deep ambivalence regarding the question: "Can it be taught?"—a question that has continued to preoccupy creative writers throughout the history of their presence in academe and continues to be in the conversation. The vast majority of discussions of the teaching of creative writing at some point mention this question of whether creative writing can be taught; it is the most discussed question in creative writing's pedagogical literature. It is a question that reveals assumptions about the writing life and the

Table 1.2 Views that cross the spectrum of perspectives in creative writing pedagogy

Generalist:	*Exclusivist:*
Everyone should have access to creative writing instruction.	Only the talented should have access to creative writing instruction.
Writers are made.	Writers are born not made.
Democratic:	*Selectivist:*
Anybody can write.	Only the genius can write.

writer's subject-position. Each iteration of this objection, D. G. Myers notes, "plays a variation on the late classical aphorism 'poets are born, not made'" which Myers relates to a eugenic "principle of 'hereditary genius.'"[118] Insofar as creative writing's institutional discourses have reinforced belief in this hereditary genius, creative writing has been accused of both elitism and of maintaining an illegitimate place in the academy—after all, if literary writers "can't be taught," what are they doing in the classroom? Creative writing's emphasis on craft can be read as a response to this situation. Defined as a body of recommendations for how to write literature well, formalized "craft"—codified and circulated—may be understood to be a means of at once democratizing and disciplining the identity of the writer. Craft is that which is accessible and "teachable" in creative writing.[119] It is also what McGurl calls a "disciplining of the egoistic authorial self with the whip of impersonal narrative form."[120]

These debates in creative writing are far from settled and they continue to shape students' experiences in literary writing classrooms. Emerging from this history, creative writing faces a key concern: how to reconcile the push and pull of populist and elitist orientations in order to serve the students who come to learn the art of literary writing today.

Exclusionary assumptions about writers and writing

In her 1965 craft text, Rebecca Caudill writes of what she has "paid for the privilege of writing."[121] Caudill constructs an idea of a writer as one who pays a material price to be able to practice literary craft, to be able to identify as a writer. It is perceived to be a high cost for this woman writer, as the title of her book—*The High Cost of Writing*—indicates. She uses the metaphor of a "coin" to describe what she has given up and what she has had to do in order to gain an identity as a writer. What has too often gone unacknowledged in creative writing is the high price our students might likewise be paying—not only in terms of tuition dollars but also in terms of cultural inheritance. Creative writing asks students to quietly adopt a set of often unspoken norms about what it means to be a writer. These norms keep a privileged group at the center of the creative writing class while naturalizing the hierarchy. In turn, the full diversity of the literary landscape remains unacknowledged by the field's entrenched prejudices.

The aesthetic traditions and pedagogical assumptions outlined above indicate how individuals come to assign meaning and value to the writing life and how they come to recognize themselves as writer-subjects. The constructions described here constitute the games of truth by which writers perceive themselves against the forms of subjectivity that have been made valid by the circulation of these discourses. The production of the literary text is always bound up with the practices of the self that this chapter describes.

These practices of the self are coupled with the continually preoccupying question of "Can it be taught?" In the next chapter I examine another side of this question: the question presupposes a standard of literary production that teachers and students are working toward. The "it" we find in the question "Can it be taught?" is a certain standard of what constitutes valid literary writing. This "it" is the focus of the next chapter, which seeks to uncover the exclusionary assumptions about literary value that circulate in the creative writing classroom. The assumptions about literary texts outlined in the next chapter dovetail with the assumptions about literary lives explored above. Together, creative writing's construction of writers and writing serve to maintain a policed sense of who and what can be respected in creative writing. This sense has kept some writers and literary formations pushed to the margins, leaving the field bereft of a robust and diverse conversation about artistic production and the relationship between aesthetics and social responsibility. In order to move toward an inclusive creative writing and a pluralized conversation about literary work, creative writing's uncritical assumptions about writing and writers must continue to be interrogated.

2

Marginalized Aesthetics

We judge their success or failure by how 'good' their work is, without adequately defining what's 'good.' We proceed as if these are indeed 'natural' concepts, without tracing how and why they came into our culture. . . . Because we were among the lucky few to figure things out does not mean our students will benefit from the same painful initiation.

Katharine Haake, "Teaching Creative Writing If the Shoe Fits"[1]

The refrain "Can it be taught?"—discussed from one angle in the previous chapter—is a launching point for another type of interrogation. The question "Can it be taught?" presupposes a standard that teachers and students are working toward: the "it" in the question signifies a certain standard of what constitutes literary writing. This "it"—which may be synonymous with "talent" or "good writing"—is a social construct, yet its specific history and social implications routinely go unmentioned in workshop conversations. This hesitance to discuss the question of value has been identified by Barbara Herrnstein Smith in her 1988 monograph *Contingencies of Value.* Herrnstein Smith theorizes that there is a general tendency in American literary studies to avoid explicitly engaging the "value question."[2] Instead, we expect students to internalize the "it" of our disciplinary taste indirectly through immersion. The work of the creative writing classroom is largely about this disciplining of taste. It is a disciplining that takes place through indirect, but nonetheless powerful, means.

What Katharine Haake calls "poorly articulated, but nonetheless prevalent, standards of 'good writing'" control much of what happens in creative writing classrooms.[3] They govern what can and cannot be said and how texts are read. It perhaps goes without saying that our encounters with stories and poems—in reading and writing—are always influenced by the aesthetic standards we have internalized—aesthetic standards being the principles which govern the choices writers make and the constitutive features of what can be considered an "ideal text" against which we assess writing.

We may discount stories and poems that do not meet our aesthetic standards, failing to consider them thoroughly. All the while these aesthetic standards are cultural constructions that are born out of specific social formations. These aesthetic standards account for some artistic producers, some communities of readers, while dismissing and marginalizing others. Creative writing has established itself as a field by systematically excluding a set of cultural aesthetics, propagating a rigid set of expectations for literary writing that, while rarely directly articulated, affects all that occurs in the literary writing classroom. This policing of taste is one part of how white supremacy within the field is maintained. This chapter seeks to uncover some of the ways that the "perpetuation of white orientation, white narrative, white dominance, white defensiveness" is maintained in creative writing.[4]

The purview and established tastes of creative writing are naturalized in our pedagogical practices—so much so that many instructors recommend activities to improve student writing without defining the successful writing the work is improving toward. When our constructs and assumptions regarding "success" are not made explicit—and when they do not become an area of inquiry both within and beyond the classroom—then the relations of power within literary spheres remain un-interrogated and unchanged. In turn, the circumstances may leave students aware of how they are being impinged upon but unable to speak about these operations in any meaningful way. Tacit expectations and untheorized preferences keep a teacher-centered hierarchy in place in the creative writing classroom, a mainstay of what Kelly Ritter calls "star" pedagogy.[5] The teacher here serves as gatekeeper, protecting and preserving the literary values of the discipline. This teacher's pedagogical practices are discipline-centered, rather than student-centered, and, as Michelene Wandor describes of these pedagogical circumstances in *The Author Is Not Dead, Merely Somewhere Else*: "Untheorised (or, at best, very under-theorised) principles of 'criticism' [are] translated into by turns brutal and patronizing exchanges" in the classroom.[6]

To counter this tendency and to move toward an inclusive curriculum that forwards diverse and versatile aesthetic knowledge and practice, creative writing must transform. Creative writing has not adequately accounted for the contingencies of literary value and the diverse ways in which literary texts are engaged by reader-writer cultures. Instead, it has maintained itself as "a privileged discourse."[7] This chapter calls attention to the policing functions of the academic creative writing curriculum and argues that the field should be reevaluated for its role in teaching students to become cultural producers and to intervene in literary-cultural spheres.

Academic creative writing has "othered" communities of practice and swaths of the literary landscape and, in so doing, has erected itself as a fundamentally exclusionary discipline. To move toward an inclusive creative writing will require excavation of the field's value system. This chapter identifies some of creative writing's "aesthetic others." I historicize the aesthetics of the creative writing workshop in order to reveal the biases and assumptions that remain operative in contemporary academic literary writing instruction. My argument is that the creative writing curriculum has, in effect, policed the student-writer's subject-position through the policing of aesthetics and literary value. I examine three sides of this policing function in turn—the policing of writers' intentions, tastes, and affect—so as to reveal the multifaceted yet intense effects of the creative writing workshop on its participants. All of these forms of policing operate at the level of social identity as they prop up the discipline's prejudices. In turn, the field becomes an unwelcoming place to many students and emerging writers who would seek it.

Policing intention: Polemics against polemics

One of the most obvious forms of taste-policing occurring in creative writing curricula is the policing of intention. Student-writers in creative writing may be discouraged from having an intention for their work at all, based on a rhetoric-versus-aesthetic binary that argues only the former mode of discourse, rhetoric, can be driven by a specific purpose.[8] Student-writers may be discouraged from having an intention for their literary work that is activist in nature. Craft texts' warn against didactic or polemical approaches to creative writing; they warn against explicitly engaging in "political" issues in literary work.

Of course, despite these pedagogical assumptions, there is a preponderance of activist work in our contemporary literary milieu that addresses specific audiences, that seeks to intervene in contemporary political situations, that advocates on behalf of communities. Take #BlackPoetsSpeakOut, for example. Or read the works of indigenous activism that are anthologized in *The Land We Are: Artists and Writers Unsettle the Politics of Reconciliation,* edited by Gabrielle L'Hirondelle Hill and Sophie McCall—a book that interrogates the relationship between "land, the role of the artist and the contested discourse of reconciliation in Indigenous cultural politics" in the context of the Canadian Truth and Reconciliation Commission.[9] Browse the fiction that depicts or responds to climate change (cli-fi), such as the edited collection *I'm With the Bears:*

Short Stories from a Damaged Planet,[10] or the many anthologies of ecopoetics. Consider the articulations of a feminist aesthetics by such writers as Rachel Blau DuPlessis, who observes that "when the phenomenological exploration of self-in-world turns up a world that devalues the female self, ... [the feminist artist] cannot just 'let it be,' but must transform values, rewrite culture, subvert structures."[11] The feminist artist that DuPlessis describes creates art as activism.[12]

The legacies of political art, critical art, awareness-raising art, guerilla art, progressive art, public art, activist art, interventionist art, and socially engaged art are long and proliferating. Yet how often are these histories and movements left beyond the scope of the creative writing class? Looking over even the cursory list above, the need to interrogate creative writing's biases against political writing becomes clear—not only because the examples of activist art-making are many, but also because of the particular privilege that comes with a denial or marginalization of these examples. To ban political writing from the study of creative writing is to potentially silence or ignore the exigencies that give rise to these forms of art-making. The alternative should be that we invite these exigencies into the classroom and ask our students to grapple with the risks and possibilities of art that has a cause.

In creative writing classes, students are often not encouraged to think about a purpose for their story or poem. Class discussions do not ask about a story or poem's use-value, the idea that someone could use a text to do something. D. G. Myers notes in his history of creative writing instruction that creative writing "has acted with hostility toward two different conceptions of literature and writing, which for convenience might be labeled the scholarly and the socially practical,"[13] the useful. Creative writing, as a field emerging in the twentieth century, has a governing ethos that rejects literature as a body of knowledge and literature as a means to an end.

There is a high/low art hierarchy at work in this value system, which stigmatizes certain forms of art. Crowley writes of the stratifying distinctions made between those "who possess the ability to discuss art ... as objects of *taste* from those who treat encounters with them as *useful or moving* experiences."[14] Creative writing craft instruction has tended to maintain an aesthetic perspective that divides high "literary" work from the socially practical—the "socially practical" here being inclusive of works intended to be entertaining and/or informative. This high/low distinction is paralleled by a rhetoric/aesthetic distinction that holds the "appeal to an audience" as to what separates rhetoric from the aesthetic. Myers notes that "Creative writing was formed by amputating 'expression' from a concern with the communication of ideas."[15] The anti-didacticism found in craft-texts, and their legacy in the aesthetic tradition, has been constitutive of creative writing as a field, yet this policing of intention serves to exclude large expanses of literary production, forms of creative work that might ultimately matter most to some of the students who would come to the field.

Countering the anti-didacticism of creative writing, Chris Green argues that "there are no such things as well-written poems, only contingently useful poems and less useful poems."[16] Green defines "use" in broad terms: "We have to be careful not to limit *use* to pragmatic utility," he writes, "but extend our consideration to other varieties: *use* might be pleasure or horror, stimulation or seduction."[17] Herrnstein Smith explains that use-value might be "hedonic, practical, sentimental, ornamental, historical, ideological, and so forth."[18] Her central argument is that "What must be emphasized, however, is that the value— the 'goodness' or 'badness'—of an evaluation … is *itself* contingent." It is a matter "of how well it performs various desired/able functions for the various people who may at any time be concretely involved with it."[19] To eschew this way of looking at texts is to discredit forms of literary writing that have specific intentions behind them, as it degrades the reading practices of many people who come to literature. The disciplinary anxiety over use manifests in formalist, decontextualized approaches to established craft principles that characterize successful literature in the classroom. We may justify these craft principles as being about scaffolding a learning experience: our students need to learn the basics, we say; they need to learn the "rules" before they can break them, before they can critique them. But to take this argument is to fail to interrogate the ways that our craft-based pedagogy has arisen from, and works to sustain, a white-dominated, male-dominated literary culture.

Stephen Dobyns, in the craft text *Best Words, Best Order,* explicitly devalues forms of political art. "We have seen antiwar poems …, radical feminist, black, gay, and Marxist poems," he writes. "Every belief has its partisan art, which either speaks to those already convinced of its truth or bullies those who aren't. The difficulty is that while extreme partisanship is easy to spot, its subtle forms can be insidious. Any kind of bias is a form of partisanship and if it enters the work, it then weakens it."[20] The optimism of the belief in a bias-less writing notwithstanding, Dobyns' view is representative of several thinkers in creative writing's craft-criticism. Warnings against didacticism and politicized or "moral" art pepper creative writing craft texts. Burroway and Weinberg's best-selling craft text *Writing Fiction,* for example, explicitly encourages writers to avoid the political: "The writer, of course, may be powerfully impelled to impose a limited version of the world as it ought to be, and even to tie that vision to a political stance, wishing not only to persuade and convince but also to propagandize. But because the emotional force of literary persuasion is in the realization of the particular," they argue, "the writer is doomed to fail."[21] In warning against this failure, Burroway and Weinberg provide no path for the writer to write with politicized intentions. The political becomes conflated with the propagandistic with Burroway and Weinberg's broad brush, foreclosing the possibility of a political literary art that offers complexity and non-programmatic critique. Surely these warnings against political art are borne of experience with reductive student texts that become "preachy" and flat in their fervor; at the same time, these warnings derive from a long history of aesthetic debate—a history that we should make known to our students and that should ground the craft recommendations we analyze in our courses.

In *Verse Writing*, Carruth describes two opposing pulls in theories of literary art: "On the one hand it has been maintained that the artist must be . . . impelled by love of beauty and the irresistible desire to express it; that he must either be wholly unconscious of any audience and the effect of his outpouring upon them [. . .] This is the doctrine of art for art's sake."[22] "On the other hand," Carruth continues, the artist is expected to "consider the effect of his product upon his fellows; that expression is only rarely and in very limited ways spontaneous, but is largely or chiefly for the sake of communication." In this second paradigm, which Carruth calls "the doctrine of art for man's sake," the artist becomes "responsible for the social influence of his output, and must accordingly calculate the moral value of his work."[23]

Evelyn May Albright, in her 1908 handbook on the writing of the short-story, represents these opposing pulls in other terms. She warns: "The short-story has no call to preach. It does not need to teach a moral truth." At the same time, a story "must never be immoral; and it rarely is quite unmoral, if it is a story worth remembering."[24]

It is worth pausing to trace several centuries of Western, Eurocentric aesthetic history to recall how these two opposing pulls came to be figured in contemporary US creative writing craft texts. As early as the writings of Homer, Beardsley notes, "The functions of poet and seer, or prophet, were already distinguished." Yet these two figures were also at times conflated: "For both the poet and the seer, like the oracle, spoke in heightened language, in words that moved and dazzled, with an inexplicable magic power."[25] The effect of this, Beardsley explains, "was to stamp Homer and Hesiod as wise men and teachers, and to link poetic greatness with epistemic value."[26] The poet becomes linked with wisdom—with the capacity to, as the Horatian dictum has it, "delight and instruct."

This dictum—to "delight and instruct"—is often repeated throughout the aesthetic tradition (along with the rhetorical tradition—Cicero also says that rhetoric and oratory should likewise "delight and instruct"). It is reiterated in works such as Sidney's famous defense of poetry. Indeed, Horace's *Ars Poetica* is a touchstone for poets and aesthetic thinkers, especially in the Renaissance and Long Eighteenth. However, the "delight and instruct" pairing was to see a split that was hinted at even in the Renaissance. Renaissance writers such as Castelvetro "denied explicitly that poetry has the aim to teach, and. . . insisted that pleasure is its sole purpose."[27]

Later, Romantic writers would take up this prioritization of pleasure and delight, rejecting didacticism in poetry. Shelley, for instance, excoriated poets who have "affected a moral aim," claiming that "the effect of their poetry is diminished in exact proportion to the degree in which they compel us to advert to this [their moral] purpose."[28] Having a moral aim diminishes "the poetical faculty" in Shelley's formulation, yet—as he is known for saying—"Poets are the unacknowledged legislators of the World."[29] Poetry strengthens "the moral nature of man," but it does so not through persuading an audience of assured moral directives. Shelley emphasizes that, "A Poet . . . would do ill to embody his own conceptions of right and wrong, which are usually those of his place and time."[30] The poet should neither participate in, nor forward, these conceptions of right and wrong, which are short-sighted and fixed in time and place. Shelley, true to the transcendent subjectivity that characterizes the Romantic period, looks toward a morality that is beyond the here and now.

This sense of a transcendent and indirect moral benefit of art, a morality that cannot be delivered in doctrine, is reflected in several Romantic and pre-Romantic period theorists of the poetic and aesthetic. These thinkers turned away from the given mandate that the artist reflect and reinforce established morals and decorum. Arguing against polemical and didactic poetry, Keats declared, "We hate poetry that has a palpable design upon us—and if we do not agree, seems to put its hand into its breeches pocket."[31]

Creative writing has inherited this legacy of skepticism toward the didactic, a legacy to which many theorists of the aesthetic have contributed. Kant is careful to differentiate aesthetic judgment from ethical thinking. He delineates the ethical, which is *interested*—invested in bringing about certain actions and dissuading other actions—from aesthetics, which are *disinterested*. Aesthetics bring about a certain type of pleasure, enlivening the mind. This type of pleasure is valued by Kant, but differentiated from the values he associates with ethics.[32] Kant's work remains influential in the common rejection of the didactic conception of literature. Literary writing is, in this view, "a good" even as it refuses to teach "the good"—a claim that Schiller underscores as well. He claims in *On the Aesthetic Education of Man* that "if we are ever to solve that political problem in practice, follow the path of aesthetics, since it is through Beauty that we arrive at Freedom."[33] Yet, while the aesthetic, in this conception, is beneficial to the political and moral life of society, it does not directly state political or moral truths. Instead, the poet satisfies "the noble impulses of his heart" by elevating society's thoughts "to the Necessary and the Eternal" and, by his creations, transforms "the necessary and the eternal into the object of [the heart's] impulses."[34]

Inheriting this objection to the Horatian dictum "to delight *and instruct*," twentieth-century craft texts often warn against didacticism in literature. Indeed, even the common workshop mantra "show, don't tell" can be understood to be a form of anti-didacticism.[35] Chekhov's often-repeated statement to his editor—"You are right to demand that the author take conscious stock of what he is doing, but you are confusing two concepts: answering the questions and formulating them correctly. Only the latter is required of an author"[36]—is likewise a warning against the didactic or polemical, an admonition against literature with a cause.

The refusal to instrumentalize art into moral or informative discourse is most famously celebrated by Oscar Wilde and proponents of the Aesthetic Movement and "art for art's sake"—a phrase dating from the nineteenth century. Beardsley explicates the "code of professional ethics" that is embedded in this concept of "art for art's sake": "the demand for freedom from external pressures was a demand for the chance to live up to the artist's own highest obligation, to his art itself."[37] This view prioritizes artistic freedom over responsibility for an artform's effect on the world. It is a view that continues to hold sway in creative writing, and there are identity politics operating here. Indeed, the logic of this "demand for freedom" parallels the "anti-PC" rhetoric of the political right. Do not limit my speech, even if my speech is a form of assault, the logic goes.

The theory of art for art's sake is tied to a white-dominated literary community. Forms of privilege are necessary to sustain this theory of art-making as transcendent, necessary to sustain this prioritization of freedom over responsibility. What gets cloaked as a demand for artistic freedom is actually a "claim that the white imagination is capable of transcendence because it is universal and not engaged and invested in its own identity politics," as Claudia

Rankine notes. This claim is core to creative writing pedagogy, as it stands today, and dismantling it will take deliberate work.[38]

As creative writers, we do well to historicize our value systems, and identify how power and privilege are at work in our positions. This critical investigation is necessary to our work on the page and in the classroom. Rather than putting a series of "dos and don'ts" before our students (e.g., don't write didactic/polemical work), we can identify how our aesthetic values and criteria came to be, who set their terms, and how these values risk keeping some works of creative production on the margins. Anti-didacticism in creative writing is tied to racism and exclusion in creative writing, as it compartmentalizes some forms of literature as "political" and simultaneously sustains a bias that reads writing by people of Color as being always political. Rather than barring activist art, we can help students gain an artistic sensitivity to navigate the problems and potentials of categories of "political literature." A graduate of creative writing should be able to discuss what it means to make an intentional intervention in art and what it means to read forms of literary production as political. A graduate of creative writing should be able to speak to a range of perspectives regarding writerly responsibility, drawing from the craft-criticism and literary output of a diverse body of writers. In turn, our students can learn to write art that makes sophisticated political interventions, art that avoids parroting party lines. The stated warnings against the didactic and polemical in the creative writing classroom are insufficient to providing this artistic education; they serve only to maintain a hierarchical system of privilege in the creative writing, which it is our collective responsibility to dismantle.

Policing taste: Ideologies of craft

As we have seen, creative writing pedagogy remains a conservative force, policing the intentions of student-writers with regards to politicized texts. The prohibition on certain forms of literary art-making serves to maintain a hierarchy within creative writing and regulates the taste of its participants.

That taste is a central, if unspoken, concern of creative writing is an inherited legacy of humanist pedagogies, which forwarded what Crowley calls a "bourgeois project of self-improvement"[39] in which "ethical instruction was conducted under the pedagogical heading of taste."[40] The pedagogical field of creative writing, with fidelity to its belletristic roots, is in large part organized around the regulation of taste. The field keeps certain preferences, assumptions, and subject-positions central while excluding others.

This pedagogy of taste is evident in fiction workshop syllabi that include statements of the unacceptability of romance, science fiction, fantasy, horror, supernatural, mystery, crime, fairy tale, thriller, war, western, or ghost stories, favoring instead "literary" fiction. The poetry workshop has its corollary—rejecting "Hallmark" and Chicken Soup poetry, along with, often, slam and spoken word poetry. The unacceptability of these genres may be explicitly stated or left implicit, but, regardless, a line is drawn to separate "high" versus "low" in literary art, as the field constructs these categories. These assumptions about high versus low art have class-based implications, and they are part of the system of privilege that structures the creative writing curriculum. The policing of taste is one way in which that system is sustained.

Craft, that which the workshop is set up to teach, is a canon of tastemaking principles. As Brent Royster notes, "the emphasis upon style and precise imagery and description [is] ever-present in the creative writing classroom."[41] Saturating the curriculum in creative writing, craft pedagogy mobilizes a set of aesthetic standards that are framed as heuristics for composing and revising literary texts. These standards are promoted as absolutes and definitive of good writing. Adrienne Perry observes, " 'Craft' has become a placeholder for an entire methodological approach to engaging with poetry and prose ... and we accept these modes of analysis without question, without attending to all of the ways they leave us wanting, the ways they have been, are, or may be bankrupt for writers of color, women writers, writers who grew up poor, are poor and working class, queer—i.e., anyone outside of the dominant cultural and economic position."[42]

Because they are presented as heuristics or tools for literary art-making, these craft principles are rarely exposed as principles of taste. Yet their function is clear: even before academic creative writing had established its disciplinary status, craft was trotted out as that which could lead the uninitiated writer to good taste. Evelyn May Albright's *Short-Story: Its Principles and Structure,* published in 1908, warns that, "Good taste cannot be taught outright," but readers can "learn to distinguish readily between the horrible and the pathetic, the ugly and the tragic"[43] by learning *craft*—that which the craft text such as Albright's is designed to teach.

The craft principles Albright's text proffers have changed little in the more than a century since her book was published. Contemporary craft texts present the same canon of principles about plot, setting, characterization, etc.—although contemporary craft texts may be less forthright about the ways that the craft curriculum is designed to reinforce the strictures of taste. This is often left unspoken, but its operations manifest nonetheless. What craft texts best provide is a picture that belies the ideologies of pedagogical creative writing. They are results of—as they are operative in sustaining—the ideology of taste that has been formative for academic creative writing.

R. V. Cassill, in his 1962 craft text, disparages the taste with which students come to the fiction workshop, though he sees some hope in their reading preferences. "Often in fiction classes I have found that the beginning writer will show much better taste and sense in his reading preferences than in the choice of material to be used in his own work," Cassill writes. "He admires and reads with pleasure the fiction of Hemingway and Faulkner ... But lo and behold, when he comes to writing his own first story, some mysterious folly leads him to choose the gaudy, sensational, and unfamiliar subject matter, something snatched from a tabloid or an old-fashioned adventure magazine." The assumptions about taste Cassill makes here have much to do with identity, as two white male writers stand in for "good taste." The "literary" is defined over and against the excesses of sensationalism, which is associated with forms of mass access (e.g., the tabloid or the magazine).

Under the heading of craft, creative writing employs both overt and subtle ways of educating students in this pedagogy of taste. Consider the discussion of the differences between high and low art in more recent bestselling craft texts such as Stephen Minot's *Three Genres* and Janet Burroway and Susan Weinberg's *Writing Fiction*. Minot attempts to do away with the labels "good" and "bad" art, but he quickly replaces them with other value-laden terms for separating high art from low: "sophisticated" and "simple." Minot is likewise uncomfortable, although not consistently so, with the term "literary" as he believes it "seems a bit pretentious when applied to contemporary work."[44] Although Minot claims that the "sophisticated" work is not "better" than the "simple," he clearly upholds a hierarchy.[45] Minot's "seven deadly sins" of fiction and poetry, for example, clearly echo his descriptions of "simple" works. Likewise, Burroway and Weinberg in *Writing Fiction* draw a line between "literary" and "genre fiction," claiming that "literary fiction differs from genre fiction fundamentally."[46] They continue,

> There is a strong tendency—though it is not a binding rule—of genre fiction to imply that life is fair, and to let the hero or heroine, after great struggle, win out in the end; and of literary fiction to posit that life is not fair, that triumph is partial, happiness tentative, and the heroine and hero are subject to mortality. Literary fiction also strives to reveal its meaning through the creation of unexpected or unusual characters, through patterns of action and turns of event that will surprise the reader. Genre fiction, on the other hand, tends to develop character stereotypes and set patterns of action that become part of the expectation, the demand, and the pleasure of the readers of that genre.[47]

While theorists such as Jim Collins warn against "any kind of bifurcation of literary cultures"—as in "Populist Amazon.com vs. Elitist *New York Times*"—because "their respective arenas overlap far too extensively,"[48] creative writing's pedagogical texts tend to maintain this binary. Collins argues that literary culture and popular culture overlap to an extent that they are ultimately indistinguishable. At this moment, in Collins' view, "refined taste, or the information needed to enjoy sophisticated cultural pleasures, is now easily accessible outside a formal education."[49] Nonetheless, creative writing's institutional discourses continue to work to police a binary between the "refined" and the less-than. The contemporary moment has blurred the boundaries between the literary and the mass market, as it has created a situation where many people participate in literary culture as writers, using modes such as fan-fiction to engage with reading experiences as writers. The field of creative writing has yet to fully allow these phenomena to influence its curriculum and teaching practices.

Rather than teaching students to be responsive to a diverse range of aesthetic situations—and to assess and negotiate the complex demands of tradition, convention, innovation, reader-response, artistic intention, and the organicity of texts-in-process—craft pedagogy and its accompanying handbooks exist to teach the conventions of "sophisticated" literature, to use Minot's term—or "good taste," to use Albright's. They forward certain conventions: for instance, Burroway and Weinberg's craft text holds that a plot *must* contain conflict, journey, connection, and disconnection—without critically reflecting on the values embedded in these recommendations and the forms of literature that may be excluded in the canon of craft.

The field's craft texts fail to account for the nuanced situatedness of writing and the contingencies of literary value. They elide the taste preferences, expectations, and use-values of different interpretive communities. They offer no nuanced perspective on the diverse reading practices of multiple discourse communities.

In these craft texts, "the reader" is not investigated as having a particular set of identifications. Rather, the texts call upon a "generic" or "universalized" reader to stand in place of a nuanced discussion of identity; this gesture makes normative what is assumed to be "generic" in the reader—a "generic" that is implicitly raced, gendered, and classed, even as these factors are neglected. Stephen Dobyns, for instance, universalizes poetry's audience as he uses synonymously "the world" and "the reader" when he speaks of how a text will be received, believing that "a poem should address as wide an audience as possible."[50] He ignores the existence of poet*ries* ranging from deaf poetry to the Gurlesque to what Maria Damon calls "micropoetries"—none of which are necessarily designed to reach the widest audience possible, as Dobyns argues all poetry should. Dobyns ignores how writing "for 'anyone who reads me'" must be accompanied by an awareness that, in Nadine Gordimer's words, "'anyone' excludes a vast number of readers who cannot 'read' you or me because of concerns they do not share with us in grossly unequal societies."[51]

Chris Green notes that creative writing assumes a "sublime reader" who is assumed to be white, educated, non-disabled, and middle class. This sublime reader invoked by creative writing's pedagogical discourse reads for craft.[52] Dobyns' conception of writing is evidence of this tendency. In assuming that the craft canon will reach "the widest audience possible," Dobyns' construction of craft makes a set of values normative. These naturalized craft values assume the universal, as they simultaneously occlude how creative writing pedagogy severely limits what can be written and formed within its domain. Thus, craft-based instruction is fundamentally exclusionary. The ideology of craft keeps a certain kind of writing centered in the creative writing class, barring manifold forms of literary production.

Naturalized as they are, these craft principles are presented as objective—as empirical as the craft principles of carpentry: an imbalanced chair will be, by nature, a less useful chair, just as an aberrational plot will be a less perfect plot, as is the supposed "nature of things." In these metaphors, we are made to assume that what is presented as the "craft of narrative" is as objective and universal as a law of physics. This is a maneuver of an ideology of taste which, in Crowley's terms, "assigns socially constructed differences to 'nature,' thus rendering its judgments true, right, and inevitable" as it simultaneously "covers over the real social work it performs, which is to maintain and harden class distinctions" that are represented in the difference between "high" and "low" art.[53] Literary education sustains itself and its biases through these hardened distinctions. It replicates itself by, Herrnstein Smith argues, providing students "with 'necessary backgrounds,' teaching them 'appropriate skills,' 'cultivating their interests,' and, generally, 'developing their tastes.'..." In so doing, "the academy produces generation after generation of subjects for whom the objects and texts thus labeled do indeed perform the functions thus privileged, thereby insuring the continuity of mutually defining canonical works, canonical functions, and canonical audiences."[54]

Creative writing students are asked to display a particular construction of "educated taste," an ability to distinguish between literary discourse and all other forms of discourse. This pedagogy of taste is white-centered and male-centered and class-based, and it vigilantly maintains its biases. In its history, this pedagogy of taste has functioned as "a policing mechanism. It is the means through which young men were taught to internalize the marks and limits of bourgeois subjectivity," as Crowley demonstrates in her study of legacies of writing instruction. "[T]his mark distinguishes him from the others who are not so disciplined, those who are so roughened by toil and hard circumstance that they ignore beauty altogether."[55]

This "pedagogy of taste" also operates as a "pedagogy of shame," which is preoccupied with outsider/insider status. We see this shame manifest when we talk about the "archive consisting of anything we feel guilty not to have read." That which we feel guilty about not having read can be called creative writing's canon, and, as Perry observes, the canon maintains a particular set of literary biases: "[n]early all of these texts we should have read are in English or are English translations in which we gloss over the translator's name and labor."[56]

Creative writing's pedagogy of shame molds workshop cultures, which are known for their competitiveness, a culture that is reinforced as students are sometimes positioned to actually compete for funding and scholarships. They compete not to be most prolific or to engage the broadest audience; they compete to be judged as sufficiently literary, as capable of producing something that will best secure for them the subject-position of "author," as it is constructed by the field. This pedagogy of taste depends upon the status one gains by entering the discourse community of literary writers.

Drawing on Sartre, Tom Kerr explains of the "pedagogy of shame," which he finds endemic in English departments:

> one feels shame only in relation to another who makes or knows the rules—the ideological standard—by which a person is judged, and so it depends on a relational, cultural, *institutional* context. Both Plato and Aristotle understood this perfectly well; the former argued that students in order to learn must first be reduced to a state of shame.... the latter noted that 'once we are on a given level, it makes us ashamed not to be as well educated, say, as the rest are; and similarly, with respect to all else.'[57]

Inheritor of this legacy, creative writing likewise works to police student subjectivity—inducting students to a pedagogy of taste that determines what is required for belonging to the literary community. For example, the academy's "demonization of the marketplace," to use Collins' phrase,[58] makes the question, so often on students' minds, an embarrassing one: How does one write in a way that will sell? How does one write literatures that will matter to the lives of diverse communities? That these questions are embarrassing in creative writing is indicative of the power and force of a pedagogy of shame.[59]

Academic creative writing monitors the extent to which a student is disciplined into the craft canon. Craft, as Jeri Kroll notes, "is often trotted out in order to support a restrictive approach to teaching; a will to disregard theory as well as historical knowledge."[60] "Mastery" of craft is considered reflective of the extent to which the student adequately affirms the value of literary culture as it is constructed in the workshop. This plays out beyond the classroom as well. In the publishing industry, as Collins demonstrates, one of the ways a writer demonstrates belonging to literary culture is to affirm literature as a special form of discourse in the texts they write and publish. Collins finds that award-winning literary texts are likely to embed affirmations of the importance and uniqueness of the literary life in their plotlines or in their characterization. The finding is perhaps not surprising, but it is telling: celebrating the status of the literary community may buy one entrance—and sanctioning in the form of prizes—in literary culture.[61] This is one of several ways that literary culture sustains its own hierarchies, continually replicating itself in the publishing industry, in its award system, and in the classroom. Creative writing students are asked to perform a set of values and align themselves with a set of constructions of the literary. They are presented with performances of the writer-self discussed in the previous chapter—identifications of the writer's lifestyle (e.g., attending a residency to find a "place apart" from common life). These acts of identification also play out in the values these students represent in their written texts.

Institutions of creative writing work to (either literally or figuratively) certify literary writers as being worthy of entrance into the literary community, in some ways similar to the first-year composition course which has historically been positioned to verify that students are deserving of entrance into the academy. What Crowley writes of composition is also characteristic of creative writing's gatekeeping function: "University and college faculty imagine composition as the institutional site wherein student subjectivity is to be monitored and disciplined. The continuing function of the required composition course has been to assure the academic community that its entering members are taught the discursive behaviors and traits of character that qualify them to join the community."[62] Creative writing parallels this in teaching the discursive behaviors and traits of character that define an idea of the literary community.

Of course, creative writing has a very different place in the academy than that of composition, and it disciplines its students in different ways, with different assumptions. Indeed, Susan Miller in *Textual Carnivals* argues that it is because of the existence of composition that "literary authorship could be openly compared to the inadequacies of popular writing and especially to inadequate student authorship. [...] [I]nstitutionalized writing-as-composition could be implicitly demeaned as unequal to writing from the advanced elect."[63] The "good student" of composition, who might be encouraged to send a letter to an editor, is put in contrast with the "advanced elect" literary writer who is sanctioned to publish in forums that are deemed to be "literary." While composition may have a pedagogy of shame of its own, it is unlike creative writing in that it does not uphold the subject-position of the literary writer as an "ideological standard" to the same extent. It is not assumed that first-year composition students are pursuing the ideal subject-position of the literary writer. Crowley puts it this way: "throughout its long history, the technology of disciplinary power that is the universally required composition course has not been considered to produce a postdisciplinary subjectivity that might be called 'the writer.'"[64] When the creative writing curriculum takes up this production of subjectivity, it centers a particular construction of the literary-writer as an exceptional being who produces texts that are exceptional in their "literariness." Even for pedagogies outlined in the previous chapter that have a universalizing belief in the creative capacities of our humankind—that is, even for proponents of the idea that "everyone's a writer"—the exclusive status of the literary text and the literary community is maintained and naturalized. What counts as "literary" still often remains coded to privilege the white, educated, non-disabled, middle class participant.

Creative writing students are asked to identify with a predominant aesthetic that, McGurl observes, "defines itself largely against the cultural forms ... consumed by the lower middle class from whom it struggles to separate itself—sentimental literature, genre fiction, and television."[65] McGurl's observation is exemplified in Burroway and Weinberg's *Writing Fiction*, which demeans writing for television, warning the students who come to their handbook: "The trouble is that if you learn fiction from television, or if the kind of story you know and like best is genre fiction—science fiction, fantasy, romance, mystery—you may have learned about technique without having learned anything about the unique contribution you can make to such a story."[66] Television writing is portrayed as inescapably formulaic and vacuous of unique thematic content, which only the literary writers can bring with their unique voices, provided that these unique voices conform to craft-based standards of literary production.

These constructions of literary vs. television writing are indicative of a larger issue that has been definitive for the field of creative writing: its aversion to instrumentality in the form of entertainment or in the form of rhetoric. Again, as D. G. Myers notes in his history of the field, creative writing "has acted with hostility toward"[67]—writing tied to scholarly knowledge and argument and writing tied to the socially practical uses of leisure, entertainment, escape, or otherwise.

Creative writing operates with what Herrnstein Smith calls the "binarized reifications of 'culture' and 'economy,' their polarized opposition-segregation into separate discourses of value."[68] Associated with "culture" are questions of reputation. Associated with economy are questions of popularity and salability. Many pedagogies of creative writing—professionalizing approaches being the exception—maintain the binary and stay on the side of culture. This culture/economy binary is then paralleled by an aesthetic/rhetoric binary. Myers notes that "Creative writing was formed by amputating 'expression' from a concern with the communication of ideas"[69]—communication between a rhetor and an audience. Rhetorical discourses are instrumentalized and are thus akin to the mass-market paperback which communicates directly to a particular market, rather than being merely overheard by a "literary and little" readership—an audience that is a mere aftereffect of the literary text's life. In these constructions of culture versus economy, literary versus mass-market, and the aesthetic versus rhetorical, we can identify a high/low distinction that separates those "who possess the ability to discuss art ... as objects of taste from those who treat encounters with them as useful of moving experiences," as Crowley observes."[70]

We can look to the biases of the Western aesthetic tradition to better understand this legacy that situates creative writing. A type of misanthropy is threaded through this tradition, manifest in disdain for, and distrust of, the "masses." This tradition regularly constructs the writer as being necessarily detached from society because social influence can be harmful to the writer. Perhaps best exemplifying this anxiety over social influence is Schiller's *On the Aesthetic Education of Man*. In the ninth letter, Schiller writes, "Here from the pure aether of his genius, the living source of beauty flows down, untainted by the corruption of the generations and ages wallowing in the dark eddies below."[71] Genius, it seems, must guard itself from the influences of its surroundings. Schiller is concerned to show the artist how "to protect himself against the corruption of the age which besets him on all sides ... [b]y disdaining its opinion."[72] The artist should become "a stranger to his own century" in order to "cleanse and purify it."[73] Whereas for Plato the poet was a potential menace to society, for Schiller society is a potential menace to the poet. Schiller's view is echoed in Emerson who writes to the poet: "If thou fill thy brain with Boston and New York, with fashion and covetousness, and wilt stimulate thy jaded senses with wine and French coffee, thou shalt find no radiance of wisdom in the lonely waste of the pine woods."[74] The poet will find wisdom in a lonely communion with nature, at a distance from the concerns of common society.

Wordsworth, for his part, is less concerned about the damaging effects of a poet's immersion in society. After all, the poet is a man speaking to men, in Wordsworth's view: "Poets do not write for Poets alone, but for men."[75] This requires that the poet adopt the language of common folk, in Wordsworth's words, "in order to excite rational sympathy, he [the poet] must express himself as other men express themselves...."[76] Wordsworth, as poet, must immerse himself in common life, listening to the speech and observing the lifestyles of the people who exist around him. But that poet is not of the community he documents in his poems. He is ultimately a world apart from the masses. He is fundamentally separate.

We can trace this theme further in "Mallarmé's view that the artist practices a mystery, which cannot be revealed to the masses who are not initiated to its rites."[77] We can find this theme in the use of ecstatic, religious terms for describing literary endeavors (e.g., May Sarton's claim that poets must serve poetry "as a good servant serves his master, must revere and woo it as the mystic reveres and woos God through self-discipline toward joy"), which, as Jim Collins notes, "exemplifies a longstanding tradition of marking culture as a transcendent experience within a profane society, an experience that could be enjoyed only by restricting access."[78] These long-entrenched constructions serve to maintain the exclusivity of the literary milieu, keeping literary culture separate from popular culture and denying entrance to many.

And this is where anti-institutional complaints about assembly-line fiction miss the point. Our primary concern should not be that the new "literary chic" is failing to recognize the unrecognized genius[79] (especially as the genius' unrecognized status is what, after all, defines him and gives him his cachet). Our primary concern should be instead that shared, community-based aesthetics are underrepresented in the creative writing workshop.

Because the creative writing curriculum lacks a thorough or critical engagement with a diverse aesthetic range and a nuanced understanding of how texts move in the world, the student-writer becomes compartmentalized. A writer's sense of belonging comes to be structured around over-simplified notions of what it means to produce a literary text. This should be the lament— but instead the lament more often heard, a la figures such as John Aldridge, is for the rugged individual (read white, male) genius whose authentic self is stripped by the consensus-based workshop. Aldridge's anti-institutional argument is that the glut of creative writing programs produce assembly-line fiction (with its mass production a sign of distasteful populism). The cost of the writing class is the writer's own elite inborn talent. Aldridge stays near the figure of the genius writer, as a "person of natural intelligence or talent" and that of "natural ability"—a usage first recorded in the 1640s. Sharing the etymological root "gen" ("produce") with "genesis," genius is associated with a self-generating power. The institution is correspondingly rendered as that which gets in the way of genius.

Aldridge's critique is by now a common refrain, but it misses the more significant cause for critique: institutions of creative writing are failing to deliver on promises to pluralize the academic-literary sphere in terms of what is taught, who is taught, and what is published. The presumptions behind arguments like Aldridge's are naturalized in creative writing, keeping a particular privileged-individualist subjectivity centered. That which seems most natural stands to be most dangerous as it remains beyond the realm of questioning and criticism. Creative writing's central assumptions have far-reaching effects.

Workshop maxims within the canon such as "show, don't tell" and "your protagonist must want something" are presented as self-evident and stated without regard to the situatedness of all writing and how these statements exclude different aesthetics. The larger aesthetic value systems promoted by such maxims are not examined. Meanwhile, broad categories of writing are demeaned. These categories (e.g., "genre fiction") go unquestioned, even as they are of little use in documenting the actual circulation and use-value of the texts they are supposedly meant to describe.

In the creative writing classroom, a range of literary traditions remain ignored. Creative writing craft textbooks pay little-to-no attention to, for example, feminist aesthetics, transnational poetics, Négritude, or diasporic avant-gardes. The state of the curriculum is impoverished without these modes and many others. In the field's current practice, when minoritized aesthetics are brought into the classroom at all (perhaps as supplemental to these course textbooks), they are sometimes included as only a tokenistic gesture.

While the workshop is often thought of as a form of student-centered pedagogy, it turns out that workshop conversations serve to marginalize a range of aesthetic orientations and the cultural histories to which they belong. The regulation of taste is one way that creative writing polices its borders, allowing the subject-position of the literary writer to remain an exclusive position that only a select few can access.

Policing emotion: Scorn of excess

The regulation of emotion is another means by which this hierarchy is maintained. Victor Hugo famously answered the question, "What indeed is a poet?" with the description of "A man who feels strongly and expresses his feelings in a more expressive language."[80] If literature works upon the emotions, in creative writing not all forms of affect are equally valued. Creative writing fosters some affective orientations to the exclusion of others, shunning certain excesses of emotion to keep in place specific structures of feeling. In turn, the emotions that are associated with the literary writer's life constitute a kind of affective economy as they "work to align some subjects with some others and against some others." [81] By dissociating itself from the excesses of sentimentality that is associated with popular culture, creative writing aligns itself with an affective constellation associated with "literariness," as it has been constructed within institutions of creative writing.

Sentimentality, in contrast, becomes associated with "the banality of mass culture, and a certain domestic order governed by middle-class maternalism," as Suzanne Clark notes in her study of sentimentality.[82] Melodrama is regarded similarly in creative writing discourse—as a form of emotion that the literary writer must guard against because it can tend toward "schlock and kitsch."[83] This denigration of the sentimental and the melodramatic is part of a long history of normativity in emotion. As Ahmed observes, "some emotions are 'elevated' as signs of cultivation, whilst others remain 'lower' as signs of weakness" in different cultures and at different times.[84] These value systems are both culturally and historically contingent, like any other aspect of the regulation of taste. For instance, melancholy was, Garber reports, "a highly desired emotion in the early modern period, one associated with art, learning, and privilege."[85] Melancholy may be less emphasized in today's discourses of creative writing, yet there remains an expectation that literary writers will cultivate certain forms of feeling. As such, creative writing instruction—whether in the form of a craft text or in a classroom workshop discussion—is also an affective education. The censure on the sentimental text, an inheritance of masculinized modernist aesthetic theory, is also a stigmatizing of sentimental sensibilities as these are construed in relation to certain identity categories. The writer is expected to abide in an emotional orientation that will produce what is considered in alignment with the "literary," and, to achieve this, the writer must reform one's own feeling. The literary writer is prohibited from indulging in "cheap sentimentalism," a proscription that preserves the bourgeois ideal implicit in much creative writing discourse.

These prohibitions are announced clearly in craft texts from the early decades of the twentieth century as often as we find them in craft texts from the early decades of the present century. The censure of sentimentality is expressed forcefully in Esenwein's short-story handbook, published in 1918, which draws upon Winchester's *Principles of Literary Criticism*:

> The hackneyed, vulgar, prurient and bestial treatment of love and the passions in the short-story cannot be too strongly condemned, particularly when found in a periodical for home circulation. Surely the sincere story-writer must feel a sense of his responsibly and avoid the cheap sentimentalism which, in spite of its undeserved popularity, is as ephemeral as it is inartistic. 'All forms of sentimentalism in literature,' says Winchester, 'result from the endeavor to excite the emotions of pathos or affection without adequate cause. Emotions thus easily aroused or consciously indulged for their own sake, have something hollow about them. The emotion excited by the true artist is grounded upon the deep truths of human life.'[86]

More recently, in *Burning Down the House*, Charles Baxter devotes an essay to the term "sentimentality" and its role in the creative writing workshop. And although he would ultimately put the term to rest in favor of more nuanced evaluation, Baxter allows that calling a text sentimental is apt criticism. In his words, "There is something fascist about sentimentality, even when it is used for populist or progressivist ends. It wants you to feel and not to think. It avoids thought by invoking emotion, and only emotion. . . . All its ideas exist simply to evoke an emotion, typically of tears, or rage."[87] While Baxter largely ignores how "sentimentality" has been gendered and associated with certain identity categories, we can see in Baxter's words that the issue of sentimentality is bound to the mandates against politicized literature discussed above. This prohibition on sentimentality is repeated in similar terms elsewhere in creative writing, in other craft texts and in workshops. Here we see a clear relationship between aesthetic appraisal and emotion. As they police taste, discourses of creative writing also serve to prohibit or permit certain affective orientations.[88]

Writing teachers evaluate student work with aesthetic-affective criteria, although we may rarely discuss our assessment procedures in these terms. Thomas Newkirk observes of his fellow writing teachers, "We have been taught to be 'vaguely nauseated' by the emblems of sentimentality that presuppose a corresponding emotional reaction on our part." We find sentimentality to be off-putting, Newkirk argues, and our grades reflect our responses.[89] Our tastes, Clark concurs, are "defined by the act of revulsion against [sentimentality's] excess and by denial that leads us to claim that our preferences are 'not sentimental.' The label helps us construct intellectual discourse in the academic community—sentimentalists are not allowed."[90]

Sentimentality is associated with imprecision and exaggeration, in contrast with "good art" which "is always precise."[91] Clark notes that this appeal to precision is a common feature of the fear of the sentimental. The denigration of sentimental writing is an outgrowth, Clark argues, of "a nostalgia for objectivity."[92] Dobyns' *Best Words, Best Order* exemplifies Clark's point. Borrowing from Rilke, Dobyns defines sentimentality as the mode in which artists present something as if they were saying "'I love this' instead of 'here it is.'"[93] Dobyns denigrates sentimental literature that expresses the author's desire, favoring instead an ostensibly neutral authorial stance that presents the object as what "it is." Of course, the fantasy of neutrality and objectivity is a fantasy that belongs to those who have the privilege of seeing their worldview reflected in dominant ideology. To counter the dominant ideology is to become visible as a desiring subject, which is read as excessive in creative writing's regime of taste. This is akin to the silencing experienced by those rendered "angry" (e.g., angry feminist, angry activist, etc.) and therefore irrational, not to be listened to. Construing emotion as indecorous becomes a warrant for hostility to the one who speaks. She is dismissed as being in violation of a system of emotional decorum that serves the status quo.

Because this is what is at stake in the regulation of affect, assumptions about emotion in the creative writing classroom necessitate interrogation. Historically, attacks on sentimental literature have also been attacks on women's literature. Clark calls the sentimental a "gendered and despised discourse."[94] She explains, "The term *sentimental* makes a shorthand of everything modernism would exclude, the other of its literary/nonliterary dualism. The feminization of culture as content allowed modernism to avoid responsibility for its most questionable exclusions, and its most notoriously reactionary violence."[95]

In response, women writers have negotiated this affective economy as it intersects with identity politics. Esther Schwartz, in her 1936 craft text, poses the question: "Is it a sin for an intelligent writer to write escape fiction?" Her answer is: "I don't think so. If I can give some dispirited girl or woman a moment's escape from ugly reality, I think I've done something noble. After all, that is all that our poetry has done for ages, isn't it?"[96] But Schwartz also acknowledges that not all forms of literature are regarded with equal value. She warns her reader, "Of course if you want to be the form of writer who lands in *Story*, *Harper's*, *Scribner's* and the like, the group we call the quality magazines, you must be wary of advice and help from people like me." She continues, staking an identity as a "practical" type of writer rather than an "arty" writer, intimating to her reader that "I haven't an arty bone in my body, and I am much too practical to point at a typewriter for fourteen years and then sell a recipe for red cabbage. Why not sell all the recipes I know, my experience with my children, my neighbors' stories, the jokes my children tell ... while I am waiting for success to come my way?"[97] This, from a writer who, at the time of writing her craft text, had over three hundred stories and articles in print, along with a book of verse and a forthcoming novel, in eight years of being a writer. Despite such accomplishments, Schwartz is hesitant to declare herself a writer. Schwartz thus reflects the tendency that Katherine Adams notes in her history of women's involvement in writing courses between 1880 and 1940: "Cast in the insubstantial role of Non-Writer, a subset of the care-giving woman, these writers were meant to address only women readers on narrowly defined women's topics such as homemaking while the genres and pronouncements of male Writers were shaping American intellectual culture."[98]

The Western tradition of aesthetic theory, which has influenced institutional thought in creative writing, has long been preoccupied with the question of the writer's emotional alignment. Aesthetic theorists express consternation about unfitting sentiments, citing certain forms of emotion as being dangerous or unworthy. Writers must remove these denigrated emotions from their constitution and pursue the forms of emotion that are germane to art-making. Shelley, for example, disparages emotions that are uncoupled from imagination: "sentiment and passion ... divested of imagination, are other names for caprice and appetite."[99] The writer, in Shelley's view, must be careful to filter his emotion through the faculty of imagination. Other theorists, such as Henry James, warn against *false* emotion: "the only condition that I can think of attaching to the composition of the novel is ... that it be sincere."[100] The writer is encouraged toward honesty and sincerity, as the writer is also instructed to foster right emotion within the self. Aesthetic discourses and craft textbooks construct the literary artist's emotional identity, assembling a standard by which writerly selves will be judged. A craft text by Evelyn May Albright warns that

> Possibly the greatest lack in the average short-story writer is that of pure, strong, reasonable, sustained emotion. And where does the lack appear more crudely than in the story of pathos or tragedy. Sympathy cannot be limited. A working up of the pitiful results is sentimental; and a working up of the tragic through the mere accumulation of harrowing details results too frequently in melodrama. The author must himself live through the emotion, suffering vicariously for his creatures, before he can reproduce their heart life in anything like a real way.[101]

While they must guard against excessive emotion, the writer is also a feeling subject. Discourses of creative writing, as we have seen, instruct the writer to feel. In May Sarton's words, the ability to "hug his 'feeling to him'" is what "divides the merely 'poetic' person from the poet, the maker."[102] The writer's ability to dwell in 'right feeling' is, in these craft text writers' views, thought to have a direct relationship to the emotional force of a work of literature. As Esenwein explains: "I doubt, however, if the reader can be made to feel more deeply than the author felt when he wrote the passage."[103] Writers must themselves feel, if they will be able to make the reader feel. And the reader must be made to feel a valued form of emotion. The sentimental text produces only sentimentality, whereas the text that is worthy of the name "literature," it is assumed, is the text that promotes certain other forms of emotion. In short, creative writing is an enterprise that monitors "right feeling" associated with the decorum and status of the literary sphere. In its constructions of the relationship between emotion and artistic production, the field erects normative affective positions and occludes the ways that these constructions privilege some identities over others.

The diversity of the textual landscape

Creative writing as an institution has worked as a regulative machine—policing the taste and orientations of the writers who come to it. By exposing creative writing's assumptions, we become better equipped to fulfill the goal that Lynn Domina sets before the field, that "instructors be prepared to respond intelligently and diplomatically to work which confronts their own prejudices." This idea takes on additional layers of meaning as Domina argues that "if they encourage students to write out of their passion, instructors will receive work which confronts their own prejudices."[104] The extent to which we as writing teachers have inherited the assumptions outlined above reveals the types of prejudice we may carry. We need to be wary of the tendency in the field, which Ostrom identifies: "when only the 'best' writers know best, then the world of successful creative writers—those who gain tenure-earning jobs, or publication, or enough publication to scorn tenure-earning jobs—becomes inbred, elite, and reactionary."[105]

The aesthetic inclinations that students come to a creative writing class with are not to be reformed, but rather are legitimized as one of many approaches that should be considered. No fixed set of criteria can account for all audiences, so the creative writing classroom should bring into conversation multiple aesthetics. A critical pedagogy for creative writing helps students to acknowledge this contingency and the ways that such contingency has been denied under creative writing's ideology of taste.

Our students are cultural participants who are situated in a constellation of textual communities with knowledge of a range of artforms. Each student comes to the writing class having years of experience with writing and communicating, telling stories and persuading others. What's more, many of our students are already publishing with tweets, status-updates, and posts. The digital age challenges the lore that our students are far from being able to publish anything. In fact, some of our students' Twitter feeds and Facebook accounts have a larger audience than some small-press, "literary and little" journals will ever see. Douglas Hesse, in a 2010 article, cites Kathleen Yancey's view that the twenty-first century has seen the emergence of a "writing culture." Hesse references a *Seed* magazine piece that claims we are on the verge of "nearly universal authorship"—with nearly everyone publishing work read by at least 100 people.[106]

Rigid rules regarding aesthetic value are likely to be rejected by students who are able to boldly state their literary tastes on Amazon.com, who are able to gain large readerships online. We need to be able to critically identify the aesthetic values we uphold and situate them in the textual landscape for our students. And we need to be able to think outside of them, acknowledging our own aesthetic biases. With this broadened perspective, we may find that there is far more transformative work taking place in the literary landscape than our field had at first believed.

Threshold Concepts in Creative Writing

Every discipline carries with it a set of beliefs, conventions and practices. Our creative writing classes represent similar content; we teach some of the same principles, tools, and concepts. To gather an inventory of the principles and content that often circulate in creative writing classes, in 1990 Wendy Bishop asked her graduate students to list what subject material they understood to be definitive of the field. The list that Bishop's students generated, as reported in her book *Released into Language*, is a response to the question: "What should writing teachers *cover* in a fourteen-week, mixed-genre college-level creative writing workshop?" The list the students generated is as follows:

> Images, metaphors, history of storytelling, rhythm, plot, point of view, closure, tension, detail, structure, cliché, style, characterization, experimentation, effective openings (first sentence/line/paragraph), revision, symbolism, overview of poetic forms, detail, simile, character portrait, narration, impact, development of line, sound, persona, effective repetition, active/vivid versus stale language, place/scene/setting, plot, undirected activities (free time), telling versus showing (exposition/scene), dialogue, review of proofreading/editing marks, stanza/scenes (use of white space or transitions), value of oral reading, flashback, rhyme.[1]

Bishop indicates that the list is incomplete (in subsequent pages, she adds "being a writer" to this list as well). However, although it was generated over twenty-five years ago, the inventory still largely reflects the teaching of creative writing. The list encapsulates much of what is found in even the most recent craft textbooks' indices and tables of contents. A glance at the contents of bestselling introductory-level craft texts, from the US, UK, and Australia exhibit great similarity in the topics presented: plot and dialogue in fiction, sound and rhythm in poetry, when to use scene versus summary, etc. The texts are also alike in what they leave out- the diversity of writer-reader cultures, the contingencies of literary value.

While Paul Dawson asserts that in creative writing, "unlike in traditional disciplines, there is no coherent body of knowledge to be passed on,"[2] this list provided by Bishop and her students is likely to feel familiar to participants in— or inheritors of—the creative writing discipline. Indeed, I recently sat with a group of creative writing faculty who generated a list nearly identical to this when we discussed what we wanted our creative writing courses to cover.

What are the limitations of this list? How has this list failed to help us address the problems that emerge in workshop? How is this list inadequate, for example, in helping to address misogyny, xenophobia, homophobia, racism, or ableism in a student's poem? As another example, does this list help us to sufficiently interrogate the workshop essay that sentimentalizes a disabled person as a pitiable victim and symbol of overcoming adversity? Does it help us to interrogate the workshop poem that appropriates cultural discourses with little context? Does this list give us what we need to respond when a student impugns another student's taste? What lenses could we offer writers, beyond what is cataloged here?

Not included in Bishop's students' list are issues such as how to avoid stereotyping, how to write race, how to engage in diverse literary traditions, how to respond to a range of occasions for art-making and storytelling. What is not included in this list is the relationship between aesthetics and activism, the use-values of literature in diverse communities, the assumptions of privilege embedded in cultural constructions of the writer.

Moreover, this craft canon, outlined by Bishop's students, leaves out critical questions about the topics that are listed: Which cultural traditions of oral and written storytelling are marginalized in common histories of narrative? How can a writer be considerate of the politics of appropriation in choosing to write with a persona or subject-position different from one's own? Which literary traditions are elided in common craft definitions of "effective story openings"? Instead of probing in these directions, the workshop is focused on a closed set of craft principles, which are decontextualized and presented without history. Literary theory's terminologies are borrowed without acknowledgment of the larger debates of which they are part, without consideration of the contexts and subject-positions from which they emerged. Little attention is paid to the backgrounds, orientations, and positionalities of the thinkers who generated the concepts that we mobilize in craft conversations. In turn, there is little critical thought about who and what these concepts privilege, and what is left to the periphery of what we teach in creative writing.

This chapter aims to push beyond the established canon of what is taught in the literary writing curriculum. How can we think about what is taught in our field in new ways? The following pages propose a set of concepts that can contextualize, rather than replace, the list that Bishop's students provide. The concepts I discuss in this chapter are not meant to be a new canon for creative writing; rather, they together compose a heuristic for making our conversations in creative writing more able to evolve, more able to respond to the concerns that arise in the workshop. I see these concepts as a portal that can take us deeper into conversation. But they are provisional. They are presented here as another threshold leading to further conversation and inquiry.

The concepts outlined in the following sections focus on critical principles that are important for writers to engage. These are principles that arise from the practice of writing. In focusing on the conceptual side of creative writing praxis—how the practice of composing also entails metacognition or theory about the activity of putting words on a page—this chapter confronts the critical/creative binary, the common assumption that the realm of the "critical" is anathema to the "creative" sphere. The assumption that would say "those who can write, do; those who cannot, theorize"[3] relies on a faulty binary between theory and practice. As the quoted list of what is taught in creative writing stands to show, the field already makes use of a set of concepts, which take the form of what the field calls "craft." The field already recognizes, to some extent, the need for naming our practice, identifying craft choices with a specialized lexicon. My intention here is to take the body of concepts we already teach and expand them into a more robust store of principles, to broaden what we can talk about in creative writing and to give us new tools to work with, as we approach student writing. What is widely considered in the field today to be the teachable craft canon is too narrow in its scope to do justice to what is actually at stake in the art of literary writing. The craft canon has too often elided the controversies and problems that are most central to literary cultural production.

In taking on the question of how to augment and transform what has been established as the teachable canon in creative writing, I find useful the "threshold concept," as an organizing device. The threshold concept is a way of naming facets of disciplinary thinking. A threshold concept is a statement that has the following characteristics and is particular to a discipline or discourse community. Threshold concepts are . . .

- Troublesome: Threshold concepts are difficult to grasp, contrary to prior beliefs or schemas, and potentially challenging to a learner's sense of the world or sense of self.

- Liminal: Threshold concepts will not be understood in a single moment; rather, they germinate over time and over a series of encounters that call prior beliefs and schemas into question.
- Bounded: Threshold concepts can help to focus a curriculum and define its parameters. While a threshold concept is not equivalent to a student learning outcome, these concepts can serve as a checkpoint when student learning outcomes are evaluated.
- Integrative: Threshold concepts are connected to many other concepts, and an encounter with these concepts ramifies to other understandings that are also changed. These concepts transform a learner's way of knowing.
- Irreversible: Threshold concepts become internalized in a way that is difficult to undo; they are transformative.[4] Threshold concepts are what newcomers to a field learn to internalize in order to gain membership in communities of practice.

Given these characteristics, threshold concepts cannot be encapsulated in a single abstraction or term. Rather, threshold concepts are expressed as statements that describe core beliefs. These statements reflect the complexities of a field's central preoccupations.

The threshold concept, as a tool, has proved generative to educators. A range of disciplines have worked to identify the threshold concepts that are central to their curricula. Indeed, within the past year several books have been published that are devoted to identifying the concepts of different fields, including those that neighbor creative writing.[5] In particular, the threshold concept is a tool that is getting considerable attention in writing studies, especially in conjunction with Writing about Writing (WAW) approaches.

A number of factors have contributed to the interest in identifying threshold concepts in writing studies. WAW approaches to teaching composition, which proliferated after Doug Downs and Elizabeth Wardle's 2007 *College Composition and Communication* article titled "Teaching about Writing, Righting Misconceptions: (Re)Envisioning 'First-Year Composition' as 'Introduction to Writing Studies.'"[6] In turn, composition curricula at many schools transformed to focus on providing students with the central findings of disciplinary research about writing. The argument of Downs and Wardle's 2007 article is that writing studies should teach students the core research-based and theoretical concepts of the field, rather than let the content of the composition course be dictated by first-year experience committees or student interest. The subject of writing—a subject that has been a scholarly subject of study for decades—should be the content of the first-year composition course, Downs and Wardle argue. We should be teaching writing by teaching *about* writing. The *practice of* writing goes hand-in-hand with *knowledge about* writing, knowledge built from a range of methodological and theoretical approaches in composition and rhetoric.

The emergence of WAW pedagogy occurred concurrently with interest in the Scholarship of Teaching and Learning (SoTL) regarding threshold concepts. A 2003 report from the Enhancing Teaching-Learning Environments in Undergraduate Courses Project, led by the School of Education at the University of Edinburgh and authored by Jan Meyer and Ray Land, defined the use of the "threshold concept" to help learners identify the disciplinary frameworks they were being asked to adopt.[7] The report, titled "Threshold Concepts and Troublesome Knowledge: Linkages to Ways of Thinking and Practising within the Disciplines," sought to join theory and practice because, as Kathleen Blake Yancey, Liane Robertson, and Kara Taczak note, "if we want students to practice 'better' in fields ranging from chemistry to history and even in medicine, we need to help them understand the theory explaining the practice, the logic underlying it, so that it makes sense to them."[8]

Meyer and Land's work has led over a decade of continued discussion about the knowledge that undergirds disciplinary practice. In writing studies, the threshold concept is a tool that aligns well with WAW pedagogy. Composition theorists Linda Adler-Kassner and Elizabeth Wardle's edited collection *Naming What We Know* was recently released in 2015 as a "crowd-sourced encyclopedia of threshold concepts of writing studies."[9] To compose this list of threshold concepts for writing studies, a group of forty-five writing researchers from rhetoric and composition were invited to contribute to a wiki and suggest statements that are definitive of the field's orientation and shared knowledge. The resulting text, and its accompanying classroom edition, demonstrates how to encapsulate key beliefs about writing in a way that is accessible to practitioners at all levels—both students and instructors. These beliefs can then be mobilized in the composition classroom, in writing across the disciplines, and can be subsequently transferred to new writing situations. WAW shares with threshold-knowledge pedagogy a belief that identifying the core concepts of a discipline can help students transfer their learning across situations.

Specifically, *Naming What We Know* identifies threshold concepts for writing studies, such as the following:

• Writing is a social and rhetorical activity.
• Writing is a knowledge-making activity.

- Writing addresses, invokes, and/or creates audiences.
- Writing expresses and shares meaning to be constructed by the reader.
- Words get their meanings from other words.
- Writing mediates activity.
- Writing is not natural.
- Assessing writing shapes contexts and instruction.
- Writing involves making ethical choices.
- Writing is a technology through which writers create and recreate meaning.
- Writing speaks to situations through recognizable forms.
- Writing represents the world, events, ideas, and feelings.
- Genres are enacted by writers and readers.
- Writing is a way of enacting disciplinarity.
- All writing is multimodal.
- Writing is performative.
- Texts get their meaning from other texts.
- Writing enacts and creates identities and ideologies.
- Writing is linked to identity.
- Writers' histories, processes, and identities vary.
- Writing is informed by prior experience.
- Disciplinary and professional identities are constructed through writing.
- Writing provides a representation of ideologies and identities.

The extent to which these threshold concepts, provided in *Naming What We Know*, reflect creative writing as a discipline is an open question. To date, creative writing has not been brought into the fold of "writing studies," at least as it is conceived by the scholars who contributed to *Naming What We Know*. The implications of this fact is beyond the scope of this chapter. Rather, my purpose here is to propose a set of threshold concepts tailored specifically for—and emerging from—creative writing, a set of threshold concepts that address issues of inclusion and diversity in the literary writing curriculum. The threshold concepts I propose here are meant to provide the conceptual scaffolding and shared set of beliefs that can help us to address students' literary production in meaningful ways. These threshold concepts broaden what is taught in creative writing as they also respond to the current state of the field. They provide a heuristic with which we can check what is brought to workshop—both in terms of the stories students write and the commentary they offer. These threshold concepts can also guide our curricular choices from day one of a course, from the time a syllabus is built—as we assign stories, poems, essays, and works of craft-criticism that support students' engagement with these concepts. These threshold concepts illustrate how creative writing can offer an inclusive education for a diverse body of learners; they are useful for countering the problematic assumptions of the discipline described in Chapters 1 and 2.

The threshold concepts listed below share with WAW and the accompanying Teaching-for-Transfer (TfT) movements in writing studies the goal of helping "students *think like writers*,"[10] across the range of writing situations that they undertake. However, the list I submit here is specific to creative writers—in particular those who are seeking to think about literary production with critical consciousness. Together, these threshold concepts create a course-of-study that resists mandating a particular way of writing and instead points to the varieties of artistic practices available, continually grounding them in context and exploring their theoretical influences and implications.

This chapter charts a conceptual road map with which students can navigate the texts that emerge for them on the page, as both readers and writers. The goal is to generate a map that reflects the complex topographies of the literary landscape. This metaphor of the map is suggested by Yancey, Robertson, and Taczak who write: "the mental model of writing students develop—or don't develop—can affect how they approach writing tasks. One way of thinking about this is to say that a mental map is very like a large road map that allows one to see different locations, routes to these locations, and connections among those routes. With such a map, one has a fair amount of agency in deciding where to go and how, at least in terms of seeing possibilities and how they relate to each other—precisely because one can see relationships *across* locations."[11] To create such a map in creative writing is to move far beyond the discrete, decontextualized concepts of the "craft canon," as listed by Bishop.

The goal is to help novice literary writers learn to think and work as experts in the field. Expertise, of course, is mindful of all it does not know. Expertise requires continual reappraisal of how biases and assumptions manifest and shape practice. The 2000 National Research Council-sponsored *How People Learn: Brain, Mind, Experience, and School* focused on the ways that experts behave and found the following six claims about experts to be true:

1. Experts notice features and meaningful patterns of information that are not noticed by novices.
2. Experts have acquired a great deal of content knowledge, organized in ways that reflect a deep understanding of their subject matter.

3. Experts' knowledge cannot be reduced to sets of isolated facts or propositions, but instead reflects contexts of applicability—that is, the knowledge is 'conditionalized' on a set of circumstances.

4. Experts are able to flexibly retrieve important aspects of their knowledge with little attentional effort.

5. Though experts know their disciplines thoroughly, this does not guarantee that they are able to teach others.

6. Experts have varying levels of flexibility in their approach to new situations.[12]

Based on this list, we can see that conceptual knowledge is key to becoming an expert practitioner. According to this study, "rather than collect information around discrete facts, experts organize knowledge around core concepts or 'big ideas' that guide their thinking about their domains." Rather than collect a set of criteria for evaluating the craft of a story or poem—divorced from the context and history from which these criteria emerged—students in creative writing can consider the negotiations that shape literary production.

The threshold concepts described in this chapter ask students to write thoughtfully within an array of situations. As students become more familiar with writing conventions and how texts are used in different communities, they are better able to achieve what creative writing instructors Eugene Garber and Jan Ramjerdi want for students: to be able to "make shrewd judgments about where writers in given pieces are locating themselves in the world of language games. [...] Having made that estimation, they can say interesting things about what moves are likely to be effective in just that place, that culture, at this time."[13] As a result of the creative writing course, student-writers can become more sensitive to what is at stake in each piece of writing; they can become more versatile, increasing the genres, purposes, situations they can write for and within. They can be better able to write for a variety of audiences, contexts and circumstances. The creative writing curriculum can exist to save writers time in learning the skills they need to write in a way that diverse audiences will want to engage. This orientation toward the creative writing curriculum takes seriously Chris Green's recommendation that creative writing "classes need to be structured so that students can transfer skills and knowledge to their various speech communities."[14] Creative writing can teach the techniques that will help students acquire the sensitivity and awareness that will enable them to participate in, ideally, whatever community and context they encounter.

In the framework presented below, students are asked to become theorists of textual politics as they also practice writing as a means of discovery. Students should be able to take positions on debates about the relationship between aesthetics and rhetoric as they also find opportunities to put artistic and "functional" discourses into relation. This, what I am calling a critical creative writing curriculum, provides students the means of accessing and identifying the conventions of different writing practices, as it also encourages text-making and text-circulation in all its forms. The pedagogy described in these pages prioritizes metadiscursive critical thinking about the processes a writer may utilize in composing, analyzing, and evaluating texts.

The list that follows is inevitably incomplete, and I offer it here primarily as a means of prompting further conversation about the role threshold concepts might play in how we conceive and re-conceive our practice as writers and teachers in creative writing. I hope that the recommendations that follow will not be read as dictums. A written document like this is not mutable enough for the needs and contributions of a classroom community. However, going into a classroom with a set of heuristics that foster critical thought, relevant to inclusivity in creative writing, can help to prevent some of the harms that the field is most infamous for.

Notably, the exercises described below require openness and self-reflexivity on the part of the writer. Such "habits of mind" require continuous scaffolding and modeling in the classroom. How to create and reinforce a classroom culture that supports self-reflexivity is the subject of the next chapter. The framework presented below relies on teachers' ability to demonstrate the type of nuanced and responsive thinking that we seek to teach the student-writers in our classes. We can put our message in the means by probing the subject matter that arises in the classroom. While these threshold concepts provide some grounding, our pedagogical approaches cannot be predetermined but are co-emergent with what each member of the classroom community brings to the workshop table. The following conceptual framework is meant to be a tool for approaching these in-the-moment conversations about emergent texts, readings, and identities for the writers with whom we work.

Concept 1: Attention

Creative writing involves specific modes of attention as writers learn to be close and critical observers of the world. Writers learn to account for the ethical considerations involved in perceiving and reinventing the world through their research and observation.

This threshold concept focuses on the place of research in creative writing. Research is about invention, about generating texts; it is also about examining the page against the world. The term "re-search," derived from a French term from the late sixteenth century, denotes the idea of looking intensively. [15] Several books have been written on the subject of research in creative writing, including Jen Webb's *Researching Creative Writing*, Jeri Kroll and Graeme Harper's *Research Methods in Creative Writing*, the *Developing Qualitative Inquiry* series published by Routledge, and a range of books released by Sense Publishers in the Netherlands on poetic and narrative inquiry. Such texts, and the creative writing research methodologies they represent, constitute an important part of the creative writing curriculum, which stands to teach writers the importance of going outside of the self and one's received knowledges. Research can be undertaken for the purposes of gathering and generating inspirations, authenticating details, memories, and unexpected connections. It can also be a way of discussing the risks and limits of cultural appropriation. What is available to the writer to use as material? Who stands to gain and who stands to lose from a particular example of "use"?

This threshold concept is meant to spur critical thought about the writer's relationship to lived experiences and existing knowledges. It reflects Jeffrey Schultz's argument about the inadequacy of traditional creative writing approaches to addressing cliché. "The undergraduate workshop . . . is more often than not structured around the idea of 'hammering . . . the clichés out of students.'" [16] This "hammering" often intervenes at the sentence level to "correct" the cliché, rather than going deeper into the writer's attentional field. What and how do writers pay attention? How does the writer learn to see the world for the way it is constellated with received knowledges and flattened representations? "If literature is going to have access to any hope," Schultz writes, "then the writer's critical . . . thought must penetrate, continuously, everything it encounters." [17] Schultz's thesis is that "thought, above everything else, must be taught" in creative writing, and this thought comes through a practice of attending to what is, beyond what has been said about it. This is what it means to teach attention in creative writing. It means seeing past the frame, seeing beyond the lens that is offered by dominant narratives, finding the counter-narrative, and critically evaluating a text's potential effects in the world.

Our students can sharpen their ability to detect when a poem or story fits a predetermined expression that is problematic. They can learn to pay attention to these expressions—and the realities they construct or represent—in new ways. This work should permeate the curriculum—teaching students in workshop, in their readings, and in their invention exercises to be skeptical of "what comes" to them. Discourses that are "in the air" and then internalized have served to maintain interconnected forms of oppression. To perpetuate these received discourses may be to participate in injustice.

This threshold concept can be approached in many ways in classroom praxis. One example of an exercise that occasions discussion of this concept comes after reading Jamaica Kincaid's "Girl" and Rick Moody's story "Boys." We discuss the complexities of gender performance and gender spectrums. We discuss transpoetics. Then I ask the students to write a story that calls into question a common idea about gender. After they write these drafts, we put them up for discussion and strategize ways of sharpening the writer's attention about questions of gender. This leads us to generating research questions, and we strategize how to approach these questions with the eye of a creative writer.

To learn some of the basic skills associated with research in creative writing, we take on another exercise: we work to discover "authenticating detail" (i.e., details that make a story seem more persuasive or "real") through a mixed-methods research story. I ask students to draft a story of any length that involves two characters—one who wants to take on a new profession, which the other character does not approve of. The prompt encourages writers to reveal the disapproval subtly in the subtext of the story, and show what is at stake in the relationship.

After an initial draft of this story emerges, writers sit down with a small group of fellow writers and read the story together. They then take time to reflect on each story as a group of readers. What authenticating details would add to this story? In particular, for the purposes of this exercise, what would they like to know about the characters' professions? What details and "insider knowledge" would these characters have about their professions? The students work in groups to list what "insider knowledge" they want to find. They do this for each story in the group, working together as a team of practitioners to come up with a list for each story.

The next step is to consider how they will go about finding answers to their research questions. How can you find details about your character's career? (This is one way of surreptitiously embedding some career education in to a creative writing curriculum, without making the curriculum exhaustively careerist.) I point students to O Net, the Occupational Handbook, and DataUSA as starting points. But we quickly find that websites like this can only take one so far in research. After browsing these websites for details and testimonials that might round out knowledge of the character, the students think about other strategies they have for researching a story. We collate a list of strategies like the following in a handout.

Interviews: How you would go about finding someone to interview for information about the career, about what the career means to them, about how they accessed the career and if they were barred or discouraged from it in any way. How would you go about setting up such an interview? What types of questions you would ask?

Archival Research: A library's Special Collections has boxes of letters, photographs, diaries, greeting cards, checkbooks, to-do lists, and a wide range of other materials. These materials will have signs of life all over them—coffee stains, lingering scents of perfume, torn corners, phone numbers written in the margins. As such, archives are a writer's go-to spot for finding authenticating details. Is there an archive you can access that would be relevant to your story? Visit your local public or university library's website and look for guides to Special Collections holdings. Remember also that archives do not only exist in libraries; you may have an archive of your grandmother's letters stored up in the attic, or your local elementary school may have old textbooks and teachers' notes hidden in the basement. Consider how an archive may play a role in your research process for this story.

Immersion: Is there a way you could access a setting and environment that is akin to the places where your characters dwell? Make a plan to visit such a site and spend a few hours there, recording everything you can perceive with all your senses. Your story's settings may be composites of multiple places that you visit in conducting your research. With your group, make a list of possible places to visit as you develop your story.

Observation: Charles Baxter argues in *The Art of Subtext*, "To create subtext, fiction writers must pay attention to the way people no longer pay attention." Writers have access to the tool of what might be called "micro-detailing" as they are "hyper-vigilant observers ... [able] to gaze upon the world in an abnormally attentive way."

Other Artforms: Are there other forms of cultural production (e.g., films, plays, songs, visual art, stories, poetry, etc.) that could help you gather authenticating details for your story? Look to these other artforms for their use of authenticating details. See if the authenticating details these artforms include might lead your imagination to invent authenticating details that are right for your story. Generate a list of works that might be relevant to what you are developing in this story. We discuss the ethics of these methods.

The students then revise the story to include the research they found. I remind them that they do not need to include every single detail or fact that they collected. Use only what serves the story, what is *significant* to the story. Do not overwhelm the plot or the character development with random facts; instead carefully select from your research to embed the apt description, the unanticipated object, the unexpected reference to a detail of the environment, the fitting vehicle for your metaphor. Use the details you have collected to show rather than tell the conflicts and complexities that drive your story.

We go through several iterations of these stories, drawing out the characters' complex relationships to the occupational world the students have researched and reinvented in their fiction. In these iterations, we learn how to seamlessly integrate authenticating details into a story. This provides the groundwork for the research skills necessary to complete projects that might have more at stake. After completing this project, we transition into thinking about how we would approach artistic projects like the following, using the same ethics of close, critical attention. I ask students to imagine that they feel compelled to write:

- a story that depicts a traumatic event that you never experienced.
- a story that depicts a conflict in a county you've never visited.
- a story that is useful to the Movement for Black Lives.
- a story that explores the effects of the Exxon Valdez oil spill.
- a story that presents a dialect you have overheard but do not speak yourself.
- a story about the Battle of Little Big Horn.
- a story narrated by someone with a gender identity different to yours.

Presenting these scenarios, I ask: Is it possible to undertake these projects and complete them well? How much depends upon the author's positionality? To what extent can research and critical attention make up for the gaps in one's knowledge? What ethical questions are at stake? What factors or circumstances might affect your decision-making? What process steps would you take to complete each project? How would you hone your attention? What would you do to attempt to prevent harm? What political work could these stories accomplish?

The students generate questions of their own. A sampling from students' written responses to this conversation includes questions such as: How can we write effective prefaces to our work, to help audiences make informed decisions? How can we best respect the experiences of people who have experienced oppression? How can we make our literary writing a productive conversation? How can we avoid simply recreating a story or trope as it already exists in popular thought? Will people want to be interviewed and have their story told? How can we keep people's stories their own? How can we avoid appropriating or "speaking for"? How can we ensure that the story benefits the people whose lives are affected by this story, without enacting a patronizing benevolence? How can we collaborate effectively and ethically?

Concept 2: Creativity

Writers benefit from a robust toolkit of applied theoretical frames and process heuristics for generating texts. Principles from creativity studies are useful for increasing the versatility of writers.

Katharine Haake puts the following aim before fellow teachers of creative writing: "Clearly our first goal as teachers can be that writing not end for our students."[18] To meet this goal, we teach multiple strategies for encouraging the generation of new texts—what the classical rhetoricians called "invention." The generative process requires learned flexibility in the composing process that can adjust to the demands of a particular text and that can improvise new techniques for composing when a "block" presents itself. Students come to see the composing process as recursive and they learn to attend to the intentions they may have for a text in relation to what unintended elements emerge in the process of creation.

There are many ways this threshold concept may translate to praxis: students can keep a process journal and collect information about their own and other writers' processes along with writing prompts. This process journal may be separate or integrated with a content journal for collecting material for writing, inspirations, research, and information. Students may also be responsible for presenting new process ideas to the class. They can read findings from the psychology of creativity: how do the five stages of preparation, incubation, intimation, illumination, and verification translate to creative writing, for instance?

Borrowing from creativity studies and the psychology of creativity, I invite the students to run a number of experiments to see what fosters their own creative thinking. One assignment asks them to remove something that they are used to using, to figure out how to write without it. This might mean writing with their non-dominant hands, writing without a pen or pencil, or writing without the alphabet that they learned in grade school.

We discuss what it means to create an environment for oneself that supports creativity, across different circumstances. We review Susan Straight's April 2014 *Los Angeles Times* article on learning to write without a room of one's own. We talk about what it takes for each of us to clear out time and space for our work, recognizing how our circumstances differ. We share challenges, resources, and strategies, and we talk about how we can support each other in this practice.

To further spur on their writing, I introduce students to the idea that every story can be read as a prompt, that every piece of writing is a piece of rewriting, and that every piece of writing can be imitated. The act of imitation is a means of studying literary production and gaining tools for one's own process. Trying out these principles, we use our readings to generate prompts. We imagine the rewriting process that a writer must have gone through by generating a hypothetical first draft of the story that was ultimately published. And we imitate the writer's craft choices to create a new work with different subject matter. We ask of the writing produced by these assignments: What tools are offered here for creative thinking? And what can we learn about craft?

I assign Matt Madden's *99 Ways to Tell a Story,* inspired by Raymond Queneau's *Exercises in Style,* and prompt students to find more ways of telling to add to these books' cataloging. The students write several iterations of the same story or essay, using different ways of telling: they might rewrite a story in five words; rewrite a story as a series of if-then statements; rewrite a story as a series of questions; rewrite a story as a diagram, recipe, tattoo, greeting card; rewrite a story as a list of rules for breaking rules, a disloyalty oath, a dangerous warning. We try out Oulipian constraints—lipograms, tautograms, etc. Then we discuss: What effects do we notice about the different ways of telling? How does each way of telling affect what is being told? We pose Madden's question: "Can a story, however simple or mundane, be separated from the manner in which it is told?"[19] How do form and content work together? What does it mean to put the "message in the means"? Where is context in these questions? How do audience, culture, the forum in which a piece is circulated, etc., affect the relationship between form and content?

Bearing these questions in mind and still keeping invention and creativity as a focus, I assign students another exercise: to write "counter-narratives" that question each assumption they find in a given work of literature. We watch Chimamanda Adichie's TED Talk "The Danger of a Single Story," and then we work together to identify the assumptions behind a story assigned for class, such as Ray Bradbury's "There Will Come Soft Rains." We then write a counter-narrative that puts assumptions of this story (the heteronormative nuclear family, the middle class lifestyle, the separation of human and environment, the fear of technology, the story's implicit teleology, etc.) into question. Also after discussing the idea of a "master narrative," I will offer a prompt like the following: "Think about what it might mean to challenge the 'master narratives' that circulate in common culture." I introduce Judith Roof's theory that "rather than imitating or responding to life, narrative might determine our notion of the shape of life and what is important in it—birth, love, reproduction, achievement, death." We then brainstorm common narratives that we know about birth, love, reproduction, achievement, death—and take time to rewrite these common narratives, to expose their assumptions, to identify what and whom they privilege, and to offer alternatives that re-center experiences.

The goal with all of these exercises is to understand that writers need tools for creativity and invention; the process is not something that just happens naturally to the gifted few. These exercises also demonstrate that creativity and invention do not happen in a vacuum. They cannot transcend culture or the realities of hierarchical systems. This threshold concept is meant to replace assumptions about the born literary genius with practical tools that make inventive thinking available to anyone who comes to the writing class.

This threshold concept also challenges the idea that the privileged "genius" writer should not be held responsible for their words and the effects these words have in the world. In a critical creative writing curriculum, the writer is not after creativity at all costs; rather, the writer invents and checks that invention. It is not a given that creative thinking is valuable; to be valued, creative thinking must be evaluated for what it does, how it operates on the world.

Students may have inherited assumptions about the genius literary writer from their educational experiences or cultural forms. At the beginning of a course, I ask the students to write down five things they believe to be true about the writing process. We then check these beliefs against other writers' descriptions of their own processes. We read research on writer's block and develop guiding principles for ourselves based on these findings. From researchers such as Donald Murray, Jone Rymer, and Nancy Sommers, we learn that writing is a highly complex problem-solving process; that writers who bring a more flexible approach to the writing process are less likely to experience writer's block; that some forms of delay and waiting are essential to the writing process, but so is continued work; that accomplished writers have spent many hours practicing their craft; that revision takes time; that writing is something anyone can learn to do.

We hone the "mental muscle" that is creativity. I encourage students to seek out challenging tasks, to take on projects that do not necessarily have a solution for the sake of working the imagination. We talk about why the imagination is a valued form of intelligence, about what creativity in writing has to offer readers, about how to evaluate creative thinking.

It perhaps goes without saying that students can also practice invention by producing a substantial body of text, as poetry instructors Davidson and Fraser note, "The first lesson, then can be to write often and voluminously, if only to provide a palette of colours, of textures, of language."[20] At the beginning of the course, the class can work together to set goals regarding the amount of text to be generated in the semester and strategies for achieving this goal. This threshold concept exists among those strategies. We revisit this threshold concept continually throught the course, as we generate this portfolio of textual production.

Concept 3: Authorship

Writerly identity is constructed by a range of cultural forces. Cultural messages about the identity and lifestyle of the writer can be critically examined as we gain resources for building a writing life.

In the critical creative writing course, constructs of the writer and the writing life can usefully become an object of critique, analysis, and methods-based study. Students are most likely to fully engage with writing if they come to see themselves as writers, but this does not mean that they must adopt the role uncritically or without a complex understanding of what the subject-position is and how it has been constructed.

We know that students encounter a range of assumptions about writing reflected in popular culture. It is the responsibility of the creative writing course to help student-writers negotiate these messages, to check these popular constructs against lived experiences, to become better able to critically consider what authorship means for different writers in different times and places. The creative writing class can provide students the opportunity to claim a writerly identity for themselves and to simultaneously critique received cultural ideas about the writerly life.

To better understand the power of these constructs of the writer—and, in turn, the way they are located in networks of power—we need to ask a basic question: Just what is a writer? What assumptions have historically been embedded in the subject-position of the creative writer? How are the writer and the writerly life constructed through the discourses we have encountered in and out of the academy? What do we associate with the figure of the literary writer? What are the implications of our associations? How do these preconceptions about the writer translate to preconceptions about writing? How do our common conceptions influence us when we sit down to compose? What embodiments are associated with the figure of the writer, and who has been excluded from the subject-position? Who stands to lose and who stands to gain from the assumptions we have inherited about the writer and the writerly life? How can writers construct identities, professions, and lifestyles that support literary production across a range of material situations and positionalities, thereby challenging the ways that cultural ideas may seek to limit and exclude? The goal is to uncover presumptions that we might have, which might work against us in the writing process.

To examine and critique assumptions we bring to the creative writing class about what constitutes a writer and the writing life, we attend to how students have encountered specific representations of the writer in popular culture and various media—such as films, television episodes, and books that portray writers as characters. We look at a series of Hollywood clips of films that present writer protagonists, such as *Dead Poets Society* (1989), *Poetic Justice* (1993), *Shakespeare in Love* (1998), *Wonder Boys* (2000), *Finding Forrester* (2000), *Adaptation* (2002), *Before Sunset* (2004), *Young Adult* (2011), *Midnight in Paris* (2011), *Ruby Sparks* (2012), *The Words* (2012), *Perks of Being a Wallflower* (2012). What images of the writer circulate in popular media, such as films, mass-market creative writing advice books, and internet discourse? Are writers of different enmeshments represented? How do these representations reinforce or destabilize a racist binary of "writer" versus "ethnic writer"? Or a sexist binary of "writer" versus "woman writer"?

Constructs of the writer translate to messages about what it takes to belong to the literary community, what it means to be recognizable to a community as a subject called "writer." Because these constructions of the writer come to signify belonging in this way, "the writer," as a construct, is also a site of exclusion. Katherine Adams notes how historically "both 'writer' and 'author' seemed to be terms appropriate only for men." In this context, women such as "Lydia Maria Child, Susan Warner, Maria Cummins, and Harriet Beecher Stowe were frequently identified by less respectful names: bluestockings, poetizers, authorlings, or a 'mob of scribbling women.'"[21] That these women were denied access to the subject-position of the writer (because of the exclusionary constructions operative during their careers) had significant ramifications: "In journalism and in fiction and poetry, the necessary assumption of the Non-Writer stance led to the writers' being treated as just that: as Non-Writers."[22] Whom a community is willing to call "writer" makes a difference; a community's way of constructing this subject-position serves to draw a closed circle around the writer,[23] excluding some from the professional status enjoyed by those who can claim that title.

We list the writer-characters we have encountered in various media, and in making our list, we discover that many cultural representations of the writer portray a white cis-gendered male character who is unworried by caretaking responsibilities, by social demands, by material concerns, or by vulnerability to violence. What is at stake in media presentations of the "lonely writer"—a misunderstood, set-apart, eminently interior figure—are assumptions about what constitutes the literary life and who has access to it.

To support this discussion of how constructions of the writer in Hollywood productions privilege white-male subjectivity, we might listen to Geoff Brumfiel's NPR segment from 2015 "Do Fictional Geniuses Hold Back Real Women?" and read Wendy Bishop and Stephen Armstrong's article "Box Office Poison: The Influence of Writers in Films and on Writers."[24] We then read Leslie Marmon Silko's "Language and Literature from a Pueblo Indian's Perspective," and list some of the common Western assumptions about writers this essay addresses.

Silko presents a picture of storytelling as "a whole way of being." She writes, "When I say 'storytelling,' I don't just mean sitting down and telling a once-upon-a-time kind of story. I mean a whole way of seeing yourself, the people around you, your life, the place of your life in the bigger context, not just in terms of nature and location, but in terms of what has gone on before, what's happened to other people."[25] In Silko's essay, stories are not owned by their tellers; they are co-created in a community and sustained by a community. Rather than conceiving of the author as originator and owner of a story, the storyteller in Pueblo culture has a responsibility to "give away" and to share with the community. The storyteller gives a truth in the form of a narrative, and that story takes a life of its own, carried forward by the community. This counters colonial notions of the subject-who-knows (the writer) as imparting truth to passive listeners. Silko offers a picture of storytelling as an invitation for co-creation of meaning.

Silko's essay is an opportunity to take up the questions that Nicole Cooley sees as central to the creative writing course. Cooley asks her students to reflect on "how much they think it matters who speaks and, by doing so, have them consider questions about authorship, voice, and authority."[26] Taking up such considerations, the critical creative writing classroom becomes a space to discuss the "construction of the writing subject as a universal ideal, and in the absence of 'diversity,' particularly as a raced, culturally, communally, and marginally specific subject, in the 'lore' of the workshop narrative."[27] A writing exercise to follow this discussion might prompt students to compose a story featuring a writer protagonist that offers a counter-narrative to common representations of the writer.

The goal in studying this threshold concept is to examine how "Our ability to claim particular self-constructions and to have those self-constructions recognized by others is," Stephanie Kerschbaum explains, "always mediated by the power dynamics influencing an interaction."[28] The ways that student-writers negotiate this reality belongs on the workshop table for discussion.

Concept 4: Language

Language choices are bound to issues of power. Supporting a polylingual and multimodal literary community requires deliberate attention from writers, which manifests in each writing occasion.

Multilingualism is an important value in a critical creative writing curriculum, and it is an intentional area of study. Creative writers should know language, as the material they work with, for the ways it is tied to identity, culture, history, and power.

With this threshold concept, student-writers can come to ask: How can we expand the possibilities of literary writing as we value multivocality? How can writers support linguistic diversity? And what are the risks and possibilities of writing in a language or vernacular that is not one's own? They can come to write with consciousness of the colonial history of "taming the wild other" through the erasure of languages and the forced adoption of a dominant code.

Creative writing is a site where we can think about the words we use to talk about language-use. Gloria Anzaldúa's "How to Tame a Wild Tongue" provides a useful way forward in this discussion. In this essay, Anzaldúa calls attention to the beliefs that surround language use: "we speak *poor* Spanish"; "we are told that our language is *wrong*." I ask creative writing students to list on the board the phrases they have heard or used themselves to evaluate someone's language-use: "her writing is *deficient*"; "he needs to be in a *remedial* English class"; "this writing needs to be "*cleaned up*"; "she is a *bad* writer"; "his essay is *riddled* with errors— *horrible atrocities* of language"; "this is a *violation* of good speech." What do you associate with these words—"poor," "wrong," "deficient," "remedial," "cleaned-up," etc.? In what other contexts are these words used? Do these words assume a link between "good speech" and "good character"?

This exercise provides us with the concrete material to think about how writers, "negotiate the conflicts between monolingual enforcement and multilingual experience."[29] Janet Neigh, writing of her pedagogy in the women's studies classroom, argues that "we must deconstruct the illusion of a monolingual environment" across the disciplines. To do this, we "need to devise strategies to engage different languages in classroom interactions."[30] This might mean assigning bilingual or parallel print textbooks, or asking students to work on translations. It also means putting the relationship between language and power on the syllabus for discussion. "An attention to linguistic politics in the classroom is crucial," Neigh writes, "because many college students in North America hear a variety of languages being spoken in their social environment or because they speak more than one language. Students must contend with the contradiction of experiencing multiple languages in their everyday lives, while also encountering resistance toward these voices by dominant power structures, including the university."[31]

Students note how in "How to Tame a Wild Tongue" Anzaldúa code-switches and forces the English-speaking monolingual members of her audience to accommodate her tongue. Anzaldúa writes that "as long as I have to accommodate the English speakers rather than having them accommodate me, my tongue will be illegitimate."[32] The essay's construction (e.g., its form, its use of language) supports her message. The message is in the means. In Anzaldúa's essay, we see the importance of a writer using "all the languages that create her."[33] This gives students in creative writing the opportunity to think about what it means for them to write with all the languages that create their histories and identities, and what it means to write their characters' relationships to language. The complexities of this terrain have always been present for the field of creative writing, even as many classroom conversations have skipped over this ground. It is ground that we need to honor with attention to how language moves, and how history conditions its movements.

Concept 5: Genre

There are no universal standards for "good writing"; however, there are conventions that are particular to established genres.

I often quote for my students Donald Murray's claim that in writing "[t]here are no rules, no absolutes, just alternatives."[34] This threshold concept rejects the notion that good writing requires "formulaic obedience to rules."[35] Rather, it introduces the idea of the convention—and the purposes that conventions serve in particular genres and writing situations.

The creative writing curriculum can expand the alternatives that are available to writers—and strengthen students' ability to evaluate these alternatives—by providing a window on the vast and ever-multiplying textual landscape, in all its diversity. At the same time, creative writing also teaches genre traditions and the histories that give rise to the genres we write within. The critical creative writing curriculum emphasizes narratology and poetics in order to give students a sense of the lineages they join when they adopt the conventions of the minimalist short story or the lyric poem. This gives writers a better sense of what it means to adopt these conventions, what politics might be carried in their continuance.

Translating this concept into practice, I draw attention to theories of genre early in any creative writing course. I ask students to discuss and agree or disagree with a series of theses on genre, such as the following. Note that several of these statements are intentionally problematic, and students are asked to think about what each statement assumes about the relationship between form and content, the writing process, etc.

1. Genre is a formal container for the writers' ideas.
2. Genre is a classificatory device.
3. Genre is an interpretive tool for readers.
4. Genres ties each text to precursors and influences.
5. Because genre is normalizing, it hinders writers' creativity.
6. "When professional writers write, they ordinarily do not begin with generic constraints in mind. Often they do not know what sort of piece will result from their work; sometimes they are unsure even whether it will become prose or poetry."[36]

We proceed by explicitly identifying the particular genre conventions we find in different bodies of work. Which conventions traverse multiple genres of fiction, of creative nonfiction, of poetry? Which are particular to a single author (e.g., a signature move that an author makes across all the works in their oeuvre), or a single sub-genre (such as the lyric essay or romance fiction or the Language poem)? What are the similarities and differences between, for example, science fiction, speculative fiction, futuristic fiction, dark fantasy, supernatural fiction, dystopian fiction, alt-history fiction, etc.? How do these genres arise in specific communities with specific interests and exigencies?

Concept 6: Craft

Craft choices produce effects in the reading experience. While these effects cannot be entirely predicted, writers can weigh the risks and possibilities of each craft choice.

Keeping the idea of conventions and literary traditions in mind, writers can be equipped to analyze the craft choices they make and to anticipate the potential effects of these choices. Thinking in terms of what a craft choice (for example, the choice to begin a story with an alarm clock) may *risk* and what it *makes possible* shifts the conversation away from absolutist claims to what is "right" or "wrong" in literary craft. Thinking instead in terms of possibilities allows that a writer may find ways of making use of the risks of, for example, a cliché (e.g., beginning a story with an alarm clock and a scene of waking) to achieve an aesthetic intention (e.g., establishing the story as a parodic metanarrative). Repetition, as another craft choice, risks frustrating readers with redundancy. At the same time, repetition can be used to build motifs that accumulate layers of meaning. We look at how particular texts use repetition to create patterns and break them. When we analyze these patterns, we talk about the risks and possibilities of predictability—interrogating how established conventions may serve a story by locating it in a genre, by bringing a readership to it, by offering readers a particular type of satisfaction in being able to forecast what will occur in a plot line, etc. At the same time, predictability can bore. And predictable clichés or hackneyed language can bring with them associations that the writer would rather not have embedded in the text (for example, the poem that reminds readers of an advertising slogan that is irrelevant to its orientation).

In the fiction workshop, the students discover the common risks of stories that tell what readers have already inferred, that summarize away their characters' struggles, that assume tension is best rendered through movie special effects and spectacle, that caricature rather than characterize. We talk about the common conventions of storytelling (e.g., inciting incidents, dialogue attributions, consistency of point-of-view and tense, etc.) and the purposes these conventions serve for their readers. Through the framework of craft analysis, we learn that all departures from convention should be purposeful—which means the writer must weigh the effects of these choices.

This heuristic, the craft-choice/effect dyad, fosters a particular type of textual analysis—a skill that should be developed from the introductory level onward to the critical exegesis often required in Australian and UK graduate-level writing programs. A critical exegesis gives a window to students' vision for the work and how they navigated the particular demands of the emergent text. In this reflective and analytical essay, students work to articulate the rationale behind their textual choices. Asking students to preface their work with critical writing promotes the metacognition necessary to the process of writing—the writer's evaluation of the moves a text can make, as that text comes into being. Students can be assessed for their growing abilities to contextualize, argue for, and enact craft choices that serve their emerging texts, aesthetic projects, and audiences. This aspect of the curriculum is significant preparation as it may provide the space for students to contribute to disciplinary knowledge about creative writing.

The reader-response offered in workshop also provides an occasion for deepening students' encounter with this threshold concept. The workshop conversation serves to pinpoint an element of a text and describe its effects, to imagine alternative choices, and to evaluate how the effects of different techniques may compare. Reader-response comments are descriptive accounts not just of the words on the page, but also how they are received or could be received. It may be useful to track workshop conversations using a three-column table, that identifies in each row a craft choice and what it risks, what it makes possible. Such structures for thinking and heuristics for analysis can deepen students' craft-based thought and can sharpen their attention to the complexity of a writer's decision-making process.

Concept 7: Community

Writers are formed by the communities they engage. An analysis of craft must be grounded in an understanding of the varying orientations of readerships. Diverse audiences come to their texts with diverse needs.

This threshold concept is related to the craft analysis framework described above. To provide some guidelines for understanding the risks and possibilities of a text, writers think about the diverse needs of audiences.

In the process of composing a text, a writer may pose a series of questions. Will this make sense to readers? Would it help my reader to know this about the character in paragraph one? Will my audience read this passage as an allusion to the Cold War? Will my audience see this characterizing detail as a racial marker? Have I assumed certain things about my characters' experiences based on their race, class, sexual orientation, etc., and will these assumptions resonate with readers who identify similarly? What authenticating details will members of my audience need in order to feel that this setting is real, given that some members of my audience live in this place? The creative writing class can refine students' ability to ask these types of questions and to think about their audience in complex ways, not allowing the literary audience to become monolithic.

The creative writing curriculum demands a thorough consideration of audience. In my university, we have recently created a course that focuses on the diversity of literary audiences. This course investigates, among other topics, Nadine Gordimer's observation that "differences [between writer and audience] affect profoundly the imagery, the relativity of values, the referential interpretation of events between the cultural givens of most writers."[37] To the extent that this is true, the onus is on the creative writing curriculum to expand the terms of reference that a writer can engage, so that they can move between different audiences. Thus, the creative writing curriculum has more than one reason to teach cross-cultural competency and humility.

In order for students to gain a broader understanding of audience and the potential use-values of imaginative texts, students can research a range of interpretive communities—to understand how various discourses and cultural forms are used and valued by diverse audiences. Such an assignment is designed to counter a limitation of common workshop practice that Chris Green identifies: that "the community of origin, if discussed at all, is the object of investigation: 'they' are talked about rather than talked to. Members of these communities become 'material' rather than an audience."[38] Similarly, Scott Russell Sanders warns against writing only for the specialized audience of literary scholars and critics—to limit one's audience in this way may cause a writer's world to become cramped. "The ethos of the academy is aloof, rational, dispassionate." And to the extent to which writers remain in this context, "their art is likely to suffer."[39]

"Who can access this text?" is a question I regularly pose to my students. They learn to not only question where and how the text circulates, but also to interrogate the assumptions of a text in order to answer this question.

Creative writing should exist to help students enter new readerships and interpretive communities with cultural awareness. Taking this as a learning outcome, the creative writing curriculum may provide space for community projects in which students interact directly with readers and fellow writers. Students can undertake service-learning projects such as helping community members produce zines, leading a journaling workshop, hosting poetry slam competitions at a coffee house.[40] Such projects should be undertaken with care, respectful collaboration, and thorough consideration for the intended and unintended effects. Alternative assignments may be less intensive, with a reduced demand on community partners. For example, one could write a poem in chalk on an off-campus sidewalk and observe how people respond to it as they walk by.

Such projects can shed light on different reading practices of audiences. In this discussion, we read Laura Wilder's research on common topoi of literary criticism[41] and Michael Warner's "Uncritical Writing," comparing and contrasting the different audience needs described in each work. Wilder identifies the reading practices that are taught and valued in literary writing courses, while Warner writes of the students who come to his literature classes who "read in all the ways they aren't supposed to." By this he means,

> They identify with characters. They fall in love with authors. They mime what they take to be authorized sentiment. They stock themselves with material for showing off, or for performing class membership. They shop around among taste-publics, venturing into social worlds of fanhood and geekdom. They warm with pride over national heritage. They thrill at the exotic and take reassurance in the familiar. They condemn as boring what they don't already recognize. They look for representations that will remediate stigma by giving them 'positive self-images.' They cultivate reverence and piety. They try to anticipate what the author wants, and sometimes to one-up the other students. They grope for the clichés they are sure the text comes down to. Their attention wanders; they skim; they skip around. They mark pages with pink and yellow highlighters. They get caught up in suspense. They laugh; they cry. They get aroused and (and stay quiet about it in class). They lose themselves in books, distracting themselves from everything else, especially homework like the reading I assign.[42]

"What audiences read to discover meanings that are beneath the surface of the text?" I ask. "Why do literature courses teach us to read for meanings that are not entirely explicit?" "Which audiences read to invest in a character's journey?" "Which read to increase their understanding and range of empathy?" These discussion questions shed light on how our texts may be engaged by our intended audiences and what it means to write toward these reading practices and the values upon which they are based.

This threshold concept teaches students that the literary text is a "form of activity inseparable from the wider social relations between writers and readers, orators and audiences, and as largely unintelligible outside the social purposes and conditions in which they are embedded."[43] This conception of writing emphasizes the co-constructed nature of texts, which are developed from a network of relations and intertextualities. Writers compose from what they have read and from what they understand of other writers and readers. Thus, a text cannot be divorced from the complex sociocultural and ecological communities that writing takes place within. These communities are not unified, homogeneous groups that exist prima facie for the writer to enter; rather, a writer's community may be constructed or met. Understanding this fluctuating complexity, the writer becomes more attentive to the effects of their choices and more able to make thoughtful moves in constructing their texts.

Concept 8: Evaluation

Literary value is contingent. The evaluation of literature is shaped by cultural and historical forces.

Wendy Bishop has been influential in her expressed resistance to the role of the creative writing teacher as "guardian of quality," but, as we know, eschewing this role does not entail an "anything goes" curriculum.[44] Rather, our responsibility as creative writing teachers is to help our students navigate the contingencies of literary value. Students can better understand how their writing may be used and valued in the world, recognizing that such evaluation is contingent.

The use-value of a text does not inhere in texts themselves; rather, as Barbara Herrnstein Smith notes, "any form of writing is only 'correct' with reference to the effect of its appeal, and that effect cannot be calculated determinately."[45] This concept counters the idea, as Katharine Haake does, that standards of good writing "reflect universal and enduring aesthetic values that exist somehow outside their cultural construction."[46] It also recognizes how "Questions of race . . . pervade our grammars, our styles, our forms, and above all our unstated systems of preferences, of aesthetic value," as is described in the book *The Racial Imaginary*.[47]

Our reading and engagement with diverse aesthetics needs to be primary in a critical creative writing pedagogy. This entails thoughtful and contextualized engagement with the Black Arts Movement, Créolité, Négritude, Nadaism, slam poetry, Ultraísmo, Pinoy poetics, the Misty Poets, Afro-Futurism, transpoetics, Chhayavaad, the Disability Poetics Movement and Crip poetry, and many other aesthetic traditions of written and oral literary forms, including postliterary poetries and micropoetries.[48] Students should work in written and oral modes, improvisational and occasional modes. Graduates of a creative writing program should know the Dark Room Collective, El Teatro Campesino, and the Nuyorican Poets Café, as well as they now know the New Formalists or the Imagists. Literary history is broad and multifaceted; it includes collectives, manifestos, and principles that emerge in different times and places. History conditions each of these emergences, and our students should write, read, and evaluate literature with a well-developed sense of this history.

Students in a critical creative writing classroom do not enact a universal standard of art, since any universal is but a privileging of one perspective. Rather, they uncover how literary values and expectations are produced. For example, Charles Baxter analyzes "[t]he mass-marketing of literary epiphanies and climactic endings [that] produces in editors and readers an expectation that stories must end with an insight" as an aesthetic value that is reflective of capitalist, consumerist US culture.[49] Features of writing reflect cultural values. As such, what is considered "good writing" varies from one situation to another. These variations depend, for example, on where a work is located in literary history, how it calls upon certain traditions, and how readers come to the work. What is effective for one interpretive community will not necessarily work for another. Students in creative writing need tools with which to identify these variations as they pertain to the work they read and write.

One way of introducing this topic in the creative writing class is to begin with a simple survey. I ask students how they would complete the following sentence: "I am writing for readers who value a literary text for its ..." Do their readers value a text for its capacity to entertain, capacity to promote empathy, capacity to challenge readers' beliefs, capacity to be repeated orally, capacity to preserve culture, capacity to voice the author's experience; capacity to include the audience's participation and co-creation of meaning; capacity to put readers in direct connection with the natural world; capacity to unite a community; capacity to teach. Other contingent values might include a text's complexity or simplicity, accessibility or difficulty, ambiguity or clarity, strangeness or familiarity. Then the question must be posed: How do different audiences think of these different values differently? What might be accessible to one audience, after all, might be difficult for another.

These contingent values are deeply related to the audience threshold concept, discussed above. As Andy Crockett posits, the value of an object depends on "who is deciding, what are the stakes involved in the designation, what are the pressures, who stands to gain, who stands to lose, and how are people being persuaded to the artfulness in question?"[50] These questions—who is deciding? what are the stakes? who stands to lose and who stands to gain?—are central to a critical creative writing pedagogy. How are literary expectations/values produced? To what extent, if any, are literary values trans-cultural and trans-historical?

To gain the resources for answering such questions about the contingencies of literary value, creative writing can draw from both rhetorical and aesthetic theories in order to reevaluate the standards by which students' texts are judged and to reconsider how these standards are communicated to students. These questions are central to a reading praxis in creative writing. Students can begin to identify the complexities of evaluation by learning to "read as a writer," which involves several layers. I teach three modes—craft-based, critical, and evaluative—which all contribute to reading as a writer.

Craft-based reading aims to construct how the text works. This mode entails asking: What choice is the writer making here? What other choices could the writer have made? How do the effects of these possibilities compare? What is it about the way this text is written that makes readers feel and respond the way they do?

Critical reading interrogates the ideological closures of a text (i.e., how the author cannot think beyond their own positions, how the author mobilizes commonly held assumptions, politics emerging from blindspots). This mode entails asking: To what extent does this text interrupt (or intervene in) the attitudes, beliefs, expectations, assumptions and myths that circulate among its audiences?

Evaluative reading works to judge whether the text is "good" (i.e., the extent to which it corresponds to a contingent set of values). This mode entails asking: Does the text achieve what it set out to do, within the contexts in which it might be read? How effectively does this text locate itself in the literary landscape? This form of reading is not about mere declarations of taste, which is, Jeffrey Schultz notes, "so often inserted as the artificial end-point of analysis in the workshop, the subjectivising death-rattle of conversation. Whenever workshop participants revert to the language of *liking* . . . whenever the conversation turns uncritically towards notions of taste, the conversation has already ceased."[51] To escape the tyranny of taste-based conversation, evaluative reading relies upon a critical analysis of how literature is valued and used by diverse communities. It also relies upon craft analysis that identifies the effects of textual representation, as detailed in the section that follows.

Concept 9: Representation

All forms of representation, including literary production, can be interrogated for assumptions, values, and ideologies.

Creative writing is a form of cultural production. It both reflects and stimulates culture. Our realities are constructed by common narratives. Judith Roof puts it this way: narrative might determine our notion of the shape of life and what is important in it."[52] In other words: To narrate is to know.[53] Narrative shapes our ways of knowing. How we represent something in narrative affects how that thing is known. Narratives arise from and in turn shape experiences.

There are master narratives that dominate a social imaginary, as the ideological scripts that act upon us.[54] Master narratives shape our notions of what is valuable, what is beautiful, what is right. These narratives are contingent, they can be changed, but they are powerful forces that produce material effects. The fact that "the socially dominant class has the final say in the designation of what is 'real' (what 'makes sense') and what is 'non-real' (what is 'nonsense') in a society" has everything to do with literary production and the workshop conversation, as Donald Morton and Mas'ud Zavarzadeh make clear in their essay "The Cultural Politics of the Fiction Workshop."[55] Dominant ideological scripts affect what is made legible in the workshop conversation, what is readable in a text.

Conscious of these ideological scripts and how they operate, the writer is faced with a decision: Do I write in a way that relies upon and reinforces master narratives? Or do I write to counter them? Joanna Russ elaborates this decision in her second-wave feminist text published in 1972 and titled "What Can a Heroine Do?" Russ explicates a range of plotlines as "dramatic embodiments of what a culture believes to be true—or what it would like to be true—or what it is mortally afraid may be true."[56] In turn, these stories shape us, construct our ways of knowing; "we interpret our own experience in terms of them ... we actually perceive what happens to us in the mythic terms our culture provides." Writers are therefore shaped by the cultures of which they are part, but they in turn can influence the culture. While it is true that writers "do not make up their stories out of whole cloth; they are pretty much restricted to the attitudes, the beliefs, the expectations, and above all the plots that are 'in the air,'[57] they can take what is "in the air" and counter it. The decision is thus: "the artist may either give the myth its final realization or stand it on its head."[58] The counter-narratives that call hegemonic myths into question vie for cultural cogency, to be heard.

The creative writing class has a responsibility to take into account the effects of the cultural productions that we teach—those written by our students and those assigned on our syllabi. Student texts, along with the published texts that accompany them on the creative writing syllabus, can be analyzed for the ideologies they represent. What cultural ideas does a particular text mobilize? What cultural assumptions does it call into question, and what assumptions or stereotypes does it rely upon? We can prompt our students to ask the following about their own texts and the published and peer-written texts they encounter:

- What common or established ideas does this text reinforce or destabilize?
- With every choice a writer makes, they forward an understanding of the world. How would you describe this text's understanding of the world?
- Whom or what is the text meant to speak for or about?
- What is centered and what is left to the margins of this text?
- How does the text represent its subjects? Are the representations potentially damaging, alienating, silencing, or oppressive?
- What are the potential ramifications of the text's claims? Who or what stands to gain from the text? And who or what stands to lose or be lost? Whom or what does the text serve?
- What might this text do in the world? How might it change societal understandings, representations, or beliefs?
- What exigencies does the text call upon?
- What desires does this text seem motivated by?
- Has the text avoided oversimplification? Has the text done justice to the multivalent, complex, and diverse nature of human experience with regard to the issues it invokes?
- How might this text avoid locking down its representation, avoid allowing the text to "stand in for" or reduce?
- What artistic responses might this text provoke? How can this text be generative of further artistic production and conversation?

With these questions, students come to understand how a literary text produces cultural meanings. Student-writers in the critical creative writing course learn to manage literature-as-representation with sensitivity and critical awareness. They come to understand the problems of cultural appropriation (Moody, et al., 2005), the essentializing tendencies of white audience expectations of identity aesthetics (Wang, 2014), and the trappings of a "post-identity" paradigm (Park Hong, 2014).[59] We discuss stereotype threat as it applies to writers and their characters.

How do we unlearn what we think we have learned about particular groups and identities? How do we represent the diversity and complexity of individuals' orientations and experiences, while also acknowledging the generalized condition of structural inequality, which shapes lives in different ways? How can we learn to follow our characters' cues about how best to understand them, represent them? How can we increase our cultural knowledge while remaining responsive to the emergence of each individual as they are in this time and this place?

We are always, as Stephanie Kerschbaum puts it, "yet-to-be." Our "differences are always shifting … because difference is relational" and contingent in each encounter.[60] "To communicate across difference," then, Kerschbaum continues, "people must always be looking to learn what more they do not know about the Other; they must avoid presuming they can know the Other as a totalized and whole consciousness. [...] To presume to know me is to close off interactional possibilities rather than to hold them open."[61] This is the stance with which we must come to our characters, our poems, and to each other in the workshop conversation. This openness toward the other is at the heart of how writers can usefully think about representation.

To explore these questions, we write. We represent a memory on paper. Then we reflect on our representations of these memories, reading them against Nadine Gordimer's claim that "original expression is inexorably linked to politics.[62] How might we read the politics that shape this writing? "The next question," Gordimer continues, "is what is the effect of the writer's original expression of social issues on the individual consciousness of society?"[63] How is this representation of memory operating on—or borrowing from—societal consciousness?

The creative writing course can teach the art of the counter-narrative and the process of identifying and challenging dominant narratives through representation. Some students will want to go further and write with an intended purpose of social change. Activist art and literature-as-resistance is a part of the critical creative writing curriculum because this pedagogy is shaped by the goals of social justice.

Concept 10: Resistance

Literature can forward social change and the transformation of culture. Literary production is a unique means of putting the world into question.

Students can identify purposes for their work, recognizing that literary texts can be means of social change (even as their particular rhetoricity is different from explicit argumentation). Creative writing is an occasion to consider what it means to engage literature as a form of resistance. The creative writing course can explore the intersections of art and activism.

Art-as-critique can disrupt prevailing norms, can subvert knowledges of the status quo, and can produce new ways of thinking. Art gives us something to think with, as it also shapes our structures of feeling. And art indeed can intervene.

A critical creative writing curriculum asks students to probe what it means to "create dangerously"—a phrase that Edwidge Danticat uses to name a "revolt against silence, creating when both the creation and the reception, the writing and the reading, are dangerous undertakings, disobedience to a directive."[64] Creative writing can promote such artistic disobedience to systems that perpetuate inequity and discrimination. To "create dangerously" is not to trot out a party line; it is instead a way of honoring the fact that literature, in its creation, knows more than we do.[65] We learn from the process of art's coming into being. Our task as teachers of creative writing is to foster students' access to this power of the literary text to call the world into question, to mobilize new ways of thinking. This is the difference between literature as resistance and literature as propaganda. Propaganda, in Gordimer's words, "comes from the certainty of orthodoxies and is never a quest, an individual exploration";[66] literature-as-resistance relies upon a unique mode of thought that calls the world into question in ways that cannot be predetermined, but can be intended and sought.

We should acknowledge that literature "is an active influence, reinforcing or refashioning values, beliefs, ideas, perceptions and aspirations," as Larry Diamond observes. "The teller of a story can become a powerful force in shaping the way a people think about their social and political order, and the nature, desirability and direction of change. [...] The novel, then, may be an agent of political culture."[67] A critical creative writing curriculum exposes students to this perspective and to techniques that might construct a politically effective art. Our students can learn to write art that seeks sophisticated political interventions. And, indeed, it may be imperative that they learn to do this—since the question of social change has long been at stake in literary production. Steve Westbrook has gone so far as to claim that it is much more difficult to list the names of writers who did not intend to change something with their words than it is to name writers who have written with the intention of social change. It is, as Westbrook notes, "extremely difficult to think of writers who have not acted to change culture or alter discourse in some meaningful way, however minor or major, especially when we recall that even the New Critics, who tried to isolate writing from its social function, set out to change—and successfully changed— the culture of writing instruction and the discourse of writing pedagogy."[68] Aesthetic discourse has regularly been harnessed for its power to disrupt normative practices. To mandate against didactic writing without acknowledging this is to mislead our students. Instead, our work in creative writing should be to interrogate what Westbrook has termed "the illusion of the purposeless text."[69] What are the purposes that interest our students? How can such purposes become enacted, problematized, reimagined, and interrogated through the artistic work of the creative writing class? What does it mean to participate in world-making as a creative writer?

Accepting that one may have a purpose for writing does not require that we surrender the value we place on uncertainty. Writing from a place of uncertainty allows us to go deeper into our purposes, to offer stories and poems that have more layers to excavate. We can invite our students into this work of delving into the political spheres that matter most to them—not to the exclusion of other forms and approaches to creative writing, but to no longer dismiss the significance of politicized literary production in the writing classroom.

Concept 11: Theory

Historical knowledge of aesthetic theories is important to the practice and craft of writing. Writers write within and against traditions, and thus benefit from a robust theoretical knowledgebase of cross-cultural artistic thought.

Creative writing is a discipline with a robust tradition of theory—written by writers, for writers. Students in a critical creative writing curriculum become well-versed in these theories, gaining the language to describe, critically examine, and put into practice aesthetic concepts such as Theodor Adorno's idea that writing must escape the world in order to intervene in the world, Langston Hughes' critical evaluations of how history and power relations shape the literary text, Trinh T. Minh-ha's suggestion that "knowledge for knowledge's sake is sickness" and she "who is sick with sickness" can pass on the story,[70] and many other concepts emerging from the aesthetic tradition. Examples of aesthetic theory address central questions regarding the relationship between literature and politics, between rhetoric and aesthetics.

The creative writing classroom is a place to examine how far theoretical concepts can take a writer, which forms of text-making they describe or fail to describe. The creative writing classroom can be a place where the things we think we know about writing are reevaluated and historicized.

For example, McGurl further specifies the history of several predominant ideas about the craft of fiction, which draw from prior aesthetic sources: "The installation of this ideal—whether known as the Jamesian 'scenic method' or in the homelier form of the dictum 'show don't tell' (which we might rephrase as 'dramatize don't generalize')—represents a deep penetration of narrative poetics by the techniques of dramatic writing. Taken up by Fitzgerald, Hemingway, and subsequently by a great many of the writers who would be associated with writing programs after the Second World War, the poetics of 'show don't tell' would gradually evolve into a more general understanding of *good fiction as founded on discipline, restraint, and the impersonal exercise of hard-won technique.*"[71] It is essential to discuss this positioned history, a history that is tied to identity politics.[72] How did the subject-positions of these authors contribute to their aesthetic theories?

The way we handle texts in the creative writing classroom is shaped by this history of aesthetics, and we do well to make this history—and all its contingencies—known to our students. We owe our students a nuancing of the perspectives they find in craft essays. Our evaluations will be more legible to students if they can understand the theories and assumptions that have shaped our understanding of the literary field. We can reconceive the creative writing class as an opportunity to decode literary communities for our students—to help emerging writers know how to navigate the cultures and conversations that constitute and promote contemporary literature.

Aesthetic theory teaches us that literary discourse has the unique capacity to awaken us to structural inequalities in a way that is not given over to hegemonic or official language, as art can escape the propositional. It can startle in a way that cannot be codified. Aesthetic discourse can detach us from the institutions to which we are given over. To follow this line of thinking in aesthetic theory is to open up the power of language in the communities that form in the workshop.

This threshold concept puts into conversation different theories of writing and is met with a challenge that I adopt from Hilde Hein: the challenge "not just to accommodate plurality, as any theory must, or to tolerate diversity, as liberal social theories profess to do, but to embrace that very ground of confusion—indeed to increase and intensify it."[73] Indeed, surveying conflicting theories of and intentions for literature can serve to confuse the regulating capacities of creative writing.

Concept 12: Revision

Writers learn to be responsive to what emerges in the process of creation, as they also bring a comparative literary analysis to bear on their revision process.

A critical approach to revision dismantles assumptions about "correcting" a text. It refuses to arrest the revision process into a list of do's and don'ts. We can put a range of options into conversation and ask what is possible.

In the workshop classes I teach, we complete a focused revision series in which students do a global revision of a single piece four or five times. With each iteration of the piece, they take a different approach. The goal is not to add four layers of refinement, but rather to explore four examples of what may be latent in each text.

In the process of completing this assignment, they gain a toolkit for revision that is meant to pluralize ideas of the genre's conventions. I take a comparative approach to understanding revision, to destabilize the idea that there is a single set of rules that guide revision. For example, when I teach story structure, the class period focuses on demonstrating that the Aristotelian plot arc is neither absolute nor neutral. I aim to help students gain a set of heuristics for thinking about how plots are constructed across varied literary works.

We read Janet Burroway's chapter on plot in *Writing Fiction* and then we discuss: "What does this chapter say about what Burroway values in literature?" I propose the thesis that "With every theory of craft there is a worldview at stake, a set of assumptions," and I ask the students what they notice about Burroway's worldview/assumptions. We locate Burroway as being influenced by minimalist, dramatic, and realist aesthetic traditions. We note in our analysis the value that Burroway places on individualism and the assumptions she represents (e.g., linear conception of time, belief in voluntary human action). We then outline in a column on the board her recommendations for story writing, grounding them in the contingencies of value that Burroway represents.

I then invite the students to write the major occurrences, significant moments, or salient transformations that compose their story drafts on a set of post-it notes, one event per sticky note. I print out an enlarged image of the inverted checkmark, and the students place their sticky notes on the diagram. They have extra sticky notes if they want to create additional scenes to add to their stories in a future revision.

This is where our discussion of Burroway pauses, and we start a new column on the board. The next column might detail Alice Munro's theory of story structure as a series of rooms—in which she conceptualizes story structure as creating a feeling of being inside. The metaphor of the building entails a notion of time different from what Burroway represents: the rooms are concurrent with each other, and what happens within them is juxtaposed and at times connected by motif. To give a visual for Munro's theory, I offer students another printout, to put next to Burroway's inverted checkmark: a basic blueprint of a building that has several rooms and a staircase. The students try moving their sticky notes onto this blueprint, in order to see how their story transforms with a different notion of story structure.

For homework, I have paired Burroway's chapter on plot with a story that defies some of her recommendations—Alice Munro's "Half a Grapefruit"; Jamaica Kincaid's "The Letter from Home"; an example of Lydia Davis' work, which Charles Baxter calls "Rotational";[74] Joy Harjo's "The Deer Dancer"; or Ryunosuke Akutagawa's "In a Grove," translated by Takashi Kojima. Juxtaposing readings that represent different orientations is part of a comparative approach to revision. The class session includes an examination of Leslie Marmon Silko's theory of Pueblo storytelling as a web, and the students experiment with moving their story's central events to a diagram of a spider's web that has a pronounced internal spiral.

The class is an occasion to think about what it means to revise toward textual features that Katharine Haake describes of Rachel Blau DuPlessis' work in *What Our Speech Disrupts*, including: contradiction and nonlinear movement, many-centeredness, anti-authoritarian ethics, antithesis to dominant values, porosity, fluidity, doubling, retelling the same, emotional vulnerability, blurring—between art and life, social creativity and "high" art, one's journal and one's poem, the artifact and the immersion in the experience—multivocality ...[75] Another feminist writer, Deena Metzger, embraces repetition, simultaneity, and interruption in fiction. She writes, "Plot may be convenient for the writer, but it does not necessarily correspond to the way things are. Plot demands abstraction, elimination, selection, and editing."[76] She sees the inclusion of the irrelevant or unconnected—that which does not forward the plot—as a means by which a writer may sanction under-represented experience.

As we have built the beginnings of a comparative analysis, we note Joanna Russ' claim that "the very pattern of dramatic construction which [some] take as natural, the idea that a story ought to have a beginning, a middle, and an end, that one ought to be led to something called a 'climax' by something called 'suspense' or 'dramatic tension' is in itself an Occidental myth."[77] We talk about the assumptions that different audiences might bring to a work of literature and how each mode of storytelling is culturally contingent. This comparative approach is meant to develop students' understanding of the range of possibilities available in storytelling as it also is meant to heighten their cultural awareness and sensitivity. I want them to revise knowing that their craft choices carry contingent values and assumptions.

To achieve this broadened understanding of the range of approaches to revision, students can compare examples of texts written in different styles. They can discuss the impact of different aesthetics by making translations and back translations across different conventions. The goal is to invite the complications and complexities of the creative process. As Davidson and Fraser note of the latter, "Polished poems announce: 'Look at how pristine and complete I am. Just imagine what kind of genius could sit down and produce such a work of art.' . . . we do well to remind our students to dwell within the messiness much longer than they might like."[78]

Threshold concepts and learning outcomes

This list of threshold concepts counters assumptions about creative writing that result in problematic commentary and exclusionary practices—assumptions such as "writers are born, not made"; or the idea that all writers are writing for essentially the same audience, necessitating the same set of craft principles; or the idea that revision is simply about applying universal craft principles. This list addresses the myth of the "transcendent imagination" that says critical thought and theory is deleterious to the creative process. This myth clings to the idea that the imagination is a free space, and writers can do whatever they want in the realm of creativity, unchecked by critical thought about how their representations came to be or the effects these representations will have in the world. The myth of the transcendent imagination denies and ignores the ways that our imaginations are conditioned by the societies in which we live. "We are all, no matter how little we like it," Beth Loffreda and Claudia Rankine write in the introduction to *The Racial Imagination*, "the bearers of unwanted and often shunned memory, of a history whose infiltrations are at times so stealthy we can pretend otherwise, and at times so loud we can't hear much of anything else."[79] They continue, "to argue that the imagination is or can be free of race—that it's the one region of self or experience that is free of race—and that I have a right to imagine whatever I want, and that it damages and deforms my art to set limits on my imagination—acts as if the imagination is not part of me, is not created by the same web of history and culture that made 'me.'"[80] The myth of the transcendent imagination, void of deliberate consideration of the limitations of what I know, either universalizes a particular (white) experience or imposes a single knower's understanding of the world on all subjects, able "to inhabit all, to address all"; either is a colonizing gesture. The myth of the transcendent imagination "mistakes critical response for prohibition."[81] The threshold concepts listed above emphasize critical response, hoping to put this fundamental myth of creative writing in check, make it answerable and accountable—"[t]o ask what we think we know, and how we might undermine our own sense of authority."[82]

Such threshold concepts can be translated into meaningful outcomes that lend themselves to assessment. My argument has been that the creative writing curriculum needs deliberate revision in order to move closer to a goal of an inclusive and equitable pedagogy. Assessment can be a means by which we check the status of that curricular revision process. Are there disparities in students' experience of the creative writing curriculum? Do our outcomes actively promote inclusion and equity, or are we failing to deliberately address these issues, which permeate all of our classes? It is, after all, the case that if we are not proactive in addressing these problems in the creative writing curriculum, we will continue to mobilize the same tenets of creative writing that have contributed to countless recorded and untold instances of marginalization. Assessment then becomes not about perfunctory boxes to check on an accreditation form; we need to rethink what and how we assess, in order to change a curriculum that has been systematically exclusionary.

Translating the threshold concepts to learning outcomes is a process of converting theory into practice. What do we want our students to be able to do, as a result of encountering these concepts? What behaviors and forms of production accompany these threshold concepts? I propose a list of twenty program outcomes below, which can be covered across a multi-course sequence. At my institution, for example, our course sequence in creative writing includes an introductory course, three advanced workshop classes, a special topics class in environmental writing, a research methods class, a course in literary editing and publishing, and a course on contemporary readerships. Each of these courses can address some part of this list of suggested program outcomes.

As a result of the creative writing curriculum, student-writers:

1. Demonstrate versatility in composing a body of work that shows aesthetic range.
2. Develop a habit of writing with a variety of methods, processes, and heuristics for generating and revising texts.
3. See a reading habit as deeply intertwined with a sustained writing process.
4. Employ writing as a meaning-making activity, creative-thinking practice, and research process.
5. Collaborate with fellow writers effectively, respectfully, and creatively to solve artistic problems.
6. Gain a basic practical understanding of the psychology of creativity.
7. Capture metaknowledge about writing that will sustain a writing practice and enable navigation of new writing situations.
8. Use a specialized lexicon to identify and assess craft choices and rhetorical moves in creative writing.
9. Consider the effects of specific craft choices for diverse readerships.
10. Incorporate craft analysis into a revision process.
11. Write with awareness of the controversies associated with craft and aesthetics.
12. Gain intimacy with the traditions, values, and debates that shape diverse literary communities.
13. Evaluate the representations found in texts generated and read.
14. Situate diverse texts in larger sociocultural contexts, literary traditions, and aesthetic theories.
15. Recognize and analyze the contingencies of literary value. Evaluate literature in context, with awareness of the diversity of the textual landscape.
16. Demonstrate a critical perspective about the relationship between literary, rhetorical, and multimodal texts.
17. Locate and analyze potential markets and forums for generated work.
18. Recognize the range of orientations and values represented by literary markets and readerships.
19. Demonstrate critical perspectives regarding authorship.
20. Demonstrate an understanding of literary citizenship and envision its role in a literary career.

Creative writing courses can encourage metadiscursive critical thinking and self-reflexivity. Students can be asked to position themselves within theoretical debates that pertain to aesthetic production and to consider their positionality within literary spheres. Students can work to articulate the rationale behind their textual choices, accounting for the traditions they draw upon and the readerly experiences they seek to create. In identifying threshold concepts for creative writing, the curriculum can come to encourage meta-cognition that will transfer across a range of occasions for writing and perhaps help students make sense of rejection notes and the vagaries of the submission-for-publication process. The idea that literary value is contingent and that audiences approach texts with different reading practices can help explain what happens in the publishing industry.

These are some of the benefits of a curriculum that fosters awareness of the threshold concepts that shape its disciplinary assumptions. The threshold concept is a tool that at once brings clarity about the practice of a discipline and openness to the possibilities a discipline has yet to uncover.

4

Toward an Inclusive Pedagogy

A critical creative writing pedagogy values flexibility, collaboration, and student agency. The goal is to enliven students' interest in writing in its range of forms and genres, to help them gain a fuller sense of how language works upon us and how we can act through it.

The previous chapter focused on the content of the curriculum; this chapter focuses on classroom culture. How can we establish a classroom culture that is affirming and centering for diverse writers? I share Tonya Hegamin's perspective that, "Radical inclusivity on all levels is a pedagogical commitment,"[1] and this chapter aims to explicate what those levels of commitment can be. Hegamin notes "the need for meaningful and radical inclusivity in and beyond the classroom, to incorporate different perspectives of religion, social class, language, gender, identity, national/immigrant status and physical/learning (dis)ability in all arenas of creative writing."[2]

The praxis described here is just one pathway toward the goal of creating a culture that is complementary to the goals of the threshold concepts outlined in the previous chapter. Many other strategies are described in texts such as Frank Tuitt and Chayla Haynes, *Race, Equity, and the Learning Environment*; Alicia Fedelina Chávez and Susan Diana Longerbeam, *Teaching Across Cultural Strengths*; and Kim A. Case, *Intersectional Pedagogy* and *Deconstructing Privilege: Teaching and Learning as Allies in the Classroom*.[3] This chapter follows from these pedagogical theories and focuses on strategies that are specific to the creative writing course.

Starting points

We know that the opening days and weeks of a new course are key to establishing an inclusive classroom culture. That first class session—with all its nervous, furtive energy—is where it must begin. The students enter the classroom. Some know each other and say hello. Some sit and wait. The classroom technology works or does not. The classroom feels strange; we have not made it familiar yet.

When I enter the classroom, I greet the students as writers. I welcome them and tell them that this is one community of writers that they now belong to, that they will contribute to all semester. They will shape the course in many ways, as authorized members of the community.

I then ask them to trust each other, even as we do not yet know each other, for a first exercise. "I have an unconventional way of starting the process of meeting each other. Before we even know each other's names, let's try something," I say.

The exercise is a well-known activity from the team-building repertoire. Some of the students may have participated in something like it before. They arise from their desks and follow me out to our building's foyer. The foyer has an inlaid tile square, which we circle around. I read a list of statements and ask that we (and I do participate as a member of the community) enter the square if the statement is true of us. Each statement is selected for its capacity to build common ground, to generate a sense of community, and to respect and acknowledge difference. The goal of the exercise is to build trust through the sharing of experiences that are relevant to the semester-long conversation that will follow.

"I'll read 12 statements," I say once our group is settled at the foyer of the building. "If any of these statements are true of you, you can enter the square." I add a caveat, asking our group to work together to not allow anyone to be in the circle alone. "So if you see someone is entering the circle alone, that can be an opportunity to fictionalize something about yourself," I say. Having the permission to fictionalize can provide an opening into this exercise for some students who may be more reticent. At the same time, I give the students the option to quietly choose not to participate by simply remaining in the circle and not entering the square.

I start with a few statements that are inviting. "Enter the square," I say, "if you remember a story that you encountered as a young person." "Enter the square if there are stories your family or friends tell over and over." These statements implicitly celebrate the shared value of writing or storytelling, and validate each student's experience of language. Then we move to the statements of other types of shared experiences—some of which might be more vulnerable to share.

"Enter the square if you've ever experienced writer's block." Most step in with this one, and I promise that this is a topic we will address in the weeks to follow.

"Enter the square if you've ever heard something said about writing that you disagree with." Most step in here too, and I note that we will be joining a conversation about writing this semester that is characterized by diverse viewpoints and a range of controversies. They are invited to offer their own perspectives on questions about writing that are very much open to debate.

"Enter the square if you've received a comment about your work that made you want to stop writing." "Enter the square if you've ever been in a class where someone said something that made you uncomfortable and that was not addressed." "Enter the square if you're nervous about this class." These last statements underscore the importance of establishing agreements and a classroom culture that will prevent some of the negative experiences common to creative writing. Discouragement resulting from feedback, discomfort that goes unaddressed, etc., these exigencies become important to the group as a whole through this exercise, as students identify them as problems that have lasting effects.

This "common ground" exercise leads nicely into the process of establishing agreements that will shape our practice, as a community, throughout the semester. A creative writing course demands utmost respect from everyone. Writing is a personal and vulnerable activity, and we share that vulnerability in the space of the workshop. I want it to be clear from day one that disrespectful behavior is never ok. The process of devising collective agreements provides a way forward in addressing these issues.

"Let's take a moment to define what we want to agree to, as we work to establish our community," I say as we move back into the classroom. I invite the students to introduce themselves to a partner and to begin listing on a notecard the principles that will sustain their own participation in an effective writing community. In this process, they list statements like: "We agree to step up and step back, allowing everyone space to speak and contribute." They pass in their notecards anonymously, and we discuss the agreements as I record them by typing into a blank document projected on the board. "What does this look like in practice?" I ask after many of the suggested agreements. "What would be an example of enacting versus violating this principle?"

In this process, students share anecdotes about instances when they or their peers might have felt marginalized from the conversation, and I ask students to offer their own (fictionalized or true) anecdotes about other examples of behaviors that detracted from learning and community-building. The following are a few scenarios I present, as I ask the students to consider: What agreements could we call upon to address these scenarios?

1. Student A is focused on their iPhone instead of on the workshop. This makes the writer who is up for workshop feel angry and hurt.
2. Student B dislikes science fiction, fantasy, and romance stories. When these stories come up for workshop, Student B writes a cursory response and offers only a single snide comment in the conversation.
3. Student C wants to submit a 50-page story for workshop. Other students express concern about the workload this entails for the respondents.
4. Student D does not want to have to read things that are not interesting to them. When Student D is part of a small group, they have little to contribute because they have not prepared for class by reading our shared homework assignment.
5. Student E makes a joke about how women can not write. This makes several people in the class feel demeaned.
6. Student F makes a racist comment about one of the characters in a story that we read together as a class.

I invite the students to invent some of their own scenarios, if they wish to add to this list. The list is meant to provide a way of checking that the agreements we have generated account for a range of concerns that can arise in the creative writing classroom.

These scenarios need to be approached with empathy. At times, students will offer the "own your offense when you're offended" trope to numbers 5 and 6, so the instructor should be prepared to begin to address the issue of how power operates in the classroom with the introduction of these scenarios. When a trope like "own your offense" arises in the conversation, I will write it on the board, thanking the student for mentioning this common idea. I then ask the students to work together to unpack the values and assumptions behind this statement. We need to remember that words matter and have material effects. The word "taking" in the phrase "taking offense" reflects an ideology that says "offense" is a personal choice—something that can be taken or left at will. But in fact "offense" is an injury that is suffered. It is an injury that is tied up in structural realities. It is the onus of the one who injures to "own" the action that caused offense, to understand the implications and risks of their choice.

Spending a significant portion of time on these issues communicates to students their importance, and I stress that we will revisit and revise these agreements periodically and as needed. The agreements that emerged from my most recent fiction-writing class included the following:

- Use trigger warnings for workshop stories.
- Workshop stories should be no more than twenty pages, double spaced. Please include page numbers.
- Read always from a place of love—love of the writing of what the story can be, and love of—and empathy for—your fellow writer.
- Be conscious of difference. Use "I" statements. Acknowledge your positionality, your background—and how your cultural assumptions may not be shared.
- Make space for every voice to be heard. Step up and step back, balancing contributions.
- Do not put down your own work or apologize for it.
- It is ok to just listen, to pass, but also push yourself. Remember that stepping out of one's comfort zone is often key to the transformative experience that is learning.
- It is ok to bring food.
- We will try to take a five minute break as a group each class, but we are free to take additional breaks individually if/when we need.
- Share facts about yourself, even when not prompted. Maybe preface your reading with a random fact. Listen to others for story ideas.
- Snapping is encouraged after someone reads.
- Listen to feedback, especially when something you have said has offended someone. Don't defend ignorance—acknowledge it, and recognize that we all have points of ignorance. Be grateful for these occasions as they are essential opportunities to learn.
- Do not tell someone what is correct or incorrect about their culture.
- Stay open to criticism. Be curious about what readers have to say. Approach the craft with humility.
- Show utmost respect for both readers and writers who are offering you the gift of their perspective.

It may be useful to follow this discussion of our collective agreements with a pledge of our own, as teachers. At the front of the classroom, we should acknowledge the power we have and the way we shape the space. Omi Osun Joni L. Jones suggests the importance of a pledge of "commitment to fulfill my role as producer [program facilitator] as thoroughly and respectfully as possible," indicating to workshop participants that "I want their trust, and I can gain it by being accountable to them."[4]

I follow this agreements-setting exercise by providing students a chance to write a vision and plan for their part in the course and success in the semester, with holistic attention to their ranging interests and obligations.

The goal with these exercises is to establish from day one students' ownership of the course and their learning. I want students to see that the course is much more theirs than mine, I want them to explicitly identify how the course fits with their larger goals, and I want them to realize that they have a great deal of control over their learning experience. We check-in about these agreements, these personal vision statements, and the class ethos periodically throughout the course.

Perhaps because of the work we do on the first day to set the foundation for the conversations we will have going forward, I find that by the end of the semester, the students often want to celebrate the community they have created. I believe that this process of articulating students' investments, desired ethos, and concerns during the first week of class is key to achieving this outcome.

Across the creative writing curriculum—including the editing and publishing classes offered at my institution—I distribute a document titled "our practices" that includes the following list of agreements:

1. We read every work carefully and thoroughly. Every text is worthy of considered attention, and every submission is read from beginning to end at least twice.

2. We are generous readers, willing to follow where each piece leads. We avoid comments that would overwrite the piece—comments that seek to erase and replace the text with our vision; rather, we seek to fully engage the work that exists.

3. We acknowledge and identify our biases and tastes. We recognize that the texts we encounter sometimes challenge us, and that can be a sign of merit and value. In turn, we challenge the texts we read by asking critical questions about a text's politics, ideologies, assumptions, and representations.

4. We are mindful of the contingencies of literary evaluation. We value multiple forms of literary production and recognize that conventions differ across traditions. As we evaluate each submission, we identify the traditions and conventions that each text calls upon, seeking to locate the text in a diverse aesthetic landscape.

5. Our conversations and evaluations are respectful of the time and efforts of each writer. We treat each work with care and humility.

Many of the concepts that are invoked in this list of agreements and practices require further discussion and analysis, and time should be built into the curriculum for these conversations. This list can be seen as a means of previewing subsequent study, as it draws upon threshold concepts regarding evaluation and representation.

Other considerations go into the first week of the semester. In the process of introducing ourselves to the group, we share our preferred gender pronouns. To accomplish this, students will sometimes co-write flash-fiction stories that mention their partner both by name and by the correct gender pronoun. I also have the students write a confidential letter to me, on an index card, that responds to my question: "How can I best support you?" I ask that the students list any requested accommodations in this letter.

For homework after the first day, the students complete a writer profile that introduces their preferred genres and they introduce some of their favorite cultural works (including film, music, art, and literature) to the class. This exercise provides an initial way of mapping the constellation of reference points that the students bring to the class.

In the first week, I also have students write a letter to someone just starting out in the writing profession, following Teju Cole's "Eight Letters to a Young Writer." This positions each student as having the authority to speak about their craft. I ask the students to pull a favorite sentence from each of their peers' letters, and we generate a list of affirmations for the writing process, composed by our classroom community, that we can return to throughout the semester.

In the first weeks of the semester, I also ask students to identify some of the preconceptions about writing and the figure of the writer that they have inherited from previous classes and cultural forms, such as Hollywood films, addressing the Authorship threshold concept described in the previous chapter. I show images and clips from a range of films and ask students to identify common traits of the writer we see on the screen. We spend a class session identifying the assumptions we see embedded in popular representations of the writer in films and novels such as *Dead Poets Society, The Perks of Being a Wallflower or Wonder Boys.* What do these representations communicate? Why is it important to put a critical eye toward these representations and toward the history of creative writing in higher education? We uncover how constructions of authorship regularly privilege white male middle-class identity. We look at images from creative writing programs' current and past marketing materials, some of which I have collected from institutional archives at the University of Denver, Boston University, Middlebury College, and elsewhere. We look at images from the 1940s, 1950s, and today. Who and what is pictured in the materials that creative writing programs use to present themselves and attract participants? We then read Leslie Marmon Silko to find another way of thinking about what it means to be a storyteller. Silko's work helps us to uncover the biases carried in the common image of the writer in the garret. This discussion provides a segue into the Unpacking Privilege exercise described in Chapter 1, and we learn to adopt a practice of checking how our views are informed by our backgrounds, positionality, and enmeshments. We begin a practice of self-reflexivity that will carry us forward in our discussions throughout the semester.

Reading

I also use the opening weeks of the semester to call upon and probe students' preconceived ideas about the scope of the course. I facilitate an exercise in which students examine a set of seven or eight example works in our genre of study that demonstrate aesthetic or formal range. The set might be drawn from several relevant subgenres. In the fiction workshop, for example, this might include a creation story, a fairy tale, a work of hint fiction, a transcript of a voice message left on my phone, a radio story, an example of collaborative oral storytelling, a testimony, a fable, comic panels, a Storify story, etc. For a poetry workshop, I might use lyrics from a range of traditions, chants and incantations, a greeting card poem, an example from a slam competition, a love poem missive that I have drawn from our university archives, etc. We might call upon Ishmael Reed's *From Totems to Hip Hop* and Jerome Rothenberg's *Technicians of the Sacred: A Range of Poetries from Africa, America, Asia, Europe and Oceania*, to examine how diverse poetries can be brought together into a single anthology. In presenting students with these curated anthologies of various approaches to storytelling, poetics, or essay-writing, I am careful to include authors and storytellers who represent a range of intersectional positionalities and cultural traditions.

As they browse these anthologies, I ask the students to discuss how the words "story," "fiction," "anecdote," and "narrative" (or "poetry," "poetics," "lyric," "lines," "verse," etc.) move in the world. What are these words used to describe? Who uses these words, and for what purposes do they use them? I then ask the student-writers to think about our scope of practice in the class. What do you expect will be beyond the purview of our work together?

The purpose of this exercise is to help students consider the diversity of the textual landscape and discursive production. It is also meant to call attention to the fact that every course draws boundaries and delimits its scope. I want students to recognize that these boundaries are a construct and that we should always look around the edges. We should be continuously mindful of what our class sessions are leaving out. I want students to be conscious of what our discussions are accounting for and what textual forms are being pushed to the outside in any given conversation. It is this consciousness that will help us all consider and include a wider diversity of textual forms, as we check: what are we missing here?

We then turn to the course syllabus and analyze it as a constructed artifact. What readings are listed on our syllabus? What traditions, what writers, are not assigned? What does it mean to pluralize a curriculum? I prompt this discussion by assigning Gloria Anzaldúa's essay "How to Tame a Wild Tongue."[5] Her discussion in that text of the canon taught in academic English courses leads us to think about the canon that is put forward in creative writing. We examine readers and craft texts that are intended for creative writers, and we note the stories and poems that regularly appear across these textbooks. Then the students take on a research project in our university library of locating and naming contemporary writers who are not included in the set of craft texts that we evaluate together. The list they generate serves as our ongoing reading list, to which we will add throughout the semester. I emphasize that the small sampling of works listed on the syllabus are there because they teach something specific, but that they should be only the tip of the iceberg of the students' reading experiences. Our collective reading list should be balanced with the assigned readings, and each student is responsible for growing the collective list of recommended texts, expanding our survey of the literary landscape in its breadth and diversity.

Those texts that appear on the syllabus I have selected by thinking carefully about their orientation. What do these texts assume about their readership? How do the writers position themselves? I avoid colonizing texts, thinking about the ways that Adrienne Perry and David Mura have characterized those texts that offer a totalizing perspective. Perry defines the colonizing text as that which "positions itself as an authority.... Nothing of the world is as real as what the text has to say, and the text seeks applause for being such as it is, for demanding— no matter its subject—that we cosign on its version of reality."[6] The author of the colonizing text is also, in David Mura's words, "convinced he knows the way the world works, and he knows what respect is, and he knows what it is to tell the 'truth.'"[7] Mura is speaking specifically of David Foster Wallace here, but the statement is a characterization of a range of works. In the precious few weeks of a semester, we should focus on the texts that will challenge, rather than reinforce, the colonizing assumptions of creative writing.

An integrated and inclusive course requires more than just tokenistically including one or two writers who represent "difference." It means dismantling creative writing's white-centrism, ableism, heteronomativity, and xenophobia. All too often, as Claudia Rankine observes, addressing white instructors of creative writing directly: "white students aren't being asked, by you and the readings and visitors you arrange for them to encounter, to think harder about the assumptions they carry into and express in workshop."[8] The readings we assign must prompt this thinking, as they also communicate that a diverse body of writers with a range of perspectives are central to the literary community.

The assumptions that students and faculty bring to workshop are powerful in shaping writers' experiences. Recognizing this requires that we do more to examine these assumptions before entering the workshop space. This work of evaluating received beliefs is supported by the body of craft-criticism (i.e., reflections on writing, by writers and for writers) that thinks through the implications of cultural production. Examples of craft-criticism that can support critical discussion of the issues that may arise in workshop include: Barrie Jean Borich's "The Craft of Writing Queer"; Edwidge Danticat's *Create Dangerously*; Nadine Gordimer's "The Essential Gesture: Writers and Responsibility"; Porochista Khakpour's "The Others"; Toni Morrison's *Playing in the Dark*; Trinh T. Minh-ha's *Woman, Native, Other*; Xu Xi's "Three Commandments for Writing about Race"; the collection *Beauty is a Verb: The New Poetry of Disability*; and the PEN World Voices panel discussion titled "Inappropriate Appropriation," on cultural appropriation.[9] These texts build a shared framework that prioritizes consideration of the implications of each work of literature. They teach us to ask: What work might this text do in the world? What are the potential political, social, ecological, etc. consequences of this text? "What cultural work does this artifact or this poetic event accomplish? What does it tell us about our own situations?"[10]

Workshop

Learning to ask these types of questions is necessary. Too often these questions are elided from the workshop conversation. In their absence, what is said in workshop is often characterized by microaggressions and unchecked bias. For example:

> When I questioned my first MFA instructor in 2012 on why he didn't include a
> diversity of writers on the reading list, he said, 'I didn't think anyone would be

interested in that.' [...] I had a few other (white) teachers who might have included one book by a person of color or people who dwell in the realm of 'other,' but they were clearly unprepared to have deep conversations about the ways writing, reading and critical analysis are affected by a variety of minority perspectives.

Tonya Hegamin[11]

When a student takes the time to point out the inequality determining, governing, and policing white spaces by stating simple facts, that student is often read by white writers in positions of authority, as well as the student's white peers, as problematic, difficult, and ungrateful ... held responsible for hurting the feelings of the benevolent, pure-minded, and well-intentioned white faculty and white students.

Claudia Rankine[12]

When a white writer is questioned or confronted by writers of color about her representation of race, she responds: "I did not mean to do any harm. Or: I wanted to imagine you—isn't that good of me, haven't others said that was good of me to try? Or: I'm writing about people; they just happen to be white. Or: If I cared about politics, I would write a manifesto—what I'm trying to do is make art. Or: I have a right to imagine whatever I want. Or: I don't see color. Or: we're all human beings.

Beth Loffreda and Claudia Rankine[13]

A famous poet who had made his reputation as a voice for the urban working class in a rust belt state spoke against recruiting me to teach creative writing to students wanting to write poems. He did not reject me based on the quality or quantity of my work. After all, my first book, *Crossing the Peninsula*, had received the Commonwealth Poetry Prize in 1980; I had published a couple of other collections; and my poems were being published in both U.S. and international journals and were beginning to appear in anthologies. Instead, he could not see how I could teach poetry to American students, when I spoke English with an accent. How could I teach rhyme, rhythm, and metrical scansion? How could I teach poetry in State U classrooms without an American voice?

Shirley Geok-lin Lim[14]

One can imagine that the microaggressions that Shirley Geok-lin Lim experienced could translate also to students in the workshop who might be marked as "accented" and therefore not belonging to particular literary spheres or readerships. Indeed, if this list is a representative sample, one can imagine that many more occurrences of silencing, insult, and invalidation are present in creative writing classrooms—many of which no doubt remain ignored in conversations about creative writing pedagogy. The disavowal of racial subjectivity in white-dominated creative writing discourse—the ignorance of whitestream assumptions as being racially marked in a dominating system—has far-reaching consequences in the creative writing classroom.

When the microaggression goes unaddressed, when there is no intervention in response to the microaggressor, we deny an invitation to combat racism and xenophobia and reject the chance to grapple with the complexities of identity and power. We miss these opportunities, I suspect, because we are unprepared to have these conversations. The standard creative writing curriculum we have traditionally set before our students, the discipline that we have inherited, the academic culture we joined—all these are forces that have foreclosed these conversations before they can begin.

The imperative that workshop practices change comes across starkly in reading the list above. Racism and xenophobia must be addressed in workshop. After all, as Sara Ahmed makes clear, "Saying that race is 'too difficult' is how racism gets reproduced."[15] Saying that race is "too difficult" to talk about continues what Derald Wing Sue calls the "conspiracy of silence" that serves "to perpetuate the status quo of race relations."[16] But to change workshop practices requires that we go deep into our curricula, deep in our beliefs about what it is we teach, and interrogate what we emphasize and what we ignore. How many readings on our syllabi, for example, explicitly address the fraught issues that can arise in workshop concerning identity, embodiment, language, and power? What scaffolding have we built into our courses to support discussions about ethnocentrism and difference? What heuristics can students and teachers collectively call upon in the moments when something wrong and assaulting is said in workshop?

The workshop as it has been is not set up to support antiracist and inclusive pedagogy. Traditional workshop practices are exclusionary in more than one sense. Maria Damon finds that it would be "simply inappropriate" to run many poetic acts "through the vitiated critique-mills be they of the MFA workshop or the poststructuralist stripe.... Modernist workshop conventions are not up to the task." Damon argues that "different 'listening skills' are required for certain texts.[17]

Similarly, in "A Small Balletic Hive" and "Igniting the Inward Prodigy"—two essays found in the collection *Singing in Magnetic Hoofbeat*—Will Alexander describes his approach to the workshop as eschewing the common practice:

"texts read, choices of phrasing discussed, fleeting forays into possible forms of publication" as he finds these classroom routines to be born of a "conservative pragmatics."[18] As a radical alternative and oppositional response to this conservatism, Alexander's workshop is concerned with the "praxis of interior life": "inner fertilization," "lateral thinking" (Edward de Bono), "movement for the sake of movement," "change [to] one's ideas," the "generation of flux," the "shattering of the sequential," "self-challenge," and the provocation of the "nucleus of courage." Alexander values "suspended judgment (de Bono), which allows for the possibility for increasing new, seemingly curious approaches."[19] All of this serves to "actively attack imaginal complacency."[20] Such a poetics of flux, activated in the classroom, destabilizes the compartmentalizing tendencies of "find-your-own-voice" workshop pedagogy.

The onus is on the field to experiment with new ways of conducting workshop in order to best serve the students who come to it. For example, moving toward a more inclusive approach may include an elimination of that "cardinal rule" which insists on the writer's silence when one's work is under discussion. This rule causes the writer to become hidden behind the written product. The text is positioned as speaking for the person, which can have the ramification of prioritizing product over a writer's process. Moreover, this common convention of the silent writer too often forwards an assumption either that all students are working toward a universal aesthetic standard or that the writer's intentions for a particular text can be derived from the words on the page. Both assumptions are problematic. The first—that a universal literary standard can be implicitly assumed—ignores the contingencies of literary value and the ways in which art is context-bound. The second assumption is otherwise known as the intentional fallacy. Michelene Wandor notes of this assumption: "To build a pedagogical set of principles on 'reading' the impossible, the invisible, is to reaffirm the unteachability of the most highly desired and elusive element of creative writing: talent, and genius."[21] In traditional workshop practice, because one cannot read the impossible or deduce a student-writer's intentions, student commentators impose their own intentions on the text and overwrite it by providing prescriptive comments that manifest their biases and taste. The writer may experience this as a silencing, colonizing gesture, depending on the power dynamics in the room. The silent writer is forced into the position of passive student who cannot be trusted to speak, and the workshop becomes more hierarchical than collaborative.

To revise this practice and invite conversation between writer and readers can alleviate what Patrick Bizzaro calls "the abandonment of apprentice writers in creative-writing programs and classes to the decisions of others."[22] Bizzaro's concern about writers' abandoning their decisions to the recommendations of others is built into the structure of common pedagogical practice in university creative writing. Instead of making routine recommendations such as "this text needs to be half its length," workshop readers can learn to reflect on their reading experience, with critical attention to their positionality, taste background, and potential bias. They can then join the writer in collaboratively identifying the craft choices and moves of the text. This results in a dispersal of authority and resists any mentor–apprentice relationship as the instructor, too, avoids prescriptive commentary.

To do otherwise, to prevent students from talking about their texts in terms of strategies, purposes, and audience, is to reinforce the mysticism surrounding the literary genius author. Forcing student-writers to be silent in workshop also buttresses the idea that only the "successful" authors get to talk about their writing, their intentions and sources. Reflective statements from authors on their works abound: these metadiscursive descriptions preface the stories and poems found in literary anthologies, and they are published in the form of author-interviews. How much do we know about students' sources, intentions, and rationales?

The aim in transforming workshop practice is to avoid imposing an aesthetic on student work. Thus, comments that start with phrases such as "What this story wants to be ...,". "What it needs ...,". "What if you ...," should be replaced with questions such as "What do you want your story to be? Your rhetorical move or craft choice here has this effect on me, and I'm not sure that's in-line with your purpose. What do you think?"

Other questions can be posed to the group with the ethos of earnest, empathic, and open co-exploration. Asking the writer, "How do you imagine your readers? What informs your intended readers' approach to literature?" can correspondingly help respondents to consider: In what ways am I, as a student in a workshop class, reading with different assumptions than the writer's intended audience?; How do my enmeshments and experiences influence my reading? Some additional exploratory questions for a fiction workshop include the following:

Vision, genre, intended audience
Where do you locate this story in the textual landscape? What genres and subgenres does it seem to call upon? What audiences does it include or exclude, given the story's assumptions and conventions? What are the potential political, social, ecological, etc. consequences of this story? Are master narratives or counter-narratives at work in this piece? Where do you expect this text to

circulate? How might it be packaged? How will that packaging affect audience expectations? If you were writing the query letter for this piece, who would you pitch it to and how would you pitch it?

Development: Characterization
What does/do the main character(s) want? What compels the character(s) to action? In what ways are the central character(s) conflicted? What ambivalences arise in this story? In what ways do these character(s) embody contradiction? What do we know about the characters' positionalities (from explicit characterization, implicit markers, etc.), and what from their background influences their actions? What, for the characters, is worth fighting for, and why? What stake do the characters have in the story's central tensions? What do you notice about the politics of representing these characters? To what extent are stereotypes affirmed or dismantled in the characterization? What cultural, societal, interpersonal, interior, psychological dynamics shape the characters? How is this character shaped and formed by the inequitable systems around them/him/her?

Development: Tension and suspense
Do problems and difficulties consistently sustain this story? What does the character want, and what obstacles are in the character's path? What patterns of shifting power relations, connection/disconnection are established? Remember that readers may be most invested in central characters who act and are not merely acted upon. What decisions do the characters make? How can the tension in this story be heightened? Are there moments where the story "gives away" its tension or suspense? Does the story answer its dramatic questions too soon? What parts of the story have the most dramatic tension, and which parts have the least?

Development: Significant detail
Are transformative plot events rendered in scenes? Do these scenes have a sense of time and space, with specific bodies moving in specific places? Do you, as a reader, know enough about the story to be able to feel that the action is actually taking place? Are there opportunities for additional significant details to be added to, or layers of meaning to be embedded in the story's presentation? Does the setting seem clichéd or stereotypical? Does it feel as though the writer has done the necessary research to find significant details?

Dialogue, voice, and POV
What adjectives would you use to describe the narrator's voice, and each individual character's voice? What do you notice about the characters'

voices? Are the voices consistent throughout? Do the voices contribute to the tension of the story and make you want to read on? Does the writer avoid creating a caricature or misrepresentation of a person or group through their voices, speech patterns, etc.? Is verb tense and POV consistent, and do these choices serve the story? What do the rhythms of this text remind you of, or what do they evoke?

Theme and motif

Does the story support multiple interpretations? Does it embed layers of meaning in its content? Does it make use of subtext? Does the story offer significance that transcends the plot line? How would you describe the thematic material that the story is working with? What motifs recur in the text, and what meanings are associated with them? If Nancy Welch is right that "all stories make arguments,"[23] what arguments is this narrative making? Whom or what do those arguments serve?

Intertextuality

How is this story similar to or different from other forms of cultural production that you have encountered—literature, films, songs, etc.? What does it remind you of? What associations are you bringing to the work as a reader? You may wish to mention ideas from craft-criticism essays, authors that seem to take a similar style or approach, a poem that reflects a similar theme, etc. Help the writer to locate the piece in the textual landscape, to know how the story functions intertextually. How do the allusions and reference points invoke certain readerships? How is this writer participating in cultural, social, political, philosophical, religious discourse?

Research

Suggest ways that outside research can help to support the story. What in the story does not yet seem fully credible? What of the story's representation of people or places needs further development and complexity? How can the writer use multiple modes of research (e.g., observation, analysis, consulting secondary sources, etc.) to move beyond received ideas, common notions, cliches, and hackneyed content? Do you have sources to suggest this writer draw upon in revising this story?

These questions are directed at both readers and writers together. They are meant to spur on class discussion, and they put questions of race, identity, politics, and the diversity of readership on the table when they are so often ignored in traditional workshop conversations. These factors may be regularly ignored, but they are present in each text nonetheless. As David Mura notes in his recent *Writer's Chronicle* article, "If the very way white writers introduce their characters and the very way writers of color introduce their characters is racialized, how is it that any piece of American fiction, white or POC, escapes being racialized?"[24] These questions, and attempts to answer them, would replace the problematic dictums that so often circulate in traditional workshops— blanket generalizations like "show, don't tell" or pronouncements about what a story or poem must include. The goal is to replace any formulaic rule-imposing method with a critical conversation about the effects of different craft choices in a literary landscape.

In some ways, the workshop discussion illustrated here is similar in nature to what Eve Shelnutt described as a theoretical questioning approach, meant to replace standard workshop commentary; she reports that this course model gained much popularity among students at her university in 1989.[25] However, such critical approaches are still relatively rare in university creative writing.

The benefits of rethinking the workshop are many. By learning to ask metadiscursive questions, students will not only become better writers of creative texts, they will also be able to participate in conversations that shape literary thought. At stake in these discussions are the following questions, posed by Garber:

> [D]o writers really have the power to revise the master narratives of a culture? Are all fictions inevitably located somewhere in relation to the master narratives? Can a significant deviation from a master narrative be effected without changing the structure of the narrative? Is a master narrative as much a set of reading conventions as it is a set of textual conventions? Is the disturbance of a deviation from a master narrative greater if the deviation remains ostensibly representational? (Is serious representational fiction impossible now—all ostensibly representational fictions being essentially self-reflections on the nature of representation?)[26]

Learning to write "requires a vigorous and often painful recognition of one's own prejudice and/or vulnerabilities within the workshop space," Hegamin observes."[27] As instructors, it is our responsibility to facilitate these conversations in ways that make entry available to every student in the room, no matter how challenging the subject matter.

Evaluation and grading

The critical creative writing course supports students as they gain a vocabulary and a set of questions for analyzing craft choices and revising their own writing. The course helps students articulate the traditions they work with or against. They learn to think critically about the moves they make in their writing and the effects their texts can have in the world. The writing classroom is an opportunity to question traditions as well as learn them. With this emphasis in mind, the topic of evaluation and assessment becomes a site where students can apply what they are learning about conventions, traditions, the diversity of literary spheres, and the contingencies of value. I invite students to critically analyze the criteria I would have them meet and to examine the values that manifest in the course materials I have drafted. We collaboratively revise the baseline rubrics and heuristics that I provide, so that the students can have input on what forms of evaluation are most useful to them. In this process of discussing a rubric, we consider definitions of successful writing and analysis.

My evaluation process is focused on students' contributions to the class community over and above their performance. I prioritize their reflections on their peers' writing and how they have shared their analysis of their own work in progress. This reflective writing enables discussion, rather than unidirectional feedback from teacher to student.

To supplement group discussions, I also meet with students regularly outside of class in order to offer individualized conversations about their work where some students may feel more comfortable bringing certain questions or thoughts. These conversations are in addition to peer reviews conducted in class activities and workshop. This approach to evaluation prioritizes formative development and uses multiple modalities so that students gain ample practice in giving and receiving feedback as members of a writing community and contributing to conversations about craft.

To give students a chance to review their learning, I ask them to complete a final take-home "exam" that is written as a set of author interview questions posed to each student. I provide a bank of interview questions, and the student-author chooses a subset for their responses. The process is meant to be authorizing, as it also provides a means of assessing how well we have grappled with the twelve threshold concepts that I see as key to an inclusive creative writing curriculum. As they write, I encourage the students to think of their author interview as a way of contributing to the writerly conversation we survey in the craft-criticism we read together. For example, the types of questions that the students in a fiction workshop see in this final review include the following:

1. How can fiction writers support linguistic diversity? And what risks does a writer need to consider when writing in a voice that is not one's own?
2. What do you think about "cultural appropriation" as it applies to fiction writing?
3. How can writers write in a "responsible" way (thinking of Nadine Gordimer's use of the term in "The Essential Gesture")?
4. How can writers avoid contributing to stereotypes? How can writers avoid mobilizing limiting constructions of lives and identities?
5. "The message is in the means." "Form and content are inextricably intertwined." What do you think about either or both of these clauses in relation to fiction-writing?
6. What is the significance of the VIDA findings? What should be done about the myth of meritocracy in publishing?
7. Describe a time when you encountered a problematic representation in a work of fiction. How can readers, fellow writers, or teachers of creative writing address issues of representation in a more critical way?
8. How is research important to your process in writing fiction? How do you think about research processes and strategies in creative writing? What risks and possibilities (including ethical considerations, etc.) are involved in fiction writers' use of outside sources, including print materials, observations, and interviews?
9. How do you account for the "contingencies of literary value" when you sit down to write? What are some significant and illustrative examples of how literary value is contingent?
10. What is meant by the idea that "there are risks and possibilities to every choice a writer makes"? What is an example of a craft choice you have made and the risks/possibilities you weighed in making it?
11. What is one finding or principle from the psychology of creativity that you find useful to your process of writing fiction?
12. What methods, processes, or heuristics for generating texts (i.e., "invention") do you find most useful?
13. What methods, processes, or heuristics for revising texts do you find most valuable?
14. What might motivate a writer to imitate another work of fiction? And what is at stake in this gesture? We have said that imitation is never neutral; What political or ethical implication should a writer consider regarding imitation?

15. What does the phrase "read as a writer" mean to you? Could you offer an example of a reading (i.e., choose one story and use craft-based, evaluative, and critical approaches to analyze this story)?

16. What do you think about Hollywood representations of writer protagonists? How do these films construct the figure of the writer, and what is at stake in these representations?

17. What is the difference or relationship between fiction and creative nonfiction? Do you agree with Wendy Bishop's statement that genre is "enforced and unenforceable"?

18. How do you work with "conventions" in writing? Are there conventions that fiction writers need to know? Thinking about one of your stories, how do you work with or against convention?

19. What aesthetic theories are most important to your fiction writing?

20. How do you define "political fiction"? Is that a useful term, in your view? What does this term risk, and what does it offer?

Students submit their author interview based on these questions as prefatory material to their final portfolios. The goal is to authorize the students' viewpoints while also providing the space to grow their understanding of the central issues that the course covers by way of the threshold concepts. This final assignment emphasizes the importance of critical reflection, as it underscores the necessity of thinking about creative writing as a form of cultural production that has effects on the world. Representation, language use, and aesthetic orientation are not neutral; this author interview makes emerging writers accountable to this fact, and makes the classroom discussion leading up to the week of final assessment accountable as well.

Coda: Reimagining Creative Writing's Institutional Practices

The argument of this book has been that creative writing requires a change at the level of curricular content and workshop practice. But the need for transformation extends beyond the classroom. What happens in the classroom is one part of moving toward an inclusive creative writing, but it alone is insufficient. A more comprehensive approach is needed that dismantles prejudice and oppression on multiple levels. We need to rethink who or what gets centered in our decisions, who or what is served by our approach to our work. From decisions regarding which writers to invite next to a Visiting Writers Series to a university's faculty retention, tenure, and promotion program, we need to rethink our practice. Who are we serving, and who are we failing to serve in the choices we make, both within and outside of the classroom? Which students see their histories and identities represented in the curriculum we have constructed and the programs we offer?

As Kazim Ali notes, "The cultural and racial homogeneity of creative writing programs is self-perpetuating. Some of the issues surrounding low enrollment of students of Color in both undergraduate and graduate creative writing programs is social and cultural, but some of it is structural and pedagogical."[1] Ali makes several suggestions for how creative writing can address structural racism, including changes in admissions practices, faculty hiring, labor conditions for faculty of Color, the importance of cross-listing courses and partnering with programs in ethnic studies, critical race studies, Africana studies, Native American studies, world languages and cultures, and other departments where literary and cultural traditions are being taught.

I want to pause and briefly consider current practices in faculty hiring because it matters greatly who is doing the work of creative writing. The field's hiring practices and capacity to retain a diverse cohort of instructors demand our scrutiny.

There is evidence that some departments have worked to actively recruit faculty members who diversify their curricula. Figure 1 represents data collected from the Creative Writing Academic Jobs Wiki for the 2016 and 2015 job markets. Other terms could be included in this chart, but this represents a quick

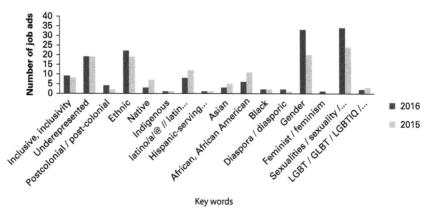

Figure 1 Number of job postings that included terms that indicate diversification of the curriculum.

snapshot of the number of programs that target writers with specialties in specific areas. Words may appear in the same ad, so the job calls represented here are relatively few—out of the 204 jobs posted on the 2016 wiki page and the 217 jobs posted on the 2015 wiki page.

Relatively few positions include these key words, and we know that those who end up in these positions, especially if they are faculty of Color or faculty who represent a minoritized identity, may face a range of obstacles, including what is known as the "minority tax" wherein faculty who represent diversity are taxed with the extra, often invisible and rarely compensated, labor of service and advising above and beyond what is required of white faculty. Such incessant demand may slow down research and creative activity, as time is snatched from the faculty member who is made to be the point of referral for all of the students of Color in a department, for example. As Sara Ahmed notes, "It is certainly the case that responsibility for diversity and equality is unevenly distributed. It is also the case that the distribution of this work is political: if diversity and equality work is less valued by organizations, then to become responsible for this work can mean to inhabit institutional spaces that are also less valued."[2] In such circumstances, it is imperative that all faculty take responsibility for "working 'on' the institutions 'at' which [we] work."[3] We can devise programs that ensure faculty time is protected in an equitable manner.

This work begins in the recruitment process. As a field, we need to address the marginalizing institutional practices that are played out year after year in academic hiring. This is an opportunity to discuss the power relationships and rhetorical maneuvers that surround one's positionality and self-presentation on the job market.

Throughout my recent job search in creative writing, I was cognizant of the many practices that underscored my privilege. The itineraries for my campus visits required me to walk up and down steep hills across large campuses, in hallways that are not wheelchair accessible, on beaches and along hiking trails. It was assumed that my body could accept such activities. The itineraries required me to socialize in rooms of people that markedly lacked diversity. I strolled through streets in towns that are only 1 percent Black, 1 percent Asian, on unceded indigenous lands fraught with violent colonial histories.

The people I met during my campus visits asked me coded questions that extracted the information they wanted to know but legally were not allowed to ask: "Are there particular industries of interest to you in our town? What forms of recreation do you and your family enjoy?"

The people I met during my campus visits followed me into restrooms and chatted with me over bathroom stalls in bathrooms that were not gender neutral. Such is the strange intimacy of the interview process, with its array of potentially marginalizing, ostracizing, and debasing customs. As a white, cisgendered women who was at the time partnered with someone who had a stable income and the flexibility to relocate, I was painfully conscious of the advantages that come with my positionality.

Hiring practices promote inequities—inequities which may be impossible for many candidates to confront, given the power differential at play in the interview situation. Each campus visit is a high-stakes moment of evaluation, and in these situations candidates may feel a type of battle fatigue most acutely.

This is all the more the case in an academic labor situation that is manifestly precarious—a precarity that is unevenly distributed among academic laborers. Today, nontenure-track instructors represent more than 70 percent of all faculty, and there is, in Sharff and Lessinger's words, a "continuing (and striking) concentration of women in [this] temporary, nontenured underclass,"[4] with women composing around 61 percent of adjunct faculty nationwide. Women are overrepresented among contingent faculty: they are 10–15 percent more likely to be in contingent positions, and earning 27 percent less than their male counterparts while there.[5] The disparity is no doubt an issue of intersectionality.

We read the pages of the Academic Jobs Wiki so tellingly titled "Universities to Fear"—the word "fear" divulges the vulnerability that one may feel in the face of institutional forces that read our bodies, our identities, as either assets or risks in our candidacy.

"Will this person be a good fit here? Will they stay?" search committees ask, without addressing the institutional features—or lack thereof—that would cause these faculty members to leave. In asking these questions, they are reading our bodies as "belonging" or not, as being "at home" in a space or not. In Ahmed's words, "Wanting to work with those who can inhabit a shared social space might seem like a rather ordinary aspiration. But the very desire for a shared social space can be a desire that *restricts to whom an institutional space is open* by imagining a social space that is not open to everyone."[6]

Such discrimination continues, even as committee members dutifully undergo their Human Resources bias trainings. What gets said by the people facilitating the interview process belies a structural system that perpetuates exclusion.

When questions of "fit" are on the interview table, the academic job search becomes problematically about building what some job descriptions call "professional relationships." Jokes get made: "we'll tenure you if we like you," which translates to a demand to "fit in"—to perform a conformity that is pleasing to the "we" that makes such statements, the "we" that is imbued with power. In this context, the job market relies upon what Arlie Hochschild calls the "emotional labor" entailed in "the management of feeling to create a publicly observable facial and bodily display."[7] This affective and stylistic display has exchange value, especially in a job market that uncritically holds on to ideas of "fit."

In this context, we should be skeptical of the boilerplate "diversity statement," conventionally appended to the bottom of a job call. The word "diverse" or "diversity" appears in over half of the job calls in both of the academic years I tracked usage, most commonly in the boilerplate institutional diversity statement.

It is of course nothing new to say we should be wary of this normative and managerial discourse of diversity. Several authors (Ahmed, 2012; Blackmore and Sachs, 2003; Lury, 2000) have noted how such discourse regularly occludes actual structural inequalities.[8] Diversity, Kerschbaum observes, becomes a kind of property or capital to be collected, which entails a particular valuation of bodies—whether those bodies are counted as faculty or students.[9] Invoking diversity in marketing copy, institutions recruit and at the same time orient toward the people recruited "as if they are raw materials that can enhance the educational products they are 'selling.'"[10] Ahmed argues in her book titled *On Being Included* that institutional statements of diversity are performative, rather than constative (using J. L. Austin's lexicon here). These diversity statements fleetingly *perform* a value; they do not state a *fact*. They discursively perform a value of diversity, while the actual levels of diversity, equity, and inclusion on a campus may be markedly lacking when measured in any material sense. There is often an extreme disconnect between the university's diversity value statement and the *fact* of who actually holds its faculty positions. When a job call states that XYZ college has a "strong commitment to diversity," this does not mean that XYZ college actually recruits and retains a diverse faculty. The structures and assumptions are hidden behind a discourse of diversity that serves to keep institutional structures in place that maintain existing hierarchies and silencing forces. "Being judged to have written an exemplary race equality policy is quickly translated into being good at race equality," Ahmed notes. "Such a translation works to conceal the very inequalities the documents were written to reveal."[11]

To look closely at the language of these job ads is to find practices that belie entrenched biases. A job call posted for the 2016 job market season had this language:

> Minimum Qualifications: Required qualifications include a terminal degree in Creative Writing (MFA or PhD) by the August 16, 2016 starting date; a strong creative writing and teaching specialization as well as an academic background in creative writing; evidence of successful teaching experience at the college/ university level; evidence of potential for excellence in teaching undergraduate and graduate courses in creative writing; significant potential for continued successful publication of creative work, as well as other scholarly, professional, and/or creative activities; and strong potential as a colleague taking part in the life and work of a unified department of English Studies (including majors in creative writing, literature, and professional writing; graduate concentrations in creative writing, literature, and rhetoric and composition, and a graduate program in technical and professional communication). *The candidate selected for this position must be able to meet eligibility requirements to work in the United States at the time the appointment is scheduled to begin and continue working legally for the proposed term of employment; excellent communication skills required.*

Note what that telling semicolon does in the italicized text—connecting one clause to another and revealing a discriminatory presumption that communication skills are tied to the matter of immigration and legal work status. Faculty members not born in this country—or whose bodies are read as "foreign"—are faced with a discriminatory skepticism, indicated by this job call's construction. They are accomplished creative *writing* faculty who are scrutinized for *basic communication skills* because of their place of birth.

Our hiring practices need greater scrutiny, as do the labor policies that support or hurt the diversity of an institution's faculty. Calling out and correcting discriminatory practices and inequitable expectations are necessary to moving toward an inclusive creative writing.

In administrative discourse, diversity is often represented in a discourse of "benign variation"—as it is in D. W. Fenza's construction of "pluralism" discussed in this book's introductory chapter. But such "benign variation" neglects inequity and power imbalances, as it can also be a form of compartmentalization. Ahmed notes how the minoritised writer, as employee of the institution, is made accountable for "being diverse and allowing institutions to celebrate their diversity."[12] In creative writing, people of Color become bound to aesthetic expectations that are particular to a racialized status. Thus responsibility for diversity becomes unevenly distributed among practicing artists, even as diversity becomes the claim of the institution (as in the AWP boast, mentioned in the introductory chapter, that the organization benefits writers of all backgrounds, economic classes, races, and ethnic origins).

This way of thinking about aesthetic pluralism, represented by Fenza's discourse in the introductory chapter, tends, as Chris Green argues, "to limit possible communities in readily available terms of demarcation (ethnicity, race, class, nationality). Undefined communities, which lie outside the language and concepts we currently use, are struggling toward definition and coherence through culture and writing."[13] While the arts have the potential to construct new publics and new collectivities, current institutional constructions of diversity tend to maintain a literary landscape that is mapped with firm boundary lines. Even discussions of the pluralist nature of creative writing programs elide questions of identity politics, as they continue to laud easy notions of "diversity" which overlook how we embody, as Kerschbaum notes, "a complex set of identifications that must be considered together, rather than independently from one another. The strength of this approach is that it broadens the range of interpretive possibilities."[14] We must remain vigilant in examining our ways of thinking about difference.

Will Alexander's writing exposes the institutional tendency to make traditions monolithic and to homogenize the readers who are grouped around a tradition. In his poetry, Alexander at once avoids the essentializing tendencies of identity aesthetics, while also avoiding the trappings of a "post-identity" paradigm that is an outgrowth of colorblind racism. In looking to the more-than-human world of particle physics and inanimate objects, Alexander rethinks the radical contingency of our social constructions and categorizations. The trance becomes not only a resource for Alexander's poetry, but also a flight of thought that vacates fixed, pre-given subject-positions. Alexander's trance poetics thus radically destabilizes the institutionalization of diversity politics, putting readers in a startling new relation to problems of inequality. While Alexander equates "artistic courage" with the "the courage to express who you really are,"[15] this becomes a matter of destabilizing expectations, rather than achieving a voice that will be recognized as one's own.

In "Igniting the Inward Prodigy," Alexander writes, "According to traditional African values, 'the person preexists and by incarnating himself . . . seeks to open himself, to grow, to insert himself always more effectively' into the larger society. The person is central in this context—not the institution, as in the West."[16] This runs in sharp contrast to the AWP marketing copy, cited in this book's introduction, that trots out individuals ("students and aspiring writers from all backgrounds, economic classes, races, and ethnic origins") in service of the institution's achievements.

In turn, Alexander's pedagogy puts students on equal footing with their teachers, as members of a community. Alexander represents the teacher as "catalyst," thereby altering the given power imbalance in the teacher–student relationship. "It is the duty of the catalyst/instructor," Alexander writes, "to stir up the life force in all students."[17] This should be our highest aim as creative writing instructors.

Through this process of igniting, there is much the catalyst/teacher does not know. The catalyst/teacher may be starkly unfamiliar with some of the readerships and communities in which students are most at home.[18] The aesthetic inclinations that students come to a creative writing class with are not to be reformed, but rather are legitimized. This form of education mobilizes identities in the classroom[19] and provides space for investigating the literary and cultural histories to which students are differentially tied.

Creative writing can be a transformative experience. The goal should be that students leave the creative writing course with a sensitivity and critical perspective that they did not have before. Students become able to think about how a text may circulate in the world, the effects it may have, the experiences it may provide for diverse audiences, the situations that give rise to it and the situations that it may in turn shape.

It is time to re-evaluate the creative writing curriculum and move literary writing pedagogy toward a more inclusive, equitable model. Creative writing can be a powerful site where cultural production is reimagined, where counter-narratives are built. It can be a place where dominant narratives are interrogated, where transformative community practices are fostered. The workshop can become a space for contesting the marginalizing tendencies of creative writing institutions and lore, where the tendencies of creative writing can be remade, where the institutional "givens" and lore of the creative writing workshop can be contested.

Creative writing can be more than it currently is. It can encourage multiple aesthetics, including those that call for activist literature and writing for social change. It can cease its longstanding practice of silencing those who do not follow the aesthetic requirements that traditional craft texts uncritically forward. It can go farther in encouraging space for conversations we have not yet had. It can encourage text-making and text-circulation in a broader set of forms.

As David Jauss notes, "There is nothing as dangerous as blank paper. [...] [T]he absence of expression is more dangerous to humanity, individually and collectively, than any form of expression can be."[20] To move toward an inclusive creative writing is to counter the blank page. It is to counter the silencing forces of our discipline, which are hundreds of years in the making—drawn from a Eurocentric aesthetic tradition and a history of writing instruction that preserves status hierarchies. To move toward an inclusive creative writing is to uncover this history and make deliberate efforts to facilitate its metamorphosis.

Our students' work is important. Their writing can be a way of countering the forces of power that would marginalize and silence. It can be a way of preserving cultural formations that are endangered by continuing cultural genocide. It can contribute significantly to dismantling and rebuilding a society that addresses disparities, and inequities. It can foster a radical pluralism. It can mobilize new ways of thinking. It can support each person's full humanity, if we no longer allow our field to foreclose these possibilities.

Appendix A—List of Craft Texts Surveyed in Chapters 1 and 2

Chapters 1 and 2 look to craft texts, along with pedagogical arguments and aesthetic theories, as sources of data for examining the assumptions of creative writing because these texts reflect the disciplinary practices of the field's pedagogies. The craft text is an extension of the institutionalized set of literary values that circulate in US creative writing instruction.

Creative writing craft texts abound. As Malcolm Bradbury notes in his article "The Bridgeable Gap," "There is, of course, no shortage at all of 'How-To' books, books telling you how to begin writing or get published (so full is the field that a recent example tells you How to Write Novels in Nigeria)."[1] My study draws from a sample selection of craft texts from the twentieth century. From the Library of Congress' database of holdings, I compiled a list of craft textbooks published by US authors (i.e., books that are explicitly intended to instruct the novice writer how to write poetry, fiction, and other genres) from the twentieth century. From this list, I chose three books from each decade of the twentieth century (see Table A.1). I included a range of texts that represent multiple genres (i.e., primarily short-stories and poetry since these are the genres that are present in nearly every academic creative writing program while creative nonfiction, graphic novels, drama, etc. are available in only some programs—these genres warrant a separate discussion that is largely beyond the scope of this project). Many of the craft texts that I analyzed went through multiple editions or saw large sales numbers, and most were written by teachers of creative writing who found employment in academia. Some of these books were written expressly for classroom use.

Craft texts are a manifestation of the ways that creative writers think about authorship and what it means to cultivate a life of writing. Some are written by professors, but are used both in and out of the classroom. When assigned in the classroom, craft texts can be considered co-teachers, of a kind. In his histories of composition, Robert Connors has noted that textbooks have, in certain times and places, provided teachers' primary means of access to disciplinary knowledge.[4] He writes,

Bereft of a theoretical discipline and a professional tradition, teachers during this period had nothing to turn to for information about their subject—except their textbooks. [...] Writing teachers became as a result the only college-level instructors who know no more of their discipline than is contained in the texts they assign their students—a sad pattern that still, alas, continues today at too many schools.[5]

Connors' description may characterize creative writing teachers of the past and present as well, since these teachers have had little in the way of a pedagogical body of scholarship to draw from. They may rely on their own experience with writing and the creative writing classroom and the principles they find in the craft textbooks they assign. McGurl writes of how the craft text contributes to the education provided in the creative writing classroom, "[s]upplementing the charismatic presence of the writer at the head of the table." In this passage, he stresses that

in order to understand the institution of creative writing in the immediate postwar period, we need to see how this 'institution' extends beyond its most literal definition as a community of common purpose housed in brick and mortar to encompass other, more obviously 'virtual' institutional forms like those textbooks, which stabilized a set of literary values even as it put them in circulation throughout the U.S. educational system.[6]

Many craft texts are marketed to non-collegiate audiences as well—as in the case of Natalie Goldberg's *Writing Down the Bones,* which targets a wide readership that includes hobbyists, therapy groups, and college classes. Some contemporary craft texts purport to provide everything a university curriculum would for a fraction of the price. The craft texts provide a window into some of the strains of thought represented in university and non-university creative writing.

According to survey data collected as part of a study of creative writing instructors' teaching practices,[7] over 50 percent of creative writing instructors report using creative writing craft texts *at least sometimes* in their classroom. While no respondents make craft texts *always* a part of their syllabi, 36 percent indicated that they *often* assign craft essays or textbooks, and 25 percent indicated that they *sometimes* do. Some instructors use creative writing craft texts in their instructional planning—in lesson plans, lectures, handouts, or in feedback to students; 18 percent indicated that they *always* use craft texts for these purposes, and 29 percent said that they *often* do.

Table A.1 Examples of creative writing instructional discourse demonstrating an exclusionary orientation

---

Smith, Lewis Worthington. *The Writing of the Short Story*, 1902

Albright, Evelyn May. *Short-Story: Its Principles and Structure*, 1908

Esenwein, J. Berg. *Writing the Short-Story; A Practical Handbook on the Rise, Structure, Writing, and Sale of the Modern Short-Story*, 1909

Fowler, Nathaniel C. *The Art of Story Writing: Facts and Information About Literary Work of Practical Value of Both Amateur and Professional Writers*, 1913

Carruth, William Herbert. *Verse Writing*, 1917

Baker, George Pierce. *Dramatic Technique*,[2] 1919

Barrett, Charles Raymond. *Short Story Writing: A Practical Treatise on the Art of the Short Story*, 1921

Wilkinson, Marguerite. *The Way of the Makers*, 1925

Bildersee, Adele. *Imaginative Writing: An Illustrated Course for Students*, 1927

Brande, Dorothea. *Becoming a Writer*, 1934

Schwartz, Esther L. *So You Want to Write!*, 1936

Ueland, Brenda. *Help from the Nine Muses (If You Want to Write)*, 1938

Buell, Robert Kingery. *Verse Writing Simplified*, 1940

Brooks, Cleanth, and Robert Penn Warren. *Understanding Fiction*, 1943

McHugh, Vincent. *Primer of the Novel*, 1950

Sarton, May. *The Writing of a Poem*, 1957

Glicksberg, Charles Irving. *Writing the Short Story*, 1953

Cassill, R.V. *Writing Fiction*, 1963

Caudill, Rebecca. *The High Cost of Writing*, 1965

Minot, Stephen. *Three Genres*, 1965

Brown, Clarence, and E. J. Heiman. *Writing Short Stories, Plays and Poems: An Introduction to Creative Writing*, 1978

Stafford, William. *Writing the Australian Crawl: Views on the Writer's Vocation*, 1978

Hugo, Richard. *The Triggering Town*,* 1979

Burroway, Janet. *Writing Fiction*,* 1982

Gardner, John. *Art of Fiction*,* 1984

Goldberg, Natalie. *Writing Down the Bones*, 1986

Hemley, Robin. *Turning Life into Fiction*, 1994

Dobyns, Stephen. *Best Words, Best Order*, 1996

Baxter, Charles. *Burning Down the House*,*[3] 1997

---

*Over 25 respondents selected one or more of these five titles from a multiple choice list of nearly 100 craft textbooks. Richard Hugo's *The Triggering Town* was the most often selected, with 43 respondents indicating that they used this text. Burroway's author website reports that *Writing Fiction* is "the most widely used creative writing text in America," across its many editions.

Appendix B—Sample Syllabus

Humboldt State University
College Arts Humanities and Social Sciences / English Department
ENGL315, Creative Writing: Fiction

Instructor:	Janelle Adsit, PhD
Email:	Janelle.adsit@humboldt.edu
Office Hours:	Wednesdays 12:30–3:30pm
Class Days/Time:	Tuesdays & Thursdays 5:00–6:50
Prerequisites:	ENGL 205
Research Guide:	http://libguides.humboldt.edu
Literary Journal Library:	Available in Founders Hall 205

Course description

We are only the stories that we tell.—Tera Maxwell

In this course, you are a writer among writers; you are a professional seeking to hone your craft. Your writing will be central to our discussions, and almost everything you write for this class will be shared with your peers. As we share our work-in-progress, we will learn from our fellow writers' approaches to the craft of fiction. This is a discussion-based course that prioritizes collaboration and learning-by-doing. Come to each meeting prepared to sustain rigorous and creative work. Both reading- and writing-intensive, this course surveys a range of perspectives on short fiction by reading short stories (and "short short" stories) alongside authors' craft-criticism (i.e., "writing about writing for writers"). You will be invited to imitate and revise the stories that we read and discuss, in order to broaden your own writerly repertoire.

Please read this document carefully. Remember that a writer's life includes following directions on grant applications, submission guidelines, and editorial processes. The guidelines included in this document should be treated with the same attention that you would give to any other professional endeavor.

Course goals and what you will learn along the way

This course is meant to propel you forward in your writing career. The course will help you think in more complex ways about the invention, revision, and circulation processes that make up a writer's practice. The following course learning objectives give language to the skills you will develop in this course.

Course learning objectives

By the end of this course, you will be able to . . .

Invent (Unit 1)

- Maintain a habit of writing with a variety of methods, processes, craft techniques, and heuristics for generating texts.
- Use a reading habit to sustain your writing processes, as a means of research and continued craft study.
- Employ fiction writing as a meaning-making activity and research process.
- Collaborate with fellow writers effectively to solve artistic problems.
- Practice literary craft with a basic understanding of the psychology of creativity.

Revise (Unit 2)

- Identify craft choices and consider their potential effects on diverse audiences and readerships.
- Incorporate craft analysis into a revision process.
- Demonstrate awareness of the controversies associated with the craft of fiction, as presented in craft-criticism.
- Gain intimacy with the assumptions, values, and debates that shape diverse literary communities.
- Recognize and analyze the contingencies of literary value. Evaluate literature in context, with awareness of the diversity of the textual landscape.

Circulate (Unit 3)

- Locate and analyze potential markets for your work.
- Recognize the range of orientations and values represented by literary markets.
- Consider the "author function" as it relates to your own participation in literary communities.
- Build from foundational knowledge about publishing and writer platforms.
- Demonstrate critical awareness of how "literary citizenship" has been constructed in the field of creative writing.

Ways of reading in creative writing

In this class, we will use the following three approaches to reading. Each entail a different purpose for reading, a different lens by which we approach the work.

Craft-Based Reading—Reading to construct how the text works (i.e., analyzing a text as an architect would analyze a building, figuring out how it is put together)

- What choice is the writer making here? What other choices could the writer have made? How do the effects of these possibilities compare? What is it about the way this text is written that makes readers feel and respond the way they do?

Critical Reading—Reading to interrogate ideological closures (i.e., how the author mobilizes commonly held assumptions, contradictions emerging in the text, politics emerging from blindspots)

- Joanna Russ argues that writers "do not make up their stories out of whole cloth; they are pretty much restricted to the attitudes, the beliefs, the expectations, and above all the plots that are 'in the air.'" To what extent does this text interrupt (or intervene in) the attitudes, beliefs, expectations, assumptions and myths that circulate among its audiences?

Evaluative Reading—Reading to judge whether the text is "good" (i.e., if it corresponds to a contingent set of values).

- Does the text achieve what it set out to do? How effectively does this text locate itself in the literary landscape?

Craft principles

As an extension of our learning outcomes, you will become familiar with the following craft principles that are characteristic of some successful stories. Keep these in mind as you take on the lens of the evaluative reader. Throughout the semester, we will discuss how the following principles are contingent, and we will investigate how these principles emerge differently in different storytelling traditions.

Literary audiences may want . . .

- To discover meanings that are beneath the surface of the text, meanings that are not entirely explicit, meanings that come through symbolism and figurative language.
- To discover meanings that are complex or paradoxical, meanings that feel new or revealing.
- To draw their own conclusions from what they see; to be guided to conclusions with concrete details and characters-in-action, rather than being told what to think or feel.
- To find details, truths, and images that they might have otherwise overlooked in the world.
- To have the world they know feel less familiar but all the more vivid.
- To invest in a journey that the character shapes through crucial decision-making.
- To understand each character's complex motivations and desires.

Literary audiences tend to become frustrated with . . .

- Redundancies in the text.
- Predictability and over-reliance on cliché or hackneyed conventions (e.g., beginning story with waking up, ending a story with a death, etc.).
- Being told what they have already inferred.
- Stories that "summarize away" or gloss over their characters' struggles.
- Stories that assume tension is best achieved through car chases and weapons. Special effects do not translate well to the page.
- Distractions from the story or confusions caused by errors and inconsistencies.
- Elements that do not seem credible within the world of the story.
- Stories that give away, or fail to maintain, their tension and suspense.
- Passive characters that lack agency. Characters who do not make decisions.
- Simplistic, predictable, stereotypical, or one-dimensional characters (caricatures).

- Characterization that does not seem empathetic or fails to do justice to human complexity. Would your characters see themselves in your presentation?

Conventions

The following are conventions of literary short stories, arising from the craft principles listed previously. If you depart from any of these conventions, be sure to thoughtfully weigh the risks and possibilities of your choice.

- The story has a unique title, and the title means more after reading the story.
- The opening paragraph offers tension and/or sets up a dramatic question.
- Significant, specific, and concrete details are employed throughout the story.
- The dialogue is punctuated and attributed according to the *Creative Writer's Style Guide* or another recognized style of your choice which serves the story.
- Blocks of dialogue are interspersed with action.
- Blocks of dialogue end on a note of tension.
- Dialogue is not used as a means of exposition.
- The characters are nuanced with distinct voices. The story does not caricature speech patterns.
- The POV, temporal distance, and verb tense is consistent.
- The story avoids clichéd or hackneyed elements (e.g., the "and then I woke up" ending).
- Repeated motifs emerge in the story that are imbued with layers of meaning.
- Style, tone, word choice, grammar, and spelling support a credible *ethos* appropriate for your audience and purpose.
- All departures from convention are purposeful and add to the story's meaning.

Classroom culture

Each person in the room depends on your unique perspective in contributing to their learning. The policies listed in this section are meant to ensure that we create a strong community in which all members are responsible to each other. Let us establish a classroom ethos that is mutually supportive. Let us work together to create a productive working space that facilitates collaboration.

It is essential that you are present for all class sessions—both for the good of the group and because this course is tailored for your professional development. As stated in the university course catalog, "Humboldt State University expects attendance at every class meeting." Every absence does matter. All projects and homework assignments are due on the date specified, regardless of whether you are present for that class meeting.

I value collaboration deeply, and this is reflected in the course expectations. You will succeed in this class by being active and engaged for the full duration of each meeting (and not distracted by a cell phone or other technology) and by being prepared for the session.

Expectations for outside of class

This course is yours, and I expect you to take ownership of your learning. The course is designed to give you the resources you need to be a critical and vital participant in literary communities as a fiction writer. Much of the work of the course takes place outside of class in your individualized study and the time you spend writing. That is, class time is only one part of your learning experience, and your outside work is just as important.

Outside of class, I am available to be a resource for you—to help you find what you need to achieve your own learning goals. I want you to come to my office, to talk with me about your career trajectory, your motivations for your writing, etc. I want to help you to gain strategies for improving your own learning experience.

Assignments and grading policy

Your final course grade will be determined by five equally weighted components: three unit projects, participation in workshop, and a final author interview. Unless otherwise specified, the following assignments will be graded using the following scale:

A 90–100% Outstanding achievement
B 80–89%   Good achievement
C 70–79%   Satisfactory achievement
D 60–69%   Minimum performance
F 0–59%   Below minimum performance

In order to achieve credit for the class, you need a grade of 70 percent. I will save detailed records of your work in the class, including your attendance and final percentage grade, for reference if you ever need a letter of recommendation in the future.

Unit 1 Project: Flash-Fiction Chapbook (20 percent, graded, due at final exam period*)

The chapbook is an opportunity to experiment with multiple processes of composing and multiple approaches to the short story. Each of the pieces of flash fiction that you collect in your chapbook should be meaningful works made more meaningful when juxtaposed with the other titles in your collection. Accompanying your sequence, include a prefatory note that describes the decisions you made in arranging your manuscript and the tools for invention you learned through this project. Additionally in this prefatory note, explore the risks and possibilities of using understatement, defamiliarization, concision, and ambiguity, which so often characterize the flash-fiction genre.

Evaluation focus: your demonstration of the craft principles listed above.

Unit 2 Project: Focused-Revision Series (20 percent, graded, due in Unit 2, dates specified in the schedule below)

Considering elements of storytelling (e.g., plot, characterization, pacing, POV, etc.) in turn, this project asks you to experiment with a series of lenses to revise and "re-see" your stories. There are four "focused revision" assignments listed in the schedule below. Revise one story these four times, demonstrating global revision. Your sequence of "focused revisions" will be prompted by the work that we do in class. By the end of Unit 2, produce several drafts of one story that employ global revision. This study will provide a set of heuristics with which to approach revision in your future work. In its last version, after completing the sequence, your focused-revision story should demonstrate the craft principles and conventions listed above, or you should take account of the risks and possibilities of any departure from these conventions. Accompanying your focused-revision series, include a prefatory note that describes your revision process and how you accounted for the craft principles we discuss in class.

Evaluation focus: your effort in the process of revision and demonstration of the craft principles and conventions listed above, with emphasis on principles six and seven.

Unit 3 Project: Story with Intended Market (20 percent, graded, due at final exam period*)

For this assignment, write a story of any length based on any prompt, form of inspiration, or exigency; the only requirement is that you compose something that you can argue is fitting for the market of your choice (e.g., a literary journal such as *Glimmer Train*). Your manuscript should be formatted so as to be ready for submission to your intended market. Include a prefatory note of at least 500 words that describes what you have learned about your intended market and why your story is appropriate for it. In this prefatory note, use specific details about your chosen publication (e.g., the publication's mission statement, submission guidelines, editorial staff, characteristics of subscribers, word-length requirements, favored themes, etc.). You are welcome to invent a zine or an alternative mode of publishing for circulating your writing. Your prefatory statement should acknowledge the range of orientations and values represented by literary markets and should reflect on the learning objectives associated with Unit 3, as listed above. (Note: this story should be a story other than what you submitted for Units 1 and 2.)

Evaluation focus: your analysis of your work in relation to the intended market.

Workshop Responses (20 percent, CR/NC each, due on workshop days as specified in collaboratively generated schedule at the end of the term)

Write a respectful, original, thorough, and thoughtful response to every story that is submitted to workshop. (Each member of the class has the option of submitting one story to workshop, so you will write between 0 and 19 responses, depending on how many people are interested in workshop.) Each of your 400–1,000-word written responses to your peers' stories will be graded on a credit/no-credit basis. In order to receive credit, these written responses must employ concepts and terms from our class discussion and must provide substantive analysis of the story by answering the questions provided in the "Heuristic for Responding to Stories Submitted for Workshop" (http://www.criticalcreativewriting.org/workshop.html).

Evaluation focus: the extent to which you can translate the craft principles listed above into your reading practice.

Author Interview (20 percent, graded, due at final exam period*)

The final "exam" asks you to write three responses to three selected prompts. The essays you generate should be of interest to writers of fiction. During this exam, you are a writer speaking to writers about the craft; you are joining the craft-critical conversation we have surveyed this semester. Each response is a work of craft-criticism that could be further revised and submitted to a venue such as *Writer's Chronicle, Poets & Writers, New Writing, TEXT, Callaloo, Assay,* etc.

The "exam" will include six prompts. You will choose three prompts from the six, and you will write a 500–1,000 word response to each. You are welcome to use any source materials that you find useful in answering the questions. Be sure to cite all words, ideas, and information that you gather from external sources.

Evaluation focus: the extent to which you can synthesize the course content (e.g., craft principles, arguments and debates in craft-criticism, etc.) in a way that is relevant to the course learning objectives. Please note that you may draft a sample answer for feedback at any point this semester, up until the week before final exams.

Submitting a story to full-class workshop (optional)

Throughout the semester there will be many opportunities for small group and partner mini-workshops. You will receive ample feedback from our writing community this semester. You additionally have the *option* to submit a story to a full-class workshop, but this is not a requirement. You can choose whether or not this is the right time for you to take part in such an opportunity. Your decision regarding whether to submit a story to workshop will have no effect on your course grade. Your grade for the workshop component of the grade (described above) is based solely on your participation as a responder and reader. Whether or not you choose to submit a story to workshop, you are asked to participate fully in each workshop conversation and to write a thorough and thoughtful response to all your peers' stories.

If you do choose to submit a story to workshop, consult with me about your preferred date and post your story to the designated forum on our learning management system at least one week before your workshop. Out of respect for your readers' time, stories that are submitted with fewer than seven days allowed for readers to engage the story will not be workshopped.

All pages should be numbered and double-spaced with adequate margins—so we will know we have all the pages and so we will have space to write notes. Your name and a title (and any contextualizing details you wish to provide, such as intended market and/or how the piece fits in to a longer manuscript) should appear in the manuscript document itself, at the top of each story. If you wish to submit a chapter or excerpt from a longer work, the excerpt you submit should stand alone well enough to be published separately from the larger project.

Please follow our workshop agreements, which we will collaboratively generate together as a class. Stories that do not follow our agreements or the specifications listed here will not be workshopped and we will use the scheduled class time for another exercise or learning opportunity.

Workshop ethos

Our approach to workshop in this class will emphasize craft-based and critical reading, above and beyond evaluative reading. In other words, our purpose is not to declare whether a story is good or bad—remembering that there is no such thing as a "good story," only a contingently valued story. It is far more helpful to a writer to understand how a story is read by diverse readers, what a story has the potential to do, how it works and the effects it has. Our workshop conversations should help the writer to locate the work in literary traditions, to make comparisons between the work and forms of cultural production, to explore the risks and possibilities of the craft choices, and to find additional possibilities for revision.

As a writer, when you submit a story for workshop, adopt an attitude of curiosity about how your work is received by a diverse group of readers. We can not calculate precisely how our writing will be read; each reading experience is idiosyncratic and readers co-create each story's meaning. Find out what happened for the readers of your story. Be greedy for these insights—but only insofar as the feedback will not deter you from completing the project you have in mind and are continuing to write. Your continued process is the priority and goal for all parts of our course, including workshop.

Reading schedule in craft-criticism

The following sets a tentative reading schedule in craft-criticism. Each week of class will also include a range of short stories and examples of flash fiction. Those works are not listed here. As a class, we will go through an exercise that will generate our reading schedule in narrative. We will work together to select the stories that will broaden our sense of the literary landscape, in its diversity. In the first weeks of the semester, we will collectively assign ourselves the stories we will read this semester, and we will learn how to never be without a story to read. The goal here is to develop a habit of reading works that challenge us, and to have the tools to continue this habit beyond the semester.

The weekly readings in craft-criticism (and by "craft-criticism," I mean "writing about writing, by writers and for writers") are related to a set of concepts or principles that are important for creative writers to grapple with. These concepts are listed in the schedule below, and the readings are organized around them. The concepts will help to focus our discussions and exercises each week, but each title listed on this schedule offers a range of ideas that we should bring to our discussion table. Read to find out what the article or book chapter says about the week's concept, but also read for whatever else resonates and challenges you in your process.

Week 1

Concept 1: Attention

Creative writing involves specific modes of attention as writers learn to be close and critical observers of the world. Writers learn to account for the ethical considerations involved in perceiving and reinventing the world through their research and observation.

Readings:

- Bruce Ziff, ed., *Borrowed Power: Essays on Cultural Appropriation* (selections from)
- Rick Moody, Chimamanda Ngozi Adichie, Patrick Roth, Tsitsi Dangarembga, Minae Mizumura, Katja Lange-Muller, Yoko Tawada, "Inappropriate Appropriation"
- Carolyn Forché, "Reading the Living Archives: The Witness of Literary Art"

Week 2

Concept 2: Creativity

Writers benefit from a robust toolkit of applied theoretical frames and process heuristics for generating texts. Principles from the psychology of creativity are useful for increasing the versatility of writers.

Readings:

- Mihaly Csikszentmihalyi, *Creativity: Flow and the Psychology of Discovery and Invention* (selections from)
- Robert D. Richardson, *First We Read, Then We Write: Emerson on the Creative Process* (selections from)
- Zadie Smith, "Fail Better"

Week 3

Concept 3: Authorship

Writerly identity is constructed by a range of cultural forces. Cultural messages about the identity and lifestyle of the writer can be critically examined as we gain resources for building a writing life.

Readings:

- Leslie Marmon Silko, "Language and Literature from a Pueblo Indian Perspective"
- Wendy Bishop and Stephen Armstrong, "Box Office Poison: The Influence of Writers in Films and on Writers"
- Alice Walker, "Saving the Life that is Your Own: The Importance of Models in the Artist's Life"

Week 4

Concept 4: Language

Language choices are bound to issues of power. Supporting a polylingual and multimodal literary community requires deliberate attention from writers, which manifests in each writing occasion.

Readings:

- Gloria E. Anzaldúa, "How to Tame a Wild Tongue"
- Kristen Harmon, "Writing Deaf: Textualizing Deaf Literature"
- Bonnie Costello, "The Plural of Us: Uses and Abuses of an Ambiguous Pronoun"

Week 5

Concept 5: Genre

There are no universal standards for "good writing"; however, there are conventions that are particular to established genres.

Readings:

- Joanna Russ, "What Can a Heroine Do? or Why Women Can't Write"
- Lev Grossman, "Literary Revolution in the Supermarket Aisle: Genre Fiction Is Disruptive Technology"
- Rachel Charlene Lewis, "Queering Gender, Queering Genre"

Week 6

Concept 6: Craft

Craft choices produce effects in the reading experience. While these effects cannot be entirely predicted, writers can weigh the risks and possibilities of each craft choice

Readings:

- Francine Prose, *Reading Like a Writer* (selections from)
- Andrew David King, Travis Macdonald, Janet Holmes, Srikanth Reddy, M. NourbeSe Philip, Matthea Harvey, David Dodd Lee, "The Weight of What's Left [Out]: Six Contemporary Erasurists on Their Craft"

Week 7

Concept 7: Community

Writers are formed by the communities they engage. An analysis of craft must be grounded in an understanding of the varying orientations of readerships. Diverse audiences come to their texts with diverse needs.

Readings:

- Chris Green, "Materializing the Sublime Reader"
- Nadine Gordimer, "The Gap Between the Writer and the Reader"
- Porochista Khakpour, "The Others"

Week 8

Concept 8: Evaluation

Literary value is contingent. The evaluation of literature is shaped by cultural and historical forces.

Readings:

- Barbara Herrnstein Smith, "Contingencies of Value"
- Natasha Sajé, "Who Are We to Judge: The Politics of Literary Evaluation"
- Claire Vaye Watkins, "On Pandering: How to Write Like a Man" (and selected responses)

Week 9

Concept 9: Representation

All forms of representation, including literary production, can be interrogated for assumptions, values, and ideologies.

Readings:

- Cathy Park Hong, "Delusions of Whiteness in the Avant-Garde"
- Roxane Gay, "A Profound Sense of Absence" and "We Are Many. We Are Everywhere"
- Ayana Mathis, "Which Subjects Are Underrepresented in Contemporary Fiction?"
- Taiye Selasi, "Stop Pigeonholing African Writers"

Week 10
Concept 10: Resistance
Literature can forward social change and the transformation of culture. Literary production is a unique means of putting the world into question.

Readings:

- Shashi Deshpande, "The Writer as Activist"
- Nadine Gordimer, "When Art Meets Politics"
- Ta-Nehisi Coates, "Writing Is an Act of Courage"
- Wole Soyinka, "Voices from the Frontier: The Plight of Writers in Exile"

Week 11
Concept 11: Theory
Historical knowledge of aesthetic theories is important to the practice and craft of writing. Writers write within and against traditions, and thus benefit from a robust theoretical knowledgebase of cross-cultural artistic thought.

Readings:

- Michael J. Hoffman and Patrick D. Murphy, eds., *Essentials of the Theory of Fiction* (selections from)

Week 12
Concept 12: Revision
Writers learn to be responsive to what emerges in the process of creation, as they also bring a comparative literary analysis to bear on their revision process.

Notes

Acknowledgments

1 Omi Osun Joni L. Jones, Lisa L. Moore, and Sharon Bridgforth, eds., *Experiments in a Jazz Aesthetic: Art, Activism, Academia, and the Austin Project* (Austin: University of Texas Press, 2010); Elee Kraljii Gardiner, Thursdays Writing Collective. Web. http://www.thursdayswritingcollective.ca/

2 Jones, Moore, and Bridgforth, eds., *Experiments in a Jazz Aesthetic*, 23.

Introduction

1 David Fenza, "The Centre Has Not Held: Creative Writing & Pluralism," *New Writing: International Journal for the Practice and Theory of Creative Writing* 8.3 (2011): 207. Fenza has been the executive director of AWP since 1995, and he has been on staff at the organization since 1988.

2 Ibid., 208.

3 Sara Ahmed, *On Being Included: Racism and Diversity in Institutional Life* (Durham: Duke University Press, 2012), 43.

4 Claudia Rankine, "In Our Way: Racism in Creative Writing," *Writer's Chronicle* (October/November 2016): 47.

5 Junot Díaz, "MFA VS. POC," *New Yorker* (April 30, 2014). Web.

6 VIDA: Women in Literary Arts, "About the VIDA Count," Vidaweb.org (February 21, 2012). Web.

7 Lynn Neary, "In Elite MFA Programs, the Challenge of Writing While 'Other,'" NPR Code Switch (August 19, 2014). Web.

8 Claudia Rankine, Beth Loffreda, and Max King Cap, *The Racial Imaginary: Writers on Race in the Life of the Mind* (Albany: Fence Books, 2015); Fred D'Aguiar, "Towards a New Creative Writing Pedagogy," *Writer's Chronicle* (October/November 2016): 85–95; Toi Derricotte, "Baring/Bearing Anger: Race in the Creative Writing Classroom," *Writer's Chronicle* (October/November 1995); Junot Díaz, "MFA VS. POC," *New Yorker* (April 30, 2014); Aminatta Forna, "Don't Judge a Book by its Author," *The Guardian* (February 13, 2015); Tonya Hegamin, "Inclusion and Diversity: A Manifesto and Interview," *Journal of Creative Writing Studies* 1.1

(2016): 1–7; Cathy Park Hong, "Delusions of Whiteness in the Avant-Garde," *Lana Turner* 7 (November 2014); Anna Leahy, ed., *Power and Identity in the Creative Writing Classroom: The Authority Project* (Clevedon: Multilingual Matters, 2005); Shirley Geok-lin Lim, "Lore, Practice, and Social Identity in Creative Writing Pedagogy: Speaking with a Yellow Voice?" *Pedagogy: Critical Approaches to Teaching Literature, Language, Composition, and Culture* 10.1 (2009): 79–93; David Mura, "Ferguson, Whiteness as Default, and the Teaching of Creative Writing," *Writer's Chronicle* (October/November 2016): 32–44; David Mura, "White Writing Teachers (or David Foster Wallace vs. James Baldwin)," *Journal of Creative Writing Studies* 1.1 (2016): 1–15; Adrienne Perry, "Writing Without Shelter," *Journal of Creative Writing Studies* 1.1. (2016): 1–6; Richard Teleky, "'Entering the Silence': Voice, Ethnicity, and the Pedagogy of Creative Writing," *MELUS* 26.1 (Spring 2001): 205–219; Dorothy Wang, *Thinking Its Presence: Form, Race, and Subjectivity in Asian American Poetry* (Stanford: Stanford University Press, 2014). Among other contributions, Mark Nowak coordinated a conference on the intersection between creative writing and critical pedagogy, hosted by the MFA program in Creative Writing at Manhattanville College, with the conference theme "Critical Creative Writing and the Pedagogy of the Oppressed." See also discussions in the 1980s and 1990s about feminist pedagogies for creative writing, such as the interchange by Katharine Haake, Sandra Alcosser, and Wendy Bishop, published in the October/November 1989 issue of the AWP *Writer's Chronicle*. See also Katharine Haake, *What Our Speech Disrupts: Feminism and Creative Writing Studies* (Urbana: NCTE, 2000).

9   As listed on the AWP website, the committee is charged with the following mission:

- To engage AWP members, member programs, and the literary community at-large in conversations about inclusion in the pedagogy, curriculum, administration, and social environment of creative writing programs, writers' conferences, and literary centers.
- To create and disseminate a set of benchmarks that offer guidance to AWP's member programs, teachers, and administrators on how to foster inclusive literary communities and how to teach effectively among diverse students.
- To engage in an ongoing review of the association's governance, policies, and projects to ensure inclusiveness and equity.

The committee consists of seven members of the Board of Trustees along with ten members of the literary community.

10 Lynn Z. Bloom, "Freshman Composition as Middle-Class Enterprise," *College English* 58.6 (October 1996): 654–675.

11 Lisa Delpit, *Other People's Children: Cultural Conflict in the Classroom* (New York: New Press, 2006); Patrick J. Finn, *Literacy with an Attitude: Educating Working-Class Children in Their Own Self-Interest*, 2nd edition (Albany: State University of New York Press, 2009); Elspeth Stuckey, *The Violence of Literacy* (New York: Heinemann, 1990).

12 Fiona Probyn-Ramsey, "Putting Complicity to Work for Accountability," in *Commitment and Complicity in Cultural Theory and Practice*, edited by Begüm Özden Firat, Sarah De Mul, and Sonja van Wichelen (Hampshire: Palgrave Macmillan, 2009), 161. Quoted in Ahmed, *On Being Included*, 5–6.

13 Hegamin, "Inclusion and Diversity," 1.

14 Eric Bennett, *Workshops of Empire: Stegner, Engle, and American Creative Writing during the Cold War* (Iowa City: University of Iowa Press, 2015); Paul Dawson, *Creative Writing and the New Humanities* (New York: Routledge, 2005); Tim Mayers, *(Re)Writing Craft: Composition, Creative Writing, and the Future of English* (Pittsburgh: University of Pittsburgh Press, 2005); Mark McGurl, *The Program Era: Postwar Fiction and the Rise of Creative Writing* (Boston: Harvard University Press, 2009).

15 Hegamin, "Inclusion and Diversity," 3.

16 Rankine, "In Our Way," 47.

17 Mura, "Ferguson, Whiteness as Default," 40.

18 Jan Meyer and Ray Land, "Threshold Concepts and Troublesome Knowledge: Linkages to Ways of Thinking and Practising within the Disciplines" (Edinburgh: School of Education, University of Edinburgh, 2003). Web. http://www.etl.tla.ed. ac.uk/docs/ETLreport4.pdf

19 Hegamin, "Inclusion and Diversity," 3.

Chapter 1

1 Marjorie Garber, *Academic Instincts* (Princeton: Princeton University Press, 2001), 80.

2 William Herbert Carruth, *Verse Writing: A Practical Handbook for College Classes and Private Guidance* (New York: Macmillan, 1934), 36.

3 Charles Raymond Barrett, *Short Story Writing: A Practical Treatise on the Art of the Short Story* (Garden City: Doubleday, Page, & Co., 1921), 209.

4 Stephanie Vanderslice, *Rethinking Creative Writing* (Cambridge, UK: Professional and Higher Partnership, 2011), 27.

5 Paul Dawson, *Creative Writing and the New Humanities* (Routledge, 2005), 49.

6 Michel Foucault, "The Culture of the Self," (University of California Berkeley, 1983).

7   And consumerism uses the identity of the writer in marketing the right accoutrements for this sought-after lifestyle. It is not difficult to find advice on buying the pens, notebooks, computer software, subscriptions, etc. that will best suit the writer's life. Consumers are provided advice on how to eat, sleep, dress, and even decorate their homes like true writers as an ever-growing body of online content addresses such topics as "Decorating Tips for Aspiring Writers." See Cassandra Neace, "Decorating Tips for Aspiring Writers," *BookRiot* (2013). Web.

8   Peggy McIntosh, "White Privilege: Unpacking the Invisible Knapsack," Working Paper 189. *White Privilege and Male Privilege: A Personal Account of Coming To See Correspondences through Work in Women's Studies* (1988). Public talk given at the University of California Berkeley, available on YouTube.

9   Claire Faye Watkins, "On Pandering," *TinHouse.org* (November 23, 2015); Kavita Das, "On Parsing," Vidaweb.org (February 6, 2016); Alison Stine, "On Poverty," KenyonReview.org (February 29, 2016).

10 Harry W. Pope, "We Do Regret Having to Advise You. . . ." *Writer's Chronicle* (18 September, 2013). Web.

11 Kenneth Goldsmith, *Uncreative Writing* (New York: Columbia University Press, 2011), 7.

12 McGurl, *Program Era*, 236.

13 Ibid., 59.

14 Ibid., 238.

15 Lynn Neary, "In Elite MFA Programs, The Challenge Of Writing While 'Other.'" National Public Radio, Code Switch. 19 August 2014. Web.

16 Hong, "Delusions of Whiteness."

17 Percy Bysshe Shelley, "From a Defense of Poetry. Or Remarks Suggested by an Essay Entitled 'the Four Ages of Poetry'," in *The Norton Anthology of Theory and Criticism*, edited by Vincent B. Leitch, 2nd edition. (New York: Norton, 1959), 595–612. The same rendering of the poet-without-audience is used as a defining marker of the poetry genre in J. S. Mill's "What Is Poetry" (1833). Mill writes, "All poetry is of the nature of soliloquy" (5). This is what differentiates poetry from "eloquence" or oratory: "eloquence is heard; poetry is overheard. Eloquence supposes an audience. The peculiarity of poetry appears to us to lie in the poet's utter unconsciousness of a listener. Poetry is feeling confessing itself to itself in moments of solitude . . . Eloquence is feeling pouring itself out to other minds, courting their sympathy, or endeavoring to influence their belief, or move them to passion or to action." In Shelley and Mill, poetry is written for its own sake and is overheard to the benefit of its listeners.

18 Shelley, "Defense of Poetry," 595.

19 Monroe C. Beardsley, *Aesthetics: From Classical Greece to the Present* (Tuscaloosa: University of Alabama Press, 1966), 284.

20 Vincent B. Leitch, ed., *The Norton Anthology of Theory and Criticism*, 2nd edition (New York: Norton, 2010), 637.

21 Phillip Lopate, "On the Necessity of Turning Oneself into a Character," *I & Eye: Contemporary Creative Nonfiction*, edited by B. Minh Nguyen and Porter Shreve (New York: Pearson Longman, 2005), 70.

22 Derald Wing Sue, *Microaggressions in Everyday Life: Race, Gender, and Sexual Orientation* (Hoboken: John Wiley and Sons, 2010), 29.

23 "The word came to be associated with poets in the mid-seventeenth century, around the time that Grub Street acquired its reputation as a place for literary hacks in England. As a result it has always been associated with hardship and penury." See Dawson, *Creative Writing and the New Humanities*, 15, 19.

24 Kelly Ritter, *To Know Her Own History: Writing at the Woman's College, 1943–1963* (Pittsburgh: University of Pittsburgh Press, 2012), 154.

25 Beardsley, *Aesthetics*, 289.

26 For those few able to secure the subset of tenure-track positions that afford time and resources for creative activity, the professorship in creative writing may allow, Weiss argues, "resident writers [to] enjoy a greater leisure than they would in most other work and a livelier relationship to literature itself. In addition, they often form a community among themselves, their students, and other interested faculty members. Such community is rare among American writers." See Theodore Weiss, "A Personal View: Poetry, Pedagogy, and Per-Versities," in *The American Writer and the University*, ed. Ben Siegel (Newark: University of Delaware Press; Associated University Presses, 1989), 153. Weiss here constructs the academy as being very similar to a residency, as Yaddo and MacDowell also offer "leisure" among writers. In his construction of the literary writing life in the academy, Weiss ignores administrative requirements that may come with such positions—perhaps because the aesthetic tradition and popular culture has constructed the writer in such a way that those demands would seem foreign to the literary life, or perhaps because some writers are able to escape such demands (by, indeed, employing these same constructs of the writer as one who does not participate in the "practical" labors of a profession). Indeed, as Ritter observes, "the figure of the creative-writer-as-artist remains set apart from other types of faculty." See Ritter, *Her Own History*, 151.

27 Hermann Hagedorn, "The Peterborough Colony: 'A Workshop, with a Wonderland Thrown in' for Creative Workers in the Seven Arts," *The Outlook* 129 (28 December 1921), 686.

28 Friedrich Schiller, *On the Aesthetic Education of Man [1794]*, translated by Reginald Snell (Mineola, NY: Dover, 2004). *On the Aesthetic Education of Man* is concerned to show the artist how "to protect himself against the corruption of the age which besets him on all sides . . . [b]y disdaining its opinion" (52). The artist should become

"a stranger to his own century" in order to "cleanse and purify it" (51). Whereas for Plato the poet was a potential menace to society, for Schiller society is a potential menace to the poet.

29 See, for example, Laren Stover, *Bohemian Manifesto: A Field Guide to Living on the Edge* (New York: Bulfinch Press, 2004). Literary bohemianism has a history in "the vagabond anti-professionalism of late nineteenth and early twentieth century writers from George E. Woodberry to Ezra Pound" (D.G. Myers, *The Elephants Teach: Creative Writing since 1880*, 1st edition (Englewood Cliffs: Prentice Hall, 1996), 22.

30 Katherine H. Adams, *A Group of Their Own: College Writing Courses and American Women Writers, 1880–1940* (Albany: State University of New York Press, 2001), 7.

31 Ibid.

32 Some women in the later part of the nineteenth century, Adams reports, legitimized themselves by emphasizing a moral calling in place of financial need (Adams, *Group of Their Own*, 9). Arguably, these women were inching closer to the subject-position of the literary author, as it is constructed in the aesthetic discourse discussed in this chapter—a literary writer being regarded as one who has a "calling." This move was perhaps enabled by the fact that women had secured a place for themselves in the world of textual production. Yet the subject-position of author was still not secured: As Adams notes, "these women were seeking the safe definition not as artist, but instead as humble and simple do-gooder, and they descried their products as anonymous types of reform documents, like religious tracts, in which the doctrine, not the quality of the prose or the personality of the writer would matter" (Adams, *Group of Their Own*, 18).

33 Myers, *Elephants Teach*, 87.

34 See Appendix. R.V. Cassill, *Writing Fiction* (New York: Permabook, 1962) 3. William Herbert Carruth, *Verse Writing: A Practical Handbook for College Classes and Private Guidance* (New York: Macmillan, 1934), 36.

35 Esther L. Schwartz, *So You Want to Write!* (New York: Phoenix, 1936), 13.

36 Cassill, *Writing Fiction*, 287.

37 Charles I. Glicksberg, *Writing the Short Story* (New York: Hendricks House, 1953), 241. For further discussion of inspiration in aesthetic theory, see Timothy Clark, *The Theory of Inspiration: Composition as a Crisis of Subjectivity in Romantic and Post-Romantic Writing* (Manchester: Manchester University Press, 1997).

38 Barrett, *Short Story Writing*, 8.

39 Spencer Trask and Katrina Trask, "Letter Addressed to the Trustees of Pine Garde," *Yaddo records, 1870–1980 at the New York Public Library*, ed. Yaddo Artists' Community. New York: Box 197, Folder 1—Establishment of Pine Garde, 1900.

40 Ibid.

41 Hermann Hagedorn, "The Peterborough Colony," 687.

42 Nathaniel C. Fowler, *The Art of Story Writing: Facts and Information About Literary Work of Practical Value to Both Amateur and Professional Writers* (New York: Sully & Kleinteich, 1913), 17.

43 Carruth, *Verse Writing*, 51.

44 For Emerson, the poet is also supremely powerful: "The poet is the sayer, the namer, and represents beauty. He is a sovereign, and stands on the centre. [. . .] Beauty is the creator of the universe. Therefore the poet is not any permissive potentate, but is emperor in his own right." Ralph Waldo Emerson, "The Poet," in *Norton Anthology of Theory and Criticism*, edited by Vincent B. Leitch. 2nd edition (New York: Norton, 2010), 622, 630.

45 Beardsley, *Aesthetics*, 285.

46 The poet is, in Wordsworth's view, "endowed with more lively sensibility, more enthusiasm and tenderness" and he "has a greater knowledge of human nature, and a more comprehensive soul, than are supposed to be common upon mankind" (8). The poet "rejoices more than other men in the spirit of life that is in him" and he is "affected more than other men by absent things as if they were present." He also has the "ability of conjuring up in himself passions, which indeed are far from being the same as those produced by real events, yet . . . do more nearly resemble the passions produced by real events, than anything which . . . other men are accustomed to feel in themselves" (8). The poet "has acquired a greater readiness and power in expressing what he thinks and feels, and especially those thoughts and feelings which . . . arise in him without immediate external excitement" (8). The poet has an exceptional emotional capacity to feel the life of the world. The poet traffics in the "general passions and thoughts and feelings of men" and is "nothing differing in kind from other men, but only in degree." The poet is "chiefly distinguished from other men by a greater promptness to think and feel without external excitement; and a greater power in expressing such thoughts and feelings are produced in him in that manner" (8). In Shelley's words, the poet is more delicately organized than other men, and sensible to pain and pleasure, both his own and that of others, in a degree unknown to them" (612). The poet's capacities make him most acutely human. "But in the intervals of inspiration," Shelley writes, "a poet becomes a man" (612). The implication here is that the poet is closer to the essence of humanity than other members of humankind. See Shelley, "Defense of Poetry"; Wordsworth, "Preface to Lyrical Ballads."

47 As in Evelyn May Albright, who asks rhetorically of the imagination: "Is it some rare, God-given faculty or talent, completed at the start, or it is a power of the mind common to us all, but in some stronger and finer and more perfectly trained?" *Short-Story: Its Principles and Structure* (New York: Macmillan Company, 1908).

48 Ben Siegel, ed., *The American Writer and the University* (Newark: University of Delaware Press; Associated University Presses, 1989), 7.

On the one hand, academic creative writing has been praised for offering students the opportunity "to enter a community of working writers" (Adams, *Group of Their Own*, 51). Weiss, for example, praises the "small, unique community" (154) that is the workshop because "rarely in our society do people live so closely and so intimately together; rarely do they share such common ... aims. Their intimacy increases as they learn to quarry and to reveal deeper and deeper parts of themselves and of the personal worlds in which they live" (155). Moreover, the place of the creative writing workshop in the academy, Weiss continues, "has provided some official status for what I [as a creative writer] do, a kind of societal approval" (154). See Weiss, "A Personal View," 149–61. The MFA program is thought to bring to the classroom a sense of fellowship among writers, as it also legitimizes the literary writer and provides sanctioned space and time for the pursuit of the literary craft. MFA programs and writer's retreats and residencies both provide these affordances. It is therefore no surprise that both types of programs are advertised in similar terms. The Bread Loaf Colony is advertised as a community that can "provide the kind of ferment in which writing goes best" ("Bread Loaf Community of International Writers"), and one hears similar slogans from the marketing materials of MFA programs. Despite this praise, the community of the workshop is understood to have accompanying risks: namely, that the community will take away from the writer's individual creative process and damage her confidence. This risk is clearly articulated in a 2008 issue of the AWP *Writer's Chronicle* in which Catherine Wallace writes to her fellow writers:

> Whether or not you know a Muse by name, I am sure you know the Harpies and all of their innumerable offspring. All of us know the Harpies. Writers contend with Harpies at every turn. [. . .] Harpies can speak through the fault-finding habits of editors, teachers, or classmates. They can speak through the fault-finding reactions of anyone to whom we show our work. Although every writer wants and needs feedback, when we do so we run the risk of Harpies.

49 Horace, "Ars Poetica," *The Norton Anthology of Theory and Criticism*, edited by Vincent B. Leitch, 2nd edition (New York: Norton, 2010), 131. He continues in response: "For my part, I don't see what study can do without a rich vein of talent, nor what good can come of untrained genius."

50 For an alternative mapping of theories of creative writing pedagogy, see Dianne Donnelly, *Establishing Creative Writing Studies as an Academic Discipline* (New York: Multilingual Matters, 2012).

51 In the eighteenth century, genius was, as Pope notes in the epigraph, a rare case—a term reserved for Shakespeare and a select few. As the editors to the *Norton Anthology of Theory and Criticism* note, "Neoclassical critics such as Alexander Pope and Johnson could exempt only a great genius like Shakespeare from external rules of literary decorum, insisting that others rely on deliberate craft" (582).

By the time of Emerson, however, the assertion could be made that "genius is not the privilege of here and there a favorite, but the sound estate of every man." Genius is the action of creation, which becomes available to the "active soul"—a most highly valued possession, though it is "in almost all men obstructed and as yet unborn." See Ralph Waldo Emerson, "From 'the American Scholar,' " 617–620.

Those who are recognized as men of genius are admired because they are more in touch with a definitive part of their human-ness. Emerson puts this claim in the following terms: "The young man reveres men of genius, because, to speak truly, they are more himself than he is. They receive of the soul as he also receives, but they more." See Ralph Waldo Emerson, "The Poet," 621.

52 This belief in the latent creative capacities of every child, or the "conviction that all children are natural poets" was expressed by Mearns. See Paul Dawson, *Creative Writing and the New Humanities*, 51–52. It can also be translated into calls for the artist to return to a more naive, childlike, or adolescent way of viewing the world. Brande, for instance, claims that the artist should be in touch with a child-like self: "the author of genius does keep till his last breath the spontaneity, the ready sensitiveness, of a child" (Dorothea Brande, *Becoming a Writer*, New York: Harcourt, Brace, and Co., 1934, 18–19). It is also expressed by Kenneth Burke who claims in *Counter-Statement* that "everyone has the artist's temper as an adolescent" (Berkeley: University of California Press, 1931, 2).

53 Mark McGurl, *The Program Era*, 88, 131. This democratization of genius is also noted by Paul Dawson in *Creative Writing and the New Humanities*. Dawson quotes J. E. Spingarn's 1917 statement that "Genius and taste no longer mean for us what they meant to the poets and critics of the Romantic period. Their halo, their mystery, their power are gone. By genius is now merely meant the creative faculty, the power of self-expression, which we all share in varying degrees" (45). This is also related to a belief in the "genius of the unconscious" (Glicksberg, *Writing the Short Story*, 20), which served to make genius an attribute, however inaccessible, of all of humanity.

54 Myers, *Elephants Teach*, 101.

55 *Creative Youth* was published because of the success of Mearns' 1923 edited collection of his students' best work, titled *Lincoln Verse, Story, and Essay*. Myers describes the success of this book, "Readers saw in *Lincoln Verse* something more than a textbook; they treated it like a manifesto. Doubleday, Page and Company immediately commissioned Mearns to write an account of his experience in teaching writing, publishing it two years later as *Creative Youth*" (Myers, *Elephants Teach*, 103).

56 Myers, *Elephants Teach*, 103.

57 Ibid., 104. See also Trentwell Mason White, "Concerning the Subject of Creative Writing," *Education* (1938): 129.

58 John Dewey, *The School and Society* (Carbondale: Southern Illinois University Press, Arcturus, 1976), 60.

59 Katharine H. Adams, *A History of Professional Writing Instruction in American Colleges: Years of Acceptance, Growth, and Doubt* (Dallas: Southern Methodist University Press, 1993), 73.

60 David R. Russell, *Writing in the Academic Disciplines: A Curricular History*, 2nd edition (Carbondale: Southern Illinois University Press, 2002), 207.

61 What David Russell calls a "stereotype" of Deweyan progressive education: the "progressive as Bohemian, the self-absorbed individualist teaching children to write avant-garde poetry under a tree while they neglected their spelling." This "expressivist, child-centered individualism" (201) was, Russell notes, a "gross caricature" of Dewey's philosophy and methods (206). It nonetheless held sway in the day.

62 Sandy Grande, *Red Pedagogy: Native American Social and Political Thought* (New York: Rowman and Littlefield, 2004), 33, 53. See Katharyne Mitchell, "Education for Democratic Citizenship: Transnationalism, Multiculturalism, and the Limits of Liberalism," *Harvard Educational Review* 71.1 (Spring 2001): 51–78. Also see John Ogbu, "Class Stratification, Racial Stratification, and Schooling," in *Race, Class, and Schooling*, edited by L. Weiss (Amherst, NY: Comparative Education Center, State University of New York, 1986), 6–35.

63 Mearns, *Creative Youth*, 28. Quoted in Myers, *Elephants Teach*, 108.

64 Colin Bulman, "Devising and Teaching a Creative Writing Course," *Critical Quarterly* 26.3 (1984): 81.

65 Carruth, *Verse Writing*, xii–xiii.

66 The Iowa Writers' Workshop, the first graduate-level creative writing program to be founded in the US, was officially established in 1936, but the beginnings of the program can be traced in the 1922 decision to begin accepting creative work as theses to fulfill graduate degree requirements and the 1930 hiring of Norman Foerster to assume control of the newly established School of Letters at the University of Iowa. (Foerster was director of this program until 1944.) Iowa offered creative writing courses prior to this founding. The first creative writing class at Iowa, "Verse-Making," was offered in the spring semester of 1897, but the creative writing program formally came to fruition under Foerster, who implemented the creative writing dissertation at the doctoral level and reconstructed the English studies curriculum to emphasize imaginative writing. At the time of this curricular reformation, Foerster dropped the category of "Rhetoric & Composition" which had served as a designation for the writing courses. This was replaced by the prefix "Imaginative Writing" so that advanced composition became "Imaginative Writing: Advanced" (see Dawson, *Creative Writing and the New Humanities*, 68). Also see the many books that have been published about the history of creative writing

at Iowa, including: Frank Conroy, *Eleventh Draft: Craft and the Writing Life from Iowa Writers' Workshop* (HarperCollins, 1999); Robert Dana, *A Community of Writers: Paul Engle and the Iowa Writers' Workshop* (University of Iowa Press, 1999); Tom Grimes, *The Workshop: Seven Decades of the Iowa Writers' Workshop* (Hyperion, 1999); Eric Olsen and Glenn Schaeffer, *We Wanted to Be Writers: Life, Love, and Literature at the Iowa Writers' Workshop* (New York: Skyhorse, 2011); the archival history by Stephen Wilbers, *The Iowa Writers' Workshop: Origins, Emergence, & Growth* (University of Iowa Press, 1980) and Milton M. Reigelman, *The Midland: A Venture in Literary Regionalism* (University of Iowa Press, 1975); and, most recently, Eric Bennett, *Workshops of Empire* (University of Iowa Press, 2015).

67 Retrieved from the *Institutional Archives*, University of Denver. See also Bernard Spilka, *The Heart of the University of Denver: A Human Approach to the Arts, Humanities, and Sciences: An Appreciation of Faculty*, edited by Steven P. Fisher (Denver, University of Denver Institutional Archives, 2007).

68 Sharon Crowley, *Composition in the University: Historical and Polemical Essays* (Pittsburgh: University of Pittsburgh Press, 1998), 13.

69 Frederick Smock, "Poetry & Compassion," *Writer's Chronicle* (February 2007). Web.

70 May Sarton, *The Writing of a Poem: An Address* (Claremont: Scripps College, 1957), 2.

71 Crowley, *Composition in the University*, 34.

72 Ibid., 35.

73 Ibid., 14.

74 Myers, *Elephants Teach*, 14.

75 McGurl, *Program Era*, 93.

76 Vanderslice, *Rethinking Creative Writing*, 35–44.

77 In 1921, Charles Raymond Barrett instructed fiction writers that, "What is worth writing and publishing is worth being paid for" (*Short Story Writing*, 227). Such claims pepper early craft texts. Schwartz provides another example as she addresses her novice audience, saying, "Yes, my dear writers, it isn't what you write, but WHAT YOU SELL that makes you a writer. Point one. And the most important point, in practical writing" (Schwartz, *So You Want to Write!*, 3). Likewise, Fowler argues, writing in 1913 (*The Art of Strong Writing*), "To refuse to discuss the making of literature commercially, or from a business point of view, would be unfair and unprofitable. [...] It is obvious that the majority of writers consider their pens as remunerative tools, and that they produce literature, or what resembles it, not wholly for fame and for the good that they may do, but because of the money received, or expected, from their work."

78 Adams, *Professional Writing Instruction*, 14.

79 Ibid., 71.

80 Jim Collins, *Bring on the Books for Everybody: How Literary Culture Became Popular Culture* (Durham, NC: Duke University Press, 2010), 51.

81 Clint Burnham, *The Only Poetry That Matters: Reading the Kootenay School of Writing* (Vancouver, British Columbia: Arsenal Pulp Press, 2011), 98.

82 Daniel Pink, "The MFA Is the New MBA," *Harvard Business Review* (February 2004): 21. Given this link between the MFA and the MBA it is worthwhile to pause over the term "workshop"—a "notably utilitarian term . . . literal versions of which [. . .] had provided for the training of their future manual laborers." See also McGurl, *Program Era*, 95.

83 Mary Ann Cain, "'To Be Lived': Theorizing Influence in Creative Writing," *College English* 71. 3 (January 2009): 229.

84 Quoted in Vanderslice, *Rethinking Creative Writing*, 51.

85 Vanderslice, *Rethinking Creative Writing*, 28–29.

86 Craig Dworkin, "Opinion: Mycopedagogy," *College English* 66.6 (2004): 604.

87 Ibid., 609.

88 Alexander Pope, "An Essay on Criticism," quoted in Beardsley, *Aesthetics*, 168.

89 Joseph Addison, "On Genius," *The Spectator* (1711).

90 Katharine Coles, "Short Fiction," *Teaching Creative Writing*, edited by Graeme Harper (New York: Continuum, 2006), 13.

91 McGurl, *Program Era*, 93.

92 Ibid., 221.

93 See Joan Retallack and Juliana Spahr, *Poetry and Pedagogy: The Challenge of the Contemporary* (New York: Palgrave Macmillan, 2006) for the references to Charles Bernstein and Derek Owens and for additional examples of experimental pedagogical approaches.

94 Louise Desalvo, *Writing as a Way of Healing: How Telling Our Stories Transforms Our Lives* (Boston: Beacon, 1999); Geri Giebel Chavis, *Poetry and Story Therapy: The Healing Power of Creative Expression* (London: Jessica Kingsley Publishers, 2011); Deborah Philips and Liz Linington, *Writing Well: Creative Writing and Mental Health* (London: Jessica Kingsley Publishers, 1999). See also James Pennebaker and John Evans, *Expressive Writing: Words that Heal* (Enumclaw: Idyll Arbor, 2014); James Pennebaker and Joshua M. Smyth, *Opening Up by Writing It Down, Third Edition: How Expressive Writing Improves Health and Eases Emotional Pain* (New York: Guilford Press, 2016).

95 Collins, *Bring on the Books*, 10.

96 Ibid., 11.

97 Myers, *Elephants Teach*, 142.

98 Marguerite Wilkinson, *The Way of the Makers* (New York: Macmillan, 1925); Adele Bildersee, *Imaginative Writing: An Illustrated Course for Students* (Boston, NY: D.C. Heath, 1927); Dorothea Brande, *Becoming a Writer* (New York: Harcourt, Brace, and Co., 1934); Esther L. Schwartz, *So You Want to Write!* (New York: Phoenix, 1936);

Margaret Widdemer, *Do You Want to Write?* (New York: Farrar & Rinehart, 1937); Brenda Ueland, *Help from the Nine Muses (If You Want to Write)* (New York: Putnam, 1938).

99 Myers, *Elephants Teach*, 145.

100 Adams, *Professional Writing Instruction*, 74.

101 Ibid., 95.

102 Kelly Ritter, *To Know Her Own History: Writing at the Woman's College, 1943–1963* (Pittsburgh: University of Pittsburgh Press, 2012), 156.

103 Jones, Moore, and Bridgforth, eds., *Experiments in a Jazz Aesthetic*, 16.

104 Barbara Herrnstein Smith, *Contingencies of Value: Alternative Perspectives for Critical Theory* (Cambridge, MA: Harvard University Press, 1988), 18.

105 Pierre Bourdieu, *The Field of Cultural Production*, translated by Randal Johnson (New York: Columbia University Press, 1993), 40.

106 McGurl, *Program Era*, 74.

107 Dorothea Brande, *Becoming a Writer* (New York: Harcourt, Brace, and Co., 1934); Robert Kingery Buell, *Verse Writing Simplified* (Stanford: Stanford University Press, 1940); Brenda Ueland, *Help from the Nine Muses (If You Want to Write)* (New York: Putnam, 1938).

108 Quoted in McGurl, *Program Era*, 131.

109 Nancy Welch, "No Apology: Challenging the 'Uselessness' of Creative Writing," *Journal of Advanced Composition* 19.1 (Winter 1999): 117–134.

110 Hans Ostrom, "Undergraduate Creative Writing: The Unexamined Subject," *Writing on the Edge* 1.1 (1989): 61.

111 Doris Betts, "Undergraduate Creative Writing Courses," *ADE Bulletin* 79 (1984): 34.

112 Nathaniel C. Fowler, *The Art of Story Writing: Facts and Information About Literary Work of Practical Value to Both Amateur and Professional Writers* (New York: Sully & Kleinteich, 1913), 17.

113 Ibid., 17.

114 Ostrom, "Undergraduate," 59

115 Vanderslice, *Rethinking Creative Writing*, 20.

116 Ron McFarland, "An Apologia for Creative Writing," *College English* 55.1 (January 1993): 34.

117 Dave Smith, "Notes on Responsibility and the Teaching of Creative Writing," *Local Assays: On Contemporary American Poetry* (Urbana, IL: University of Illinois Press, 1985), 223.

118 Myers, *Elephants Teach*, 39.

119 McFarland, "An Apologia," 34.

120 McGurl, *The Program Era*, 99, 144.

121 Rebecca Caudill, *The High Cost of Writing* (Cumberland: Southeast Community College / University of Kentucky, 1965), 9.

Chapter 2

1   Katharine Haake, "Teaching Creative Writing If the Shoe Fits," in *Colors of a Different Horse: Rethinking Creative Writing Theory and Pedagogy*, edited by Wendy Bishop and Hans Ostrom (Urbana, IL: NCTE, 1994), 89.

2   Herrnstein Smith, *Contingencies of Value*.

3   Haake, "Teaching Creative Writing If the Shoe Fits," 80.

4   Rankine, "In Our Way" 50.

5   Kelly Ritter, "Ethos Interrupted: Diffusing 'Star' Pedagogy in Creative Writing Programs," *College English* 69 (2007): 283–292.

6   Michelene Wandor, *The Author Is Not Dead, Merely Somewhere Else: Creative Writing Reconceived* (New York: Palgrave Macmillan, 2008), 131.

7   Adrienne Perry, "Writing Without Shelter," *Journal of Creative Writing Studies* 1.1 (2016): 1–6.

8   Creative writing's rejection of didactic and polemical writing is tied to a larger skepticism regarding formal reasoning, argumentation, and rhetoric. Evoking emotions in readers or causing them to experience something through the text are worthwhile intentions for the artist; but to deliberately argue something is another matter. To teach or influence readers through rhetoric runs too close to the feared possibility that art will become subsumed by established norms. Demonstrating this perspective, which transcends multiple decades of craft-text writing, Charles Glicksberg's 1953 *Writing the Short Story* argues that the writer must have a "creative truthfulness," an "unswerving integrity," and a "resistance to all forms of political coercion, to catchwords and gospels and creeds, since no commissar can presume to tell him what to write or how to write" (200). The writer, in other words, must have a vision of his or her own—a vision that transcends institutionalized discourse. Yet that vision is not meant to be translated into polemical or didactic discourse.

The complexities of this craft concept called "vision" are many, as this is a notoriously difficult concept for students in creative writing. Examining Charles Baxter's use of the term in his popular work of craft-criticism *Burning Down the House: Essays on Fiction* (St. Paul, MN: Graywolf, 2008) points to some of the term's knots: Baxter writes, "Technique must follow a vision, a view of experience. No technique can ever take precedence over vision (116). "Vision," for Baxter, is a "view of experience," but it should not be managed so calculatingly as to render a work that is overly controlled by it. "[A]rt that is overcontrolled by its meaning," Baxter writes, "may start to go a bit dead," so the artist cannot doggedly follow a vision, cannot launch a concerted argument. To Baxter, a text overly controlled by meaning would become a mere vehicle of the writer's opinions or views, something nearing propaganda. Arguing against overly manipulative writing that insists on designated emotional responses, Baxter claims the text must be true to the writer's vision, but it should not be controlled by the writer's opinions, beliefs, intended meanings or effects. Baxter's theory of artistic vision is backed by the aesthetic thought that precedes him. In the conception of "vision" offered by this craft text, Baxter echoes warnings against the potential harms of the didactic in art, while preserving the writer's artistic freedom—a value that governed the art-for-art's-sake movement—to play out his/her own vision of the world. Behind these statements in *Burning Down the House* is a rejection of approaches to art that treat literature as useful texts, or texts that are determined to deliver a particular effect. But what is at stake in these common conceptions? What forms of literature are pushed to the margins in the value system this aesthetic legacy has erected?

9 Gabrielle L'Hirondelle Hill and Sophie McCall, *The Land We Are: Artists and Writers Unsettle the Politics of Reconciliation* (Winnipeg: ARP, 2015), 1.

10 Mark Martin, *I'm With the Bears: Short Stories from a Damaged Planet* (London: Verso, 2011).

11 Rachel Blau DuPlessis, *The Pink Guitar* (New York: Routledge, 1990), 17.

12 Christina Davis' list of activist poetry collections, from her article "Is the Constitution: Some Notes on Poetry & Activism" includes, for example, M NourbeSe Philips, *Zong*; Juliana Spahr's *This Connection of Everyone With Lungs*, Claudia Rankine's *Citizen: An American Lyric*; Anne Waldman's *The Iovis Trilogy* and *Civil Disobediences*; Thomas Sayers Ellis' *Skin, Inc.: Identity Repair Poems*, Frank Smith's *Guantanamo* (trans. Vanessa Place); CD Wright, *One with Others*; Fred Moten's "The University and the Undercommons," Gabriel Gudding's forthcoming *Rivers for Animals*; poet-journalist Eliza Griswold's *I Am the Beggar of the World: Landays from Contemporary Afghanistan*, Cecilia Vicuña's *A Menstrual Quipu: The Blood of the Glaciers Journal*. And, as Davis notes, there are countless other examples. See Christina Davis, "Is the Constitution: Some Notes on Poetry & Activism," *Teachers & Writers Magazine.* (November 12, 2014). Also see anthologies such as Phil Cushway and Michael Warr, eds., *Of Poetry and Protest: From Emmett Till to Trayvon Martin* (New York: Norton, 2016).

13 Myers, *Elephants Teach*, 8.

14 Crowley, *Composition in the University*, 44, emphasis mine.

15 Myers, *Elephants Teach*, 61.

16 Chris Green, "Materializing the Sublime Reader: Cultural Studies, Reader Response, and Community Service in the Creative Writing Workshop," *College English* 64.2 (November 2001): 162.

17 Ibid., 165.

18 Herrnstein Smith, *Contingencies of Value*, 14.

19 Ibid., 22.

20 Stephen Dobyns, *Best Words, Best Order: Essays on Poetry*, 2nd edition (New York: Palgram Macmillan, 2003), 183. Dobyns scorns writing that preaches. He cautions against the "partisan poem" which might try "to gain sympathy from the reader" (181). He defines the partisan poem as one that tells us how to think and feel. Yet, although Dobyns disparages the moralizing poem, he also preserves a moral role for poetry: He writes, "It is easy to say that art has no moral role—that, basically, it is a piece of instruction for the maker. Once the poem is made and has a public life, then it is impossible to deny that social and moral aspect. The poet is not attempting to teach, but, nonetheless, the poem teaches" (339).

21 Janet Burroway and Susan Weinberg, *Writing Fiction*, 6th edition (New York: Longman, 2003), 359.

22 Carruth, *Verse Writing*, 48.

23 Ibid., 49.

24 Albright, *Short-Story*, 227. In Albright, as with Stephen Dobyns discussed in note 163 above—writers who are separated by nearly a century—we find the formulation, common to Romantic theorists, that good literature is inherently also a moral benefit to society, even as it makes no effort to preach a moral good. It is the nature of good literature to be good for society, even as the literary writer makes no explicit moral claims.

25 Beardsley, *Aesthetics*, 25.

26 Ibid.

27 Ibid., 136.

28 Shelley, "Defense of Poetry," 597.

29 Ibid., 613.

30 Ibid., 596–597.

31 Quoted in Garber, *Academic Instincts*, 11.

32 Immanuel Kant, *Critique of Judgment [1790]*, translated by James Creed Meredith, edited by Nicholas Walker (Oxford: Oxford University Press, 1978), 27.

33 Friedrich Schiller, *On the Aesthetic Education*, 27.

34 Ibid., 53.

35 Dawson, *Creative Writing and the New Humanities*, 104.

36 Quoted in Dobyns, *Best Words*, 354.

37 Beardsley, *Aesthetics*, 289. See also Oscar Wilde, *The Picture of Dorian Gray* (London: Wordsworth Editions, 1992).

38 Rankine, "In Our Way," 52.

39 Crowley, *Composition in the University*, 34.

40 Ibid., 35.

41 Brent Royster, "The Construction of Self in the Contemporary Creative Writing Workshop: A Personal Journey" (Dissertation, Bowling Green State University, 2006), 60.

42 Perry, "Writing Without Shelter," 2.

43 Albright, *Short-Story*, 204.

44 Stephen Minot, *Three Genres: The Writing of Poetry, Fiction, and Drama*, 7th edition (Upper Saddle River, NJ: Prentice Hall, 2003), 8.

45 Ibid., 149.

46 Burroway and Weinberg, *Writing Fiction*, 411.

47 Ibid.

48 Collins, *Bring on the Books*, 212–213.

49 Ibid., 8.

50 Dobyns, *Best Words*, 152.

51 Nadine Gordimer, *Telling Times: Writing and Living, 1950–2008* (London: Bloomsbury, 2010), 440.

52 Green, "Materializing the Sublime Reader."

53 Crowley, *Composition in the University*, 43

54 Herrnstein Smith, *Contingencies of Value*, 23.

55 Ibid., 42.

56 Perry, "Writing Without Shelter," 2.

57 Tom Kerr, "The Feeling of What Happens in Departments of English," in *A Way to Move: Rhetorics of Emotion and Composition Studies*, edited by Dale Jacobs and Laura R. Micciche (Portsmouth, NH: Boynton/Cook, 2003), 31.

58 Collins, *Bring on the Books*, 49.

59 Creative writing's high/low taste binaries translate into biases about reception and circulation, the "uses and abuses of literature" in society, to use Marjorie Garber's phrase. To maintain a binary distinction between "high" and "low" art as the craft texts do (e.g., Burroway's "literary" and "genre" fiction, Minot's "sophisticated" and "simple" poetry and fiction) is to deny the complex history of reception and circulation, of literary form and genre functions. Creative writing curricula rarely include courses on the sociology of the publishing industry, on reception and the practices of readers, on book history and the changing packaging of literature. Circulation is a mystified subject in many of creative writing's pedagogies. When publishing is discussed at all, it is often introduced without acknowledgment of the industry's need for transformation, in light of the findings of the VIDA Count and other studies like it.

60 Jeri Kroll, "Creativity, Craft, and the Canon: Unpacking the Cult(ure) of the Workshop," in *The and is papers: proceedings of the 12th conference of the AAWP* (2007), edited by Jen Webb and Jordan Williams: Web, http://www.aawp.org.au/publications/the-is-papers/

61 Collins finds that, "Judging by the winners and short-list nominees for the most prestigious literary prizes awarded between 2004 and 2008, the best way to ensure that a novel will be deemed a literary bestseller, and make a big splash in the awards

game, is to feature a highly self-conscious celebration of the transformative power of the written word and equally impassioned advocacy of the need for aesthetic beauty" (*Bring on the Books*, 222).

62 Crowley, *Composition in the University*, 9.

63 Susan Miller, *Textual Carnivals: The Politics of Composition* (Carbondale: Southern Illinois University Press, 1991), 54–55.

64 Crowley, *Composition in the University*, 216

65 McGurl, *Program Era*, 67.

66 Burroway and Weinberg, *Writing Fiction*, 12. Harry W. Pope's 2013 contribution to the AWP *Writer's Chronicle* provides another example. Pope quotes Styron who once said, "Loneliness is your companion for life. If you don't want to be lonely, get into TV." The facile second sentence—if you don't want the loneliness of the literary artist's life go into the entertainment business—is bound up with a high/low art divide. The special status of the literary writer pushes her into the seclusion of one who is an observer of the world that she is not part of; the TV writer, in contrast, works on a team to produce a commodity that will be enjoyed by the masses.

67 Myers, *Elephants Teach*, 8.

68 Herrnstein Smith, *Contingencies of Value*, 131.

69 Myers, *Elephants Teach*, 61.

70 Crowley, *Composition in the University*, 44.

71 Schiller, *On the Aesthetic Education*, 52.

72 Ibid.

73 Ibid., 51.

74 Emerson, "The Poet," 630.

75 William Wordsworth, "Preface to Lyrical Balads, with Pastoral and Other Poems [1802]," in *Norton Anthology of Theory and Criticism*, edited by Vincent B. Leitch, et al. (New York: Norton, 2010), 12.

76 Ibid., 14.

77 Beardsley, *Aesthetics*, 285.

78 Collins, *Bring on the Books*, 20. Sarton, *The Writing of a Poem*, 17 .

79 John Aldridge, "The New American Assembly-Line Fiction: An Empty Blue Center," *The American Scholar* 59.1 (Winter 1990): 17–38; John Aldridge, "*Talents and Technicians: Literary Chic and the New Assembly-Line Fiction* (New York: Scribner's, Maxwell Macmillan International, 1992).

80 Quoted in Beardsley, *Aesthetics*, 248.

81 Sara Ahmed, *The Cultural Politics of Emotion* (Edinburgh: Edinburgh University Press, 2004), 42.

82 Suzanne Clark, "Rhetoric, Social Construction, and Gender: Is It Bad to Be Sentimental?" *Writing Theory and Critical Theory*, edited by John Clifford and John Schilb (New York: Modern Language Association, 1994), 97.

83   Baxter, *Burning Down the House*, 139.

84   Ahmed, *Cultural Politics of Emotion*, 3.

85   Garber, *Academic Instincts*, 141. In 1913, a craft text by Fowler provides an example of creative writing discourse that upholds melancholy as a valuable emotional state for the writer to cultivate. Fowler writes, "many attempt to write verse because of the real and worthy vein of sentiment in every human heart, which makes impassioned expression,—and that is what poetry is essentially,—natural to every one when deeply stirred. The lover is always, at moments, a poet, though he be tongue-tied. *He who is melancholy for any reason, serious or trivial, drinks for the moment of the fountains which ever feed the souls of the poet and philosopher*" (emphasis mine). See Fowler, *The Art of Story Writing*, 49–50.

86   J. Berg Esenwein, *Writing the Short-Story; a Practical Handbook on the Rise, Structure, Writing, and Sale of the Modern Short-Story* (New York: Hinds, Hayden & Eldridge, 1918), 184.

87   Charles Baxter, *Burning Down the House: Essays on Fiction* (St. Paul, MN: Graywolf, 2008), 228.

88   Some forms of *sentiment*, as opposed to sentimentality, are more often valued in discourses of creative writing instruction. Lewis Turco makes a distinction between sentiment and sentimentality in another popular craft text, *The Book of Forms*, 3rd edition (Hanover: University Press of New England, 2000). He writes, a "distinction is to be made between the terms sentiment and sentimentality. The former is a feeling of tenderness, whereas sentimentality is an excess of sentiment, overstated sympathy" (67). There is great agreement among creative writers that the literary traffics in the realm of emotion, as Esenwein states unequivocally "there can be no sustained human interest without emotion"—thus fiction requires emotion. See J. Berg Esenwein, *Writing the Short-Story*, 183.

89   Thomas Newkirk, *The Performance of Self in Student Writing* (Portsmouth, NH: Boynton/Cook, Heinemann, 1997), 36, 28.

90   Clark, "Rhetoric, Social Construction, and Gender," 96.

91   Baxter, *Burning Down the House*, 218.

92   Clark, "Rhetoric, Social Construction, and Gender," 105.

93   Dobyns, *Best Words*, 354.

94   Clark, "Rhetoric, Social Construction, and Gender," 96.

95   Suzanne Clark, *Sentimental Modernism: Women Writers and the Revolution of the Word* (Bloomington: Indiana University Press, 1991), 9.

96   Schwartz, *So You Want to Write!* 27.

97   Ibid. 3.

98   Adams, *Group of Their Own*, 1. It is in this context that we read Schwartz's mention of the fact that her "earnings have averaged about a thousand dollars a year while … Joseph Hergesheimer wrote for fourteen years before he made his first sale, and

then it was a check for a few dollars for his wife's recipe for red cabbage" (*So You Want to Write!*, 1). Schwartz imagines an audience for her craft text as a group of women writers who may be hesitant to act on their literary aspirations—aspirations that may involve the writing of "practical" or "escapist" material. Schwartz not only condones this work, she finds the space to compare herself to a fellow male writer.

99   Shelley, "Defense of Poetry," 599.

100 Henry James, "The Art of Fiction," in *The Norton Anthology of Theory & Criticism*, 758.

101 Albright, *Short-Story*: 205. Albright asserts the lack of genuine emotion in sentimentality: "It was the attempt to force the emotional element into fiction that brought about that tremendous amateurish blunder of *sentimentalism* in eighteenth century fiction." To avoid sentimentality, Albright claims, the writer must have true emotion in sufficient supply—and this cannot be forced, nor can it be taught. She continues, "the young writer whose work lacks emotional power can do little more than trust time to broaden and deepen his emotional experiences. If he has eyes to see, mind to judge, and heart to feel the human life about him, emotions will arise in him spontaneously. They cannot be prematurely forced" (188).

102 May Sarton, *The Writing of a Poem*, 5, 4.

103 Esenwein, *Writing the Short Story*, 195.

104 Lynn Domina, "The Body of My Work Is Not Just a Metaphor," in *Colors of a Different Horse: Rethinking Creative Writing Theory and Pedagogy*, edited by Wendy Bishop and Hans Ostrom (Urbana, IL: NCTE, 1994), 34.

105 Hans Ostrom, "Introduction: Of Radishes and Shadows, Theory and Pedagogy," *Colors of a Different Horse: Rethinking Creative Writing Theory and Pedagogy* (Urbana, IL: NCTE, 1994), xiii.

106 See Douglas Hesse, "The Place of Creative Writing in Composition Studies," *College Composition and Communication* 62.1 (2010): 45. In this article, Hesse cites Kathleen Blake Yancey, "*Made Not Only in Words: Composition in a New Key*," *College Composition and Communication* 56.2 (2004), and Denis G. Pelli and Charles Bigelow, "A Writing Revolution," *Seed Magazine* (2009), 17 January 2013.

Chapter 3

1   Wendy Bishop, *Released into Language: Options for Teaching Creative Writing* (Urbana, IL: NCTE, 1990), 39.

2   Dawson, *Creative Writing and the New Humanities*, 178.

3 Hans Ostrom, "Introduction: Of Radishes and Shadows," xiv.

4 Jan Meyer and Ray Land, "Threshold Concepts and Troublesome Knowledge: Linkages to Ways of Thinking and Practising within the Disciplines," Occasional Report 4, Enhancing Teaching-Learning Environments in Undergraduate Courses Project (Higher and Community Education, School of Education, University of Edinburgh, Coventry and Durham, 2003).

5 Patricia, Bravender, Hazel McClure, and Gayle Schaub, *Teaching Information Literacy Threshold Concepts: Lesson Plans for Librarians* (Washington, D.C.: American Library Association, 2015); Timothy Clark, *Ecocriticism on the Edge: The Anthropocene as a Threshold Concept* (New York: Bloomsbury Academic, 2015); Christie Launius and Holly Hassel, *Threshold Concepts in Women's and Gender Studies: Ways of Seeing, Thinking, and Knowing* (New York: Routledge, 2015).

6 Doug Downs and Elizabeth Wardle, "Teaching about Writing, Righting Misconceptions: (Re)Envisioning 'First-Year Composition' as 'Introduction to Writing Studies,'" *College Composition and Communication* 58.4 (June 2007): 552–584.

7 Meyer and Land, "Threshold Concepts and Troublesome Knowledge."

8 Kathleen Blake Yancey, Liane Robertson, and Kara Taczak, *Writing Across Contexts: Transfer, Composition, and Sites of Writing* (Logan: Utah State University Press, 2014), 4.

9 Linda Adler-Kassner and Elizabeth Wardle, *Naming What We Know: Threshold Concepts of Writing Studies* (Boulder: University Press of Colorado, 2015) 3.

10 Yancey, Robertson, and Taczak, *Writing Across Contexts*, 4.

11 Ibid., 41.

12 Quoted in ibid., 39.

13 Eugene Garber and Jan Ramjerdi, "Reflections on the Teaching of Creative Writing: A Correspondence," in *Colors of a Different Horse: Rethinking Creative Writing Theory and Pedagogy*, edited by Wendy Bishop and Hans Ostrom (Urbana, IL: NCTE, 1994), 21.

14 Green, "Materializing the Sublime Reader," 161.

15 Jen Webb, *Researching Creative Writing* (Suffolk: Frontinus, 2015), 6.

16 Jeffrey Schultz, "Cliché as Reification: Nurturing Criticality in the Undergraduate Creative Writing Classroom," *New Writing: The International Journal for the Practice and Theory of Creative Writing* 12.1 (2015): 79.

17 Ibid., 82.

18 Haake, "Teaching Creative Writing If the Shoe Fits," 93.

19 Matt Madden, *99 Ways to Tell a Story* (New York: Chamberlain Brothers, 2005).

20 Chad Davidson, and Gregory Fraser, "Poetry," in *Teaching Creative Writing*, edited by Graeme Harper (New York: Continuum, 2006), 23.

21 Adams, *Group of Their Own*, xiv.

22 Ibid., 23.

23 Ibid., xvii.

24 Wendy Bishop and Stephen Armstrong, "Box Office Poison: The Influence of Writers in Films on Writers (in Graduate Programs)," in *Can It Really Be Taught? Resisting Lore in Creative Writing Pedagogy*, edited by Kelly Ritter and Stephanie Vanderslice, 1st edition (Portsmouth: Boynton / Cook, Heinemann, 2007), 91–105.

25 Leslie Marmon Silko, "Language and Literature from a Pueblo Indian Perspective," in *Contemporary Creative Nonfiction: I & Eye*, edited by Bich Minh Nguyen and Porter Shreve (New York: Pearson, 2004), 179–185.

26 Nicole Cooley, "Literary Legacies and Critical Transformations: Teaching Creative Writing in the Public Urban University," *Pedagogy: Critical Approaches to Teaching Literature, Language, Composition, and Culture* 3.1 (2003): 102.

27 Shirley Geok-lin Lim, "Lore, Practice, and Social Identity in Creative Writing Pedagogy: Speaking with a Yellow Voice?" *Pedagogy* 10.1 (Winter 2010): 84.

28 Stephanie Kerschbaum, *Toward a New Rhetoric of Difference* (Urbana: National Council of Teachers of English, 2014), 10.

29 Janet Neigh, "Dreams of Uncommon Languages: Transnational Feminist Pedagogy and Multilingual Poetics," *Feminist Formations* 26.1 (Spring 2017): 71.

30 Ibid., 72.

31 Ibid., 75.

32 Gloria Anzaldúa, *Borderlands/La Frontera: The New Mestiza*, 3rd edition (San Francisco: Aunt Lute Books, 2007), 81.

33 Julie Jung, *Revisionary Rhetoric, Feminist Pedagogy, and Multigenre Texts* (Carbondale: Southern Illinois University Press, 2005), 35.

34 Donald Murray, "Teach Writing as a Process Not Product," in *Cross-Talk in Comp Theory*, edited by Victor Villanueva, 2nd edition (Urbana: NCTE, 2003), 6.

35 William A. Covino, "Rhetorical Pedagogy," in *A Guide to Composition Pedagogies*, edited by Gary Tate, Amy Rupiper, and Kurt Schick (New York: Oxford University Press, 2001), 37.

36 Sharon Crowley, *A Teacher's Introduction to Deconstruction* (Urbana, IL: NCTE, 1989), 30.

37 Gordimer, *Telling Times*, 444.

38 Green, "Materializing the Sublime Reader," 161.

39 Scott Russell Sanders, "The Writer in the University," *ADE Bulletin* 99 (Fall 1991): 24.

40 See Katharine Coles, ed., *Blueprints: Bringing Poetry into Communities* (Salt Lake City: University of Utah Press; Chicago: Harriett Monroe Poetry Institute, 2011). Also see Terry Ann Thaxton, *Creative Writing in the Community: A Guide* (London: Bloomsbury, 2014).

41 Laura Wilder, *Rhetorical Strategies and Genre Conventions in Literary Studies: Teaching and Writing in the Disciplines* (Carbondale: Southern Illinois University Press, 2012).

42 Michael Warner, "Uncritical Reading," in *Polemic: Critical or Uncritical (Essays from the English Institute)*, edited by Jane Gallup (New York: Routlege, 2004), 13.

43 Terry Eagleton, *Literary Theory: An Introduction* (Minneapolis: University of Minnesota Press, 1996), 206.

44 Wendy Bishop, "Teaching Undergraduate Creative Writing: Myths, Mentors, and Metaphors," *Journal of Teaching Writing* 7.7 (1988): 91.

45 Herrnstein Smith, *Contingencies of Value*, 45.

46 Haake, "Teaching Creative Writing If the Shoe Fits," 80.

47 Rankine, Loffreda, and Cap, eds., *The Racial Imaginary*, 31.

48 Maria Damon, *Postliterary America: From Bagel Shop Jazz to Micropoetries* (Iowa City: University of Iowa Press, 2011).

49 Baxter, *Burning Down the House*, 49.

50 Andy Crockett, "Straddling the Rhet Comp/Creative Writing Schism," *Writing on the Edge* 9.2 (Spring 1998): 88.

51 Schultz, "Cliché as Reification," 88.

52 Judith Roof, *Come as You Are: Sexuality and Narrative* (New York: Columbia University Press, 1996), 8.

53 Judith Summerfield, "Is There a Life in This Text? Reimaging Narrative," in *Writing Theory and Critical Theory*, edited by John Clifford and John Schilb (New York: Modern Language Association of America, 1994), 180.

54 Toni Morrison, interview with Bill Moyers, *World of Ideas* television series (March 1990). Quoted in Ileana Jiménez, *The Feminist Teacher: Educating for Equity and Justice (April 13, 2014)*. Web. https://feministteacher.com/2010/04/13/exposing-the-master-narrative-teaching-toni-morrisons-the-bluest-eye/

55 Donald Morton, and Mas'ud Zavarzadeh, "The Cultural Politics of the Fiction Workshop," *Cultural Critique* 11 (Winter 1988–1989): 157.

56 Joanna Russ, "What Can a Heroine Do? Or Why Women Can't Write," in *Images of Women in Fiction; Feminist Perspectives*, ed. Susan Koppelman Cornillon (Bowling Green, OH: Bowling Green University Popular Press, 1972), 4.

57 Ibid., 4.

58 Ibid., 16.

59 Rick Moody, Chimamanda Ngozi Adichie, Patrick Roth, Tsitsi Dangarembga, Minae Mizumura, Katja Lange-Muller, and Yoko Tawada, "Inappropriate Appropriation: A Believer Nighttime Event. PEN American World Voices Festival, 2005." Web. https://pen.org/conversation/inappropriate-appropriation; Cathy Park Hong, "Delusions of Whiteness in the Avant-Garde"; Dorothy Wang, *Thinking Its Presence*.

60 Kerschbaum, *Toward a New Rhetoric of Difference*, 69.

61 Ibid., 70.

62 Gordimer, *Telling Times*, 550.

63 Ibid.

64 Edwidge Danticat, *Create Dangerously: The Immigrant Artist at Work* (New York: Vintage, 2011), 11.

65 Rankine, Loffreda and Cap, *Racial Imaginary*, 20.

66 Gordimer, *Telling Times*, 548.

67 Larry Diamond, "Fiction as Political Thought," *African Affairs* 88 (July 1989): 352, 435.

68 Steve Westbrook, "Just Do It™: Creative Writing Exercises and the Ideology of American Handbooks," *New Writing: International Journal for the Practice and Theory of Creative Writing* 1.2 (2004): 142.

69 Ibid., 143.

70 Trinh T. Minh-ha, *Woman, Native, Other: Writing Postcoloniality and Feminism* (Bloomington: Indiana University Press, 1989), 2.

71 Emphasis mine. McGurl, *The Program Era*, 99, 144.

72 This is a modification of an idea presented in Lisa Delpit, *Other People's Children*. In Delpit's classroom, a diverse array of textual traditions are contrasted and analyzed. The teacher in this classroom knows how to ask the questions and scaffold student insights regarding writing conventions and context.

73 Hilde Hein, "Refining Feminist Theory: Lessons from Aesthetics," in *Aesthetics in Feminist Perspective*, edited by Hilde Hein and Carolyn Korsmeyer (Bloomington: Indiana University Press, 1993), 4.

74 Baxter, *Burning Down the House*, 57.

75 Haake, *What Our Speech Disrupts*, 209.

76 Deena Metzger, "In Her Image," *Heresies* 1 (1977): 7.

77 Russ, "What Can a Heroine Do?," 11.

78 Davidson and Fraser, "Poetry," 24.

79 Rankine, Loffreda, and King Cap, eds., *The Racial Imaginary*, 13.

80 Ibid., 15.

81 Ibid., 16.

82 Ibid., 18.

Chapter 4

1 Hegamin, "Inclusion and Diversity," 3.

2 Ibid., 1.

3 Frank Tuitt and Chayla Haynes, *Race, Equity, and the Learning Environment: The Global Relevance of Critical and Inclusive Pedagogies in Higher Education* (Sterling,

VA: Stylus, 2016); Alicia Fedelina Chávez and Susan Diana Longerbeam, *Teaching Across Cultural Strengths: A Guide to Balancing Integrated and Individuated Cultural Frameworks in College Teaching* (Sterling, VA: Stylus, 2016); Kim A. Case, *Intersectional Pedagogy: Complicating Identity and Social Justice* (New York: Routledge, 2017); Kim A. Case, *Deconstructing Privilege: Teaching and Learning as Allies in the Classroom* (New York: Routledge, 2013).

4 Omi Osun Joni L. Jones, Lisa L. Moore, and Sharon Bridgforth, eds., *Experiments in a Jazz Aesthetic*, 8.

5 Anzaldúa, *Borderlands/La Frontera: The New Mestiza*, 75–86.

6 Perry, "Writing without Shelter," 4.

7 Mura, "White Writing Teachers," 7.

8 Rankine, "In Our Way," 48.

9 Barrie Jean Borich's "The Craft of Writing Queer," *Brevity* 40 (Fall 2012); Edwidge Danticat, *Create Dangerously: The Immigrant Artist at Work* (New York: Vintage, 2011); Nadine Gordimer, "The Essential Gesture: Writers and Responsibility," *Granta* 15 (1985): 137–150; Porochista Khakpourt's "The Others" *Guernica* (2011); Toni Morrison, *Playing in the Dark: Whiteness and the Literary Imagination* (New York: Vintage, 1992); Trinh T. Minh-ha, *Woman, Native, Other* (Bloomington: Indiana University Press, 1989); Xu Xi's "Three Commandments for Writing about Race," *Brevity* 53 (Fall 2016); Sheila Black and Jennifer Bartlett, *Beauty is a Verb: The New Poetry of Disability* (El Paso: Cinco Puntos Press, 2011); Rick Moody, Chimamanda Ngozi Adichie, Patrick Roth, Tsitsi Dangarembga, Minae Mizumura, Katja Lange-Muller, and Yoko Tawada, "Inappropriate Appropriation: A Believer Nighttime Event," panel conversation, 2005 PEN World Voices Festival of International Literature, New York, available on http://pen.org (also appears in PEN America 7: World Voices).

10 Maria Damon, "Post-Literary Poetry, Counterperformance, and Micropoetries." *Poetry & Pedagogy: The Challenge of the Contemporary*, edited by Joan Retallack and Juliana Spahr (New York: Palgrave Macmillan, 2006) 143, 146).

11 Hegamin, "Inclusion and Diversity," 2.

12 Rankine, "In Our Way," 51.

13 Rankine, Loffreda, and Cap, eds., *The Racial Imaginary*, 20.

14 Lim, "Lore, Practice, and Social Identity," 83.

15 Ahmed, *On Being Included*, 4.

16 Derald Wing Sue, *Race Talk and the Conspiracy of Silence: Understanding and Facilitating Difficult Dialogues on Race* (Hoboken: Wiley, 2015), xvi.

17 Damon, "Post-Literary Poetry," 143.

18 Will Alexander, *Singing in Magnetic Hoofbeat: Essays, Prose Texts, Interviews and a Lecture, 1991–2007*, edited by Taylor Brady (Ithaca: Essay Press, 2012), 12.

19 Ibid., 21.

20 Ibid., 15.

21 Wandor, *The Author Is Not Dead*, 147.

22 Patrick Bizzaro, "Research and Reflection in English Studies: The Special Case of Creative Writing," *College English* 66.3 (January 2004): 305–306.

23 Nancy Welch, "No Apology: Challenging the 'Uselessness' of Creative Writing," *Journal of Advanced Composition* 19.1 (Winter 1999): 124.

24 Mura, "Ferguson, Whiteness as Default," 40.

25 Eve Shelnutt, "Transforming Experience into Fiction: An Alternative to the Workshop," in *Creative Writing in America Theory and Pedagogy*, edited by Joseph M. Moxley (Urbana, IL: National Council of Teachers of English, 1989), 151–168.

26 Garber, *Academic Instincts*, 21.

27 Hegamin, "Inclusion and Diversity," 2.

Coda

1 Kazim Ali, "Addressing Structural Racism in Creative Writing Programs," *Writer's Chronicle*. Web.

2 Ahmed, *On Being Included*, 4.

3 Ibid., 5.

4 Jagna Wojcicka Sharff and Johanna Lessinger, "The Academic Sweatshop: Changes in the Capitalist Infrastructure and the Part-Time Academic," *Anthropology of Work Review* 15.1 (2008): 3.

5 Judith M. Gappa, Ann E. Austin, and Andrea G. Trice, *Rethinking Faculty Work* (San Francisco: Jossey-Bass, 2007). Quoted in Janelle Adsit, Sue Doe, Marisa Allison, Paula Maggio, and Maria Maisto, "Affective Advocacy: Answering Institutional Productions of Precarity in the Corporate University," Special Issue: Institutional Feelings: Practicing Women's Studies in the Corporate University, edited by Jennifer Nash and Emily Owens, *Feminist Formations* 27.3 (December 2015): 21–48.

6 Ahmed, *On Being Included*, 39.

7 Arlie Russell Hochschild, *The Managed Heart: Commercialization of Human Feeling* (University of California Press, 2003). See also Jennifer Sano-Franchini, "It's Like Writing Yourself into a Codependent Relationship with Someone Who Doesn't Even Want You! Emotional Labor, Intimacy, and the Academic Job Market in Rhetoric and Composition," *College Composition and Communication* 68.1 (September 2016): 98–124.

8 Sara Ahmed, *On Being Included: Racism and Diversity in Institutional Life* (Durham: Duke University Press, 2012); Jill Blackmore and Judyth Sachs, "Managing Equity Work in the Performative University," *Australian Feminist Studies* 18.41 (2003): 141–162; Celia Lury, "The United Colors of Diversity," in *Global Nature, Global*

Culture, edited by Sarah Franklin, Celia Lury, and Jackie Stacey (London: Sage, 2000), 147–187.

9 Stephanie Kerschbaum, *Toward a New Rhetoric of Difference* (Urbana: National Council of Teachers of English, 2014), 32.

10 Ibid., 37.

11 Ahmed, *On Being Included*, 100.

12 Ibid., 43.

13 Green, "Materializing the Sublime Reader," 169.

14 Kerschbaum, *Toward a New Rhetoric of Difference*, 10.

15 Alexander, *Singing in Magnetic Hoofbeat*, 20,

16 Ibid., 19.

17 Ibid., 21.

18 Ostrom, "Introduction: Of Radishes and Shadows," xiii.

19 Paul Moya writes that "a truly multi-perspectival, multicultural education will work to *mobilize* identities in the classroom" (96). Quoted in Kerschbaum, *Toward a New Rhetoric of Difference*, 15.

20 David Jauss, "Articles of Faith," in *Creative Writing in America: Theory and Pedagogy*, edited by Joseph M. Moxley (Urbana, IL: National Council of Teachers of English, 1989), 64.

Appendix A

1 Malcolm Bradbury, "The Bridgeable Gap: Bringing Together the Creative Writer and the Critical Theorist in an Authorless World," *Times Literary Supplement* (January 1992): 8.

2 This is the only text in this list that is devoted to playwriting. The most famous of the early attempts to teach playwriting was George Pierce Baker's "47 Workshop." Baker won fame as the teacher of Eugene O'Neill, Philip Barry, John Dos Passos, and Thomas Wolfe. The first meeting of English 47 was held in 1906. *Dramatic Technique* is an outgrowth of these workshops.

3 Baxter's *Burning Down the House* is not intended to be a craft text. Making his intentions explicit, Baxter tells his readers that he "didn't want to write a how-to book" (xii) and that his "intention was never to give any kind of direct advice. I hoped the talks would stimulate the listener to think about a social and literary matter in a way that would be naggingly helpful" (xvi). He places the book in the genre of "literary criticism with a few glances at the culture at large" (xi). Nonetheless, the book is used in creative writing classrooms as a guide to the writing of fiction, like other craft texts.

4 Robert J. Connors, *Composition-Rhetoric: Backgrounds, Theory, and Pedagogy* (Pittsburgh, PA: University of Pittsburgh Press, 1997), 69.

5 Quoted in Sharon Crowley, *The Methodical Memory: Invention in Current-Traditional Rhetoric* (Carbondale: Southern Illinois University Press, 1990) 72.

6 McGurl, *Program Era*, 132.

7 Laura Wilder and Janelle Adsit, "Borders Crossed: A Nationwide Survey on the Influence of Rhetoric and Composition on Creative Writing" (manuscript under review).

Index

#BlackPoetsSpeakOut 51

Academic Jobs Wiki 137–139
Academy of American Poets 13
Adams, Katherine 27, 37, 42, 71, 92,
    168 n.30–32, 170 n.48, 172 n.59,
    173 n.78–79, 175 n.100–101, 182 n.98,
    184 n.21–23
Adichie, Chimamanda Ngozi 89, 158,
    185 n.59, 187 n.9
Adler-Kassner, Linda 79, 183 n.9
Adorno, Theodor 108
Afro-Futurism 102
Ahmed, Sara 2, 68, 128, 138, 140–142,
    163 n.3, 165 n.12, 180 n.81, 181 n.84,
    187 n.15, 188 n.2, 188 n.6, 189 n.8
Akutagawa, Ryūnosuke 111
Albright, Evelyn May 54, 58, 60, 147,
    169 n.47,178 n.24, 179 n.43,182 n.101
Aldridge, John 66–67, 180 n.79
Alexander, Will 128–129, 142–143,
    188 n.18, 189 n.15
Ali, Kazim 137, 188 n.1
Anzaldúa, Gloria E. 94–95, 125, 159,
    184 n.32, 187 n.5
Aristotle 62
Asian American Writers' Workshop 8
Association of Writers and Writing
    Programs (AWP) 1, 4, 19, 36, 142–143,
    163 n.1, 164 n.9, 170 n.48
Austin Project x, 42, 163 n.1
Austin, J.L 141

Barrett, Charles Raymond 13, 28, 147,
    165 n.3, 165 n.38, 173 n.77
Baudelaire, Charles 24, 40
Baxter, Charles 69, 86, 102, 111, 147,
    176 n.8, 181 n.83
Beardsley, Monroe 23, 25, 54, 56, 166 n.19,
    167 n.5, 169 n.45, 174 n.88, 178 n.25,
    178 n.37, 180 n.77, 180 n.80,
Beat Poetry 8

Bernstein, Charles 40, 174 n.93
Betts, Doris 44, 175 n.11
Bildersee, Adele 41, 147, 174 n.98
Bishop, Wendy 75–77, 81, 93, 101, 136, 159,
    164 n.8, 182 n.1, 184 n.24, 185 n.44
Bizzaro, Patrick 129, 188 n.22
Black Arts Movement 8, 102
Borich, Barrie Jean 126, 187 n.9
Boston University ix, 123
Bradbury, Malcolm 145, 189 n.1
Bradbury, Ray 90
Brande, Dorothea 41, 147, 171 n.52,
    174 n.98, 175 n.107
Bulman, Colin 34, 172 n.64
Burnham, Clint 37, 174 n.81
Burroway, Janet 53–54, 59–60, 64, 110, 111,
    147, 178 n.21, 179 n.46, 179 n.59, 180 n.66

Cage, John 20, 39
Cain, Mary Ann 38, 174 n.83
CantoMundo 8
Carruth, William Herbert 13, 30, 34–35,
    54, 147, 165 n.2, 168 n.34, 169 n.43,
    172 n.65, 178 n.22
Cassill, R.V. 28, 59, 147, 168 n.34, 168 n.36
Caudill, Rebecca 47, 147, 175
Cave Canem 8
Chang, Lan Samantha 4
Chavis, Geri Giebel 41, 174 n.94
Chekhov, Anton 56
Chhayavaad 102
Clark, Suzanne 68–70, 181 n.82, 181 n.95
cli-fi 51
Cole, Teju 123
Coles, Katharine 174 n.90, 184 n.40
Collins, Jim 41, 60–63, 66, 174 n.80,
    174 n.95, 179 n.48, 179 n.58, 180 n.61,
    180 n.78
Connors, Robert 145–146, 190 n.4
Cooley, Nicole 94, 184 n.26
counter-narrative 84, 89, 90, 94, 105–106,
    130, 143

Créolité 102
Crip 102
Crockett, Andy 103, 185 n.50
Crowley, Sharon 35–36, 52, 57, 61–64,
    173 n.68, 173 n.71, 177 n.14, 178 n.39,
    180 n.62, 180 n.64, 180 n.70, 184 n.36,
    190 n.5

D'Aguiar, Fred 4, 163 n.8
Damon, Maria 60, 128, 185 n.48, 187 n.10,
    187 n.17
Danticat, Edwidge 107, 126, 186 n.64,
    187 n.9
Dark Room Collective 102
Davidson, Chad 91, 112, 183 n.20,
    186 n.78
Davis, Angela 7
Davis, Lydia 111
Dawson, Paul 14, 24, 27, 33, 76, 165 n.14,
    165 n.5, 167 n.23, 171 n.52, 171 n.53,
    172 n.66, 178 n.35, 183 n.2,
de Bono, Edward 129
deaf poetry 60, 159
Delpit, Lisa 6, 165 n.11, 186 n.72
Derricotte, Toi 4, 163 n.8
Desalvo, Louise 41, 174 n.94
Dewey, John 33–34, 172 n.58, 172 n.61
Diamond, Larry 107, 186 n.67
Díaz, Junot 2, 4, 163 n.5, 163 n.8
Disability Poetics Movement 102, 126,
    187 n.9
Dobyns, Stephen 53, 60–61, 70, 147,
    178 n.20, 178 n.24, 178 n.36, 179 n.50,
    181 n.93
Domina, Lynn 72, 182 n.104
Downs, Doug 78–79, 183 n.6
DuPlessis, Rachel Blau 52, 111, 177 n.11
Dworkin, Craig 39, 174 n.86

ecopoetics 52
El Teatro Campesino 102
Emerson, Ralph Waldo 23, 30, 38, 65, 158,
    169 n.44, 171 n.51, 180 n.74
Engle, Paul 43, 173 n.66
Esenwein, J. Berg 69, 72, 147, 181 n.86,
    181 n.88, 182 n.103

Fenza, D.W. 1–2, 142, 163 n.1
Finn, Patrick 6, 165 n.11

Fitzgerald, F. Scott 109
Flaubert, Gustave 25
Foerster, Norman 34–36, 172 n.66
Forna, Aminatta 4, 163 n.8
Foucault, Michel 14–15, 165 n.6
Fowler, Nathaniel C. 30, 44–45, 147,
    169 n.42, 173 n.77, 175 n.112, 181 n.85
Fraser, Gregory 91, 112, 183 n.20, 186 n.78

Garber, Eugene 82, 183 n.13
Garber, Marjorie 13, 68, 133, 165 n.1,
    178 n.31, 179 n.59, 181 n.85, 188 n.26
Glicksberg, Charles Irving 28, 147,
    168 n.37, 171 n.53, 176 n.8
Goldberg, Natalie 41, 146–147
Goldsmith, Kenneth 20, 166
Gordimer, Nadine 61, 99, 106–107, 126,
    135, 160–161, 179 n.51, 186 n.62,
    186 n.66, 187 n.9,
Grande, Sandy 34, 172 n.62
Green, Chris 53, 61, 82, 99, 142, 160,
    177 n.16, 179 n.52, 183 n.14, 184 n.38,
    189 n.13
Gurlesque 60

Haake, Katherine 49, 88, 101, 111, 164 n.8,
    176 n.1, 176 n.3, 183 n.18, 185 n.46,
    186 n.75
Hagedorn, Hermann 25, 29, 167 n.27,
    168 n.41
Harjo, Joy 111
Harlem Renaissance 8
Harper, Graeme 84
Harvard Business Review 38
Haynes, David 4
Hegamin, Tonya 4, 8, 11, 117, 127, 163 n.8,
    165 n.13, 165 n.15, 165 n.19, 186 n.1,
    187 n.11, 188 n.27
Hemingway, Ernest 59, 109
Hermotimus 14–15
Hesse, Douglas 73, 182 n.106
Hill, Gabrielle L'Hirondelle 51, 177 n.9
Hochschild, Alie 140, 188 n.7
Hong, Cathy Park 4, 23, 106, 161, 164 n.8,
    166 n.16, 185 n.59
Horace 31, 55, 170 n.49
Hughes, Langston 108
Hugo, Victor 68
Humanism 32, 34–36, 43, 45, 57

Imagism 102
Institute of American Indian Arts 8

Jauss, David 144, 189 n.20
Johns Hopkins University 46
Jones, Omi Osun Joni L. x, 121, 163 n.1,
   163 n.2, 175 n.103, 187 n.4

Kameen, Paul 39
Kant, Immanuel 55–56,178 n.32
Keats, John 55
Kelly, Mary 27
Kerchval, Jesse Lee 38
Kerr, Tom 62, 179 n.57
Kerschbaum, Stephanie 94, 106, 140, 142,
   184 n.28, 186 n.60, 189 n.9, 189 n.14,
   189 n.19
Kincaid, Jamaica 85, 111
King, Amy 23
Kroll, Jerri 63, 84, 179 n.60

Lambda Literary 8
Land, Ray 9–10, 79, 81, 165 n.18, 183 n.4,
   183 n.7
Leahy, Anna 4, 164 n.8
Lessinger, Johanna 139, 188 n.4
Lim, Shirley Geok-lin 4, 127, 164 n.8,
   184 n.27
Linington, Liz 41, 174 n.94
Lloyd, Carol 38
Loffreda, Beth 4, 113, 127, 163 n.8,
   185 n.47, 186 n.65, 186 n.79,
   187 n.13
Longinus 30
Lopate, Phillip 24, 167 n.21
Lorde, Audre 7
Los Angeles Times 89

MacArthur Foundation 13
MacDowell Colony 25, 28–29, 167
Madden, Matt 89, 183 n.19
Mallarmé, Stéphane 30, 66
Mathis, Ayana 3, 161, 163 n.7
McCall, Sophie 51, 177 n.9
McFarland, Ron 45–46, 175 n.116,
   175 n.119
McGurl, Mark 22, 33, 37, 43, 47, 64, 109,
   146, 165 n.14, 166 n.12, 171 n.53,
   173 n.75, 174 n.82, 174 n.91, 175 n.106,

   175 n.108, 175 n.120, 180 n.65,
   186 n.71, 190 n.6
McIntosh, Peggy 17, 166 n.8
Mearns, William Hughes 33–34, 171 n.52,
   171 n.55, 172 n.63
melodrama 6, 68, 71
Mestizo Arts & Activism Collective 8
Metzger, Deena 111, 186 n.76
Meyer, Jan 4, 113, 127, 163 n.8, 185 n.47,
   186 n.65, 186 n.79, 187 n.13
Middlebury College ix, 123
Miller, Susan 63, 180 n.63
Minot, Stephen 59–60, 147, 179 n.44,
   179 n.59
Misty Poets 102
Moody, Rick 85, 106, 158, 185 n.59,
   187 n.9
Morton, Donald 104, 185 n.55
Munro, Alice 111
Mura, David 4, 125, 133, 164 n.8,165 n.17,
   187 n.7, 188 n.24
Murray, Donald 90, 96, 184 n.34
Myers, D.G. 33, 36, 41, 47, 52, 65, 168 n.29,
   168 n.33, 171 n.54–57, 172 n.63,
   173 n.74, 174 n.97, 175 n.99, 175 n.118,
   177 n.13, 177 n.15, 180 n.67, 180 n.69

Nadaism 102
National Council of Teachers of English 33
National Public Radio (NPR) 3, 22, 93,
   163 n.7
National Research Council 81
Native American Literature Symposium 8
Négritude 67, 102
Neigh, Janet 95, 184 n.29
New Criticism 108
New Formalist 102
New York Times 3, 60
Newkirk, Thomas 69, 181 n.89
Nowak, Mark 4, 164 n.8
Nuyorican Poets Café 102

Oliver, Mary 36
Oprah 12, 41
Orozco, Daniel 5
Ostrom, Hans 44–45, 72, 175 n.110,
   175 n.114, 182 n.105, 183 n.3, 189 n.18
Oulipo 89
Owens, Derek 40, 174 n.93

PEN America 8, 126, 185 n.59, 187 n.9
Perry, Adrienne 4, 58, 62, 125, 164 n.8,
    176 n.7, 179 n.42, 179 n.56, 187 n.6
Pink, Daniel 38, 174 n.82
Pinoy poetics 102
Philips, Deborah 41, 174 n.94
Plato 62, 65, 168 n.28
Poe, Edgar Allan 24, 40
Pope, Alexander 40, 170 n.51, 174 n.88
Pope, Harry W. 19, 166 n.10, 180 n.66
Pound, Ezra 40
Probyn-Ramsey, Fiona 7, 165 n.12
progressive education 6, 32–34, 43, 172 n.61

Queneau, Raymond 89

Ramjerdi, Jan 82, 183 n.13
Rankine, Claudia 2, 4, 9, 57, 113, 126–127,
    163 n.4, 163 n.8, 165 n.16, 176 n.4,
    177 n.12, 178 n.38, 185 n.47, 186 n.65,
    186 n.79, 186 n.80, 187 n.8, 187 n.12,
    187 n.13,
Reed, Ishmael 124
Rich, Adrienne 7
Rickert, Thomas 39
Rilke, Rainer Maria 70
Ritter, Kelly 24, 42, 50, 167 n.24, 167 n.26,
    175 n.102, 176 n.5
Robertson, Liane 79, 81, 183 n.8,
    183 n.10–11
Roof, Judith 90, 104, 185 n.52
Rothenberg, Jerome 124
Royster, Brent 58, 179 n.41
Royster, Jacqueline Jones 6
Russ, Joanna 104, 112, 150, 159,
    185 n.56–58, 186 n.77
Rymer, Jone 90

Sanders, Scott Russell 99, 184 n.39
Sarton, May 15, 36, 66, 72, 147, 173 n.70,
    180 n.78, 182 n.102
Sartre, Jean-Paul 62
Schiller, Friedrich 23, 25, 38, 56, 65,
    167 n.28, 178 n.33, 180 n.71
Scholarship of Teaching and Learning
    (SoTL) 9, 79
Schultz, Jeffrey 84, 103, 183 n.16, 185 n.51
Schwartz, Esther 28, 41, 70–71, 147,
    168 n.35, 173 n.77, 174 n.98, 181 n.96–98

sentimentality 6, 22, 53, 64, 68–72, 76
Sharff, Jacna Wojcicka 139, 188 n.4
Shelley, Percy Bysshe 23, 30, 55, 71,
    166 n.17–18, 169 n.46, 178 n.28,
    182 n.99
Shelnutt, Eve 133, 188 n.25
Silko, Leslie Marmon 93–94, 111, 123–124,
    159, 184 n.25
Sirc, Geoffrey 39
slam poetry 5, 12, 18, 58, 100, 102, 124
Smith, Barbara Herrnstein 16, 49, 53, 61,
    101, 160, 175 n.104, 176 n.2, 177 n.18,
    179 n.54, 180 n.68, 185 n.45
Smith, Dave 46, 175 n.117
Smock, Frederick 36, 173 n.69
Sommers, Nancy 90
spoken word 8, 12, 58
Straight, Susan 89
Stuckey, Elspeth 6, 165 n.11
Sue, Derald Wing 24, 128, 167 n.22,
    187 n.16
Swallow, Alan 35

Taczak, Kara 79, 81, 183 n.8, 183 n.10–11
Teaching for Transfer (TfT) 81
Teleky, Richard 4, 164 n.8
threshold concept 3, 9–11, 75, 77–83,
    112–115, 123
Tolstoy, Leo 27
transpoetics 85, 102
Trask, Spencer and Katrina 28–29,
    168 n.39
Trinh T. Minh-ha 109, 126, 186 n.70,
    187 n.9

Ueland, Brenda 41, 147, 175 n.98,
    175 n.107
Ulmer, Gregory 39
Ultraísmo 102
University of California-San Francisco 25
University of Chicago 33
University of Denver ix, 35, 123, 173 n.67
University of Edinburgh 79
University of Iowa Writers' Workshop 35,
    172 n.66

Vanderslice, Stephanie 13, 37–38, 45,
    165 n.4, 173 n.76, 174 n.84, 174 n.85,
    175 n.115

VIDA Women in Literary Arts 2–3, 8, 11, 15–16, 29, 135, 163 n.6, 179 n.59
Vitanza, Victor 39
voice 5, 16, 21–23, 42, 64, 94–95, 102, 121, 124, 127, 129, 131–132, 135, 143, 152, 161, 164 n.8

Wallace, David Foster 125, 164 n.8
Wandor, Michelene 50, 129, 176 n.6, 188 n.21
Wang, Dorothy 4, 19, 164 n.8, 185 n.59
Wardle, Elizabeth 78–79, 183 n.6, 183 n.9
Warner, Michael 100, 185 n.42
Watkins, Claire Faye 19, 160, 166 n.9
Webb, Jen 84, 183 n.15
Welch, Nancy 44, 132, 175 n.109, 188 n.23

Westbrook, Steve 108, 186 n.68
Widdemer, Margaret 41, 175 n.98
Wilde, Oscar 56, 178 n.37
Wilder, Laura 100, 185 n.41, 190 n.7
Wilkinson, Marguerite 41, 147, 174 n.98
Wordsworth, William 30, 66, 169 n.46, 180 n.75
Writing about Writing (WAW) 78–81

Xi, Xu 126, 187 n.9

Yaddo ix, 28–29, 167 n.26, 168 n.39
Yancey, Kathleen Blake 73, 79, 81, 182 n.106, 183 n.8, 183 n.10–11

Zavarzadeh, Mas'ud 104, 185 n.55